THE BEST OF
FRASIER ™

THE BEST OF
FRASIER™

**FIFTEEN COMPLETE SCRIPTS OF THE
FINEST FRASIER EPISODES**

CHANNEL 4 BOOKS

First published in 1999 by Channel 4 Books, an imprint of **Macmillan Publishers Ltd**,
25 Eccleston Place, London, SW1W 9NF and Basingstoke
www.macmillan.co.uk

Associated companies throughout the world

ISBN 0 7522 1394 6

5 7 9 8 6 4

A CIP catalogue record for this book is available from the British Library

Typeset by SX Composing DTP, Rayleigh, Essex

Printed by Mackays of Chatham plc, Chatham, Kent

CONTENTS

INTRODUCTION

Twenty-four Wednesdays every year, about sixty people gather in a conference room at Paramount Studios in Hollywood. Among these sixty are an affable, rambunctious five. These are the cast of *Frasier*. Also among them are an ashen, nail-biting ten. This is the writing staff of *Frasier*.

The occasion is the 'table reading.' This is the first reading aloud of that week's *Frasier* script by the cast. The episode won't be shot until the following Tuesday, after five days of rehearsal and rewriting, a honing process which can result in the script being overhauled entirely (hence the nail-biting and ashening of faces). But the table reading sets the tone for the week and also marks that time when the script ceases to be merely words on a page and becomes a living thing, a play.

As at most such births, a range of emotions is on display: fear, joy, laughter, tears. And not all the babies are beautiful. Some are flabby, or misshapen, or just too long. But every now and then there's one that's just right. And everyone who's there knows it. Certainly that was the case with the fifteen shows in this volume.

Something about each one – whether it was the particular story we were telling, or the way we were telling it – just struck a nerve with everyone. So with this book you have the ability to imagine yourself at those fifteen charmed table readings. You simply need to summon the glorious baritone of Kelsey Grammer, the flinty counterpoint of David Hyde Pierce, the rasp of John Mahoney, the airy lilt of Jane Leeves, and the smoky twang of Peri Gilpin and you've got all the tools you need.

Frasier has, in its way, been charmed since the start. 'The Good Son', the pilot script for the show, had a lot to do with that. The table reading for that show was in fact the first time all five cast members had been in the same room together and so there was a natural trepidation about what sort of chemistry there would be. But by the time Kelsey Grammer and David Hyde Pierce had played their first scene together (and since we are talking about chemistry, I will even be scientific enough to pinpoint the exact moment; it's when Frasier says: 'When was the last time you had an unexpressed thought?' to which Niles responds: 'I'm having one now.') there was little doubt that these two would be brilliant together.

In fact all the actors worked brilliantly together, and not just in the comedic scenes. Toward the end of the second act Martin (John Mahoney) and Frasier finally have the confrontation that has been brewing since the start and it's a long, angry, mean, and very true-sounding fight. That doesn't happen in sitcoms very often. It happens in pilot scripts even less, the thinking presumably being that we are trying to get our audience to like these people and maybe having them say harsh hurtful things to each other for a *long* time isn't the best way to do that. But the scene played beautifully, and it taught us as writers that we never had to shy away from a dramatic scene – these actors would make such scenes compelling, even in the framework of a comedy. I think what the scene ultimately taught the audience was that this was a program which promised not just to be funny, but also perhaps to be poignant and true.

One hundred and fifty episodes later we are still trying to deliver on that promise: to be funny, first, but also to be true to these characters, to explore their wants and needs in ways that occasionally achieve something like poignancy. The other scripts in this book represent various approaches we've taken to that end. There's flat-out farce ('The Matchmaker', 'The Ski Lodge') and old-fashioned romantic comedy ('Mixed Doubles'). There's also swashbuckling ('An Affair To Forget'), dancing ('Moon Dance'), parody ('Slow Tango in South Seattle'), and something akin to a silent movie ('Three Valentines'). It has always been a point of pride at *Frasier* that we can write – or perhaps more properly, that the vast talent of our actors allows us to write – in a broad range of styles and this book should demonstrate that. Many of these scripts have won individual awards for writing and all have been instrumental in *Frasier*'s winning the Emmy award for best comedy an unprecedented five years consecutively.

On behalf of the many writers who have contributed to *Frasier* over the years and whose work is represented here, let me say it is a privilege to be published in Britain, the birthplace of sophisticated comedy. We enjoyed writing these shows and we hope you enjoy reading them.

Christopher Lloyd
Executive Producer of *Frasier*

THE CAST

Frasier Crane. . . . . Kelsey Grammer
Martin Crane. . . . . John Mahoney
Niles Crane. David Hyde Pierce
Daphne Moon . . . . Jane Leeves
Roz Doyle. . . . . Peri Gilpin
Bulldog Brisco . . . . Dan Butler
Eddie . . . . Moose

ADDITIONAL CAST MEMBERS

The Good Son
Russell (V.O.). . . . . Jeremy Lawrence
Waitress. . . . . Gina Ravarra
Deliveryman . . . . Cleto Augusto
Claire (V.O.) . . . . Mimi Savage

Call Me Irresponsible
Hank (V.O.) . . . . Eddie Van Halen
Marco (V.O.) . . . . Bruno Kirby
Catherine . . . . Amanda Donohoe

A Midwinter Night s Dream
Eric . . . . Dean Erickson

Slow Tango In South Seattle
Steven (V.O.) . . . . James Spader
Thomas Jay Fallow. . . . . John O'Hurley
Amber Edwards . . . . Susan Brown
Gil Chesterton . . . . Edward Hibbert
Mrs Warner. . . . . Myra Carter
Clarice. . . . . Constance Towers
Man. . . . . David Sederholm

The Matchmaker
Tom O'Connor . . . . Eric Lutes

An Affair To Forget
Gretchen (V.O.). . . . . Glenne Headley
Marta . . . . Irene Olga Lopez
Gunnar. . . . . Brian Cousins

Moon Dance
Lacey Lloyd . . . . Christine McGraw

Andrew Lloyd . . . . Hank Stratton
Conductor. . . . . Michael G. Hawkins
Claire Barnes . . . . Nancy Stafford

The Two Mrs Cranes
Gil Chesterton . . . . Edward Hibbert
Clive. . . . . Scott Atkinson

Mixed Doubles
Adelle. . . . . Allison MacKie
Rodney. . . . . Kevin Farrell

Ham Radio
Gil Chesterton . . . . Edward Hibbert
Ian . . . . Jack Betts
Mel White . . . . Richard Easton
Noel Shempsky. . . . . Patrick Kerr
Maxine . . . . Hope Allen

Perspectives On Christmas
Masseur . . . . Albert Macklin
Albert . . . . Conrad Janis
Doris. . . . . Brooks Almy
Jane. . . . . Marilyn O'Connor
Woman . . . . Jennifer Williams
Man. . . . . Mark Capri
Sally . . . . Jamie Alexis
Billy . . . . JB Gaynor
Vic. . . . . Zachary McLemore

Room Service
Lilith . . . . Bebe Neuwirth
Waiter. . . . . John Ducey
Betsy (V.O.). . . . . Hale Berry

The Ski Lodge
Annie . . . . Cynthia Lamontagne
Guy James . . . . Patrick Stuart
Connie . . . . Lisa Robinson

Three Valentines
Cassandra Stone . . . . Virginia Madsen
Violinist . . . . Peter Waldman
Mario . . . . Armando Molina
Maître d' . . . . Dan Kern
Waiter . . . . Lawrence Lowe

SEASON ONE

THE GOOD SON

#60181-098

Created and Written by David Angell & Peter Casey & David Lee
Directed by James Burrows

ACT ONE

Scene A

A BLACK SCREEN. IN WHITE LETTERS APPEARS "THE JOB."

Man #1 (V.O.): I'm a long-time listener, first-time caller. My problem began when I . . .

FADE IN:

MONTAGE – (V.O.'S) – DAY/1

INT. CAB – DAY

A CABBIE IS LISTENING TO HIS RADIO.

Woman #1 (V.O.): I don't know him anymore. It's like living with a stranger. Take yesterday . . .

CROSS FADE TO:

INT. KITCHEN – DAY

A MESSY KITCHEN, A FRAZZLED HOUSEWIFE AND A SCREAMING INFANT IN A HIGHCHAIR. THE RADIO IS ON.

Man #2 (V.O.): At least I thought I had a normal childhood. Aw, hell, who knows what's normal anymore. I . . .

CROSS FADE TO:

EXT. PARK – DAY

A MAN JOGS IN THE PARK. HE'S LISTENING TO HIS WALKMAN.

Woman #2 (V.O.): (BLUBBERING) I'm sorry, I thought I had this under control. I, I, I . . . Give me a minute.

THE JOGGER ROLLS HIS EYES.

CROSS FADE TO:

EXT. NEWSSTAND – DAY

A NEWS-STAND, FEATURING A PORTABLE RADIO NEXT TO THE CASH REGISTER. A COAT HANGAR IS USED AS AN ANTENNA.

Woman #3 (V.O.): (THICK MIDDLE EASTERN ACCENT) I tell him, "I'm a human being. I'm a human being. You can't treat me like a dog." You've got to help me, Dr. Crane.

CROSS FADE TO:

Scene B

INT. RADIO STUDIO – DAY – DAY/1
(Frasier, Roz, Russell [V.O.])

KACL – A TYPICAL RADIO STUDIO: TWO ROOMS SEPARATED BY A GLASS PARTITION AND A DOOR. ON ONE SIDE, <u>FRASIER CRANE</u> IS SEATED AT A DESK WITH A MULTI-LINE PHONE AND MICROPHONE. HE IS WEARING HEADPHONES. ON THE OTHER SIDE OF THE GLASS IS HIS CALL SCREENER, <u>ROZ DOYLE</u>. ANOTHER GLASS PARTITION IN THE STUDIO LOOKS OUT INTO THE HALLWAY. THE LIGHTS ARE LOW. FRASIER IS IN THE MIDDLE OF ANSWERING A CALLER.

Frasier: (FIRMLY, WITH CONCERN) Listen to yourself, Bob. You follow her to work. You eavesdrop on her calls. You open her mail. The minute you started doing those things, the relationship was over. Thank you for your call.

HE PUNCHES A BUTTON ON THE CONSOLE.

Frasier (CONT'D): Roz, do we have time for one more?

ROZ SPEAKS INTO THE MICROPHONE IN THE BOOTH IN A SOOTHING RADIO VOICE.

Roz: Yes, Dr. Crane. On line four we have Russell from Kirkland. He feels like he's caught in a rut.

FRASIER PUSHES A BUTTON ON THE PHONE.

Frasier: This is Dr. Frasier Crane. I'm listening.

Russell (V.O.): Well, I've been feeling, sort of, you know, depressed lately.

Frasier: For how long?

Russell (V.O.): Oh, the last seven or eight years.

Frasier: Go on.

Russell (V.O.): I don't know, my life's not going anywhere. It's not that it's bad. It's just the same old apartment, the same old job, the same old people, day after day. Sometimes I just . . .

ROZ SIGNALS FROM THE BOOTH THAT TIME IS RUNNING SHORT AND FRASIER HAS TO WRAP THIS UP.

Frasier: Russell, we're nearing the end of our hour. Let me see if I can cut to the chase by using myself as an example. Six months ago I was living in Boston. My wife had left me, which was very painful, then she came back, which was excruciating. I thought I could look past her indiscretion but I was only kidding myself. On top of that, my practice had grown stagnant and my social life consisted of hanging around a bar night after night. Suddenly I realized I was clinging to a life that wasn't working anymore. I knew I had to do something, anything. So I put an end to the marriage and moved back here to my hometown of Seattle. Go Seahawks! I took action, Russell and you can too. Move, change, do something. If it's a mistake, do something else. Will you do that, Russell? Will you? Russell? (TURNING TO ROZ) I think we lost him.

Roz: No, we cut to the news about thirty seconds ago.

FRASIER TAKES OFF HIS HEADSET, GETS UP AND HEADS INTO ROZ'S CONTROL ROOM.

Frasier: Oh, for crying out loud. I finally bare my soul to all of Seattle and they're listening to "Chopper Dave's Rush-Hour Roundup"? At least the rest of the show was good. (THEN) It was a good show, wasn't it?

Roz: Here. (HANDS HIM A SLIP OF PAPER) Your brother called.

Frasier: You know, in the trade, we call that avoidance. Don't change the subject. What did you think?

SHE POINTS TO HER CONSOLE.

Roz: Did I ever show you what this button does?

Frasier: I'm not a piece of Lalique. I can handle criticism. How was I today?

Roz: Let's see. You dropped two commercials, you left a total of twenty-eight seconds of dead air, you scrambled the station's call letters, you spilled yogurt on the control board and you kept referring to Jerry with the identity crisis as "Jeff."

Frasier: (PAUSE) You say my brother called.

CUT TO:

Scene C

A BLACK SCREEN. IN WHITE LETTERS APPEARS "THE BROTHER."

Niles (V.O.): So I said to the gardener, "Yoshi, I do not need a Zen garden in my backyard.

FADE IN:

EXT. SEATTLE STREET – DAY – DAY/1 – 2ND UNIT
(Niles [V.O.])

A CITY BUS IS STOPPED, PICKING UP PASSENGERS. ON THE SIDE OF THE
BUS IS A LARGE ADVERTISEMENT. ON IT IS FRASIER'S SMILING FACE AND
THE WORDS "DR. FRASIER CRANE. HE LISTENS. KACL – 780 AM." THE BUS
PULLS AWAY TO REVEAL "CAFE NERVOSA," ONE OF SEATTLE'S POPULAR
COFFEE HOUSES.

Niles (V.O.) (CONT'D): If I want to rake gravel every ten minutes to maintain my inner
harmony, I'll move to Yokohama."

CUT TO:

INT. COFFEE HOUSE – CONTINUOUS – DAY/1
(Niles, Frasier, Waitress, Extras)

FRASIER AND HIS BROTHER, DR. NILES CRANE, STAND AT THE COUNTER.
FRASIER HAS HIS NOSE IN A MENU.

Niles (CONT'D): Well, this offends him so he starts pulling up Maris' prized camellias
by the handful. I couldn't stand for that, so I marched right into the morning room and
locked the door until he cooled down. Tell me you would have handled it differently,
Frasier.

AFTER A BEAT, FRASIER LOOKS UP.

Frasier: Oh, I'm sorry, Niles, I didn't realize you'd stopped talking.

Niles: You haven't heard a word I said.

Frasier: Niles, you're a psychiatrist. You know what it's like to listen to people prattling
on endlessly about their mundane lives.

Niles: Touché. And on that subject, I heard your show today.

Frasier: And?

Niles: You know what I think about pop psychiatry.

Frasier: Yes, yes, I know what you think about everything. When was the last time you
had an unexpressed thought?

Niles: I'm having one now.

THEY BOTH CHUCKLE GOOD-NATUREDLY. A WAITRESS APPROACHES.

Waitress: You guys ready?

Frasier: (TO WAITRESS) Two cafe latte supremos.

NILES MOVES TO A CHAIR AND BEGINS TO DUST IT OFF WITH A HANDKERCHIEF. HE OFFERS IT TO FRASIER.

Frasier (CONT'D): No, thank you.

Niles: So, Frasier, how are you doing on your own?

Frasier: I'm fine. I love my new life. I love the solitude. I miss Frederick like the dickens, of course. He's quite a boy. He's playing goalie on the pee wee soccer team now. He's a chip off the old block.

Niles: You hated sports.

Frasier: And so does he, but the fresh air's good for him.

THEY BOTH LAUGH AT THIS.

Niles: This has been fun, Frasier, but we have a problem. That's why I thought we should talk.

Frasier: Is it Dad?

Niles: I'm afraid so. One of his old buddies from the police force called this morning. He went over to see him. Found him on the bathroom floor.

Frasier: Oh my God.

Niles: No, it's okay, he's fine.

Frasier: What? His hip again?

NILES NODS.

Niles: Frasier, I don't think he can live alone anymore.

Frasier: What can we do?

Niles: Well, I know this isn't going to be anyone's favorite solution, but I took the liberty of checking out a few convalescent homes for him.

HE REACHES INTO HIS BRIEFCASE AND TAKES OUT A PILE OF PAMPHLETS.

Frasier: A home? He's still a young man.

Niles: Well, you certainly can't take care of him. You're just getting your new life together.

Frasier: Absolutely. Besides, we've never been sympatico. I remember a car trip as a child. We drove from Seattle to Spokane and the only thing he said to me was, "I think we've got a problem with your brother Frasier."

Niles: Yes, well, and, of course, I can't take care of him.

Frasier: Yes, of course, of course. (BEAT) Why?

Niles: Dad doesn't get along with Maris.

Frasier: Who does?

Niles: I thought you like my Maris.

Frasier: I do. I like her from a distance. You know, the way you like the sun. Maris is like the sun . . . except without the warmth.

Niles: Well then, I guess we're agreed on what to do with Dad.

NILES PICKS UP A PAMPHLET FROM THE TABLE.

Niles (CONT'D): (READING) "Golden Acres. We care so you don't have to."

Frasier: It says that?

Niles: It might as well.

Frasier: (RESIGNED) Alright, I'll make up the guest room.

Niles: You're a good son, Frasier.

Frasier: Oh God, I am, aren't I?

FRASIER BURIES HIS HEAD IN HIS HANDS AS NILES COMFORTS HIM. THE WAITRESS BRINGS THEM THEIR COFFEE.

Waitress: Two cafe supremos. Anything to eat?

Frasier: No. I've lost my appetite.

Niles: I'll have a large piece of cheesecake.

CUT TO:

Scene D

A BLACK SCREEN. IN WHITE LETTERS APPEARS "THE FATHER."

FADE IN:

INT. FRASIER'S LIVING ROOM – DAY – DAY/2
(Frasier, Niles, Martin, Deliveryman)

IT'S A SMART, CLEAN, METICULOUSLY DECORATED CONDO. THE
FURNISHINGS LEAN TOWARD THE CONTEMPORARY, WITH WELL CHOSEN
PIECES OF ART AND SCULPTURE. CENTER IS A VIEW OF THE SEATTLE
SKYLINE. THERE IS A <u>KNOCK</u> AT THE DOOR. FRASIER, AT THE PIANO, GOES
TO THE DOOR. HE STEELS HIMSELF AND OPENS THE DOOR. NILES IS
STANDING THERE WITH A FEW SUITCASES IN HIS HAND.

Niles: We finally made it.

<u>NILES ENTERS</u> FOLLOWED BY THEIR FATHER, <u>MARTIN</u>, USING A WALKER.

Frasier: Ah, Dad, welcome to your new home. You look great.

Martin: Don't B.S. me. I do not look great. I spent Monday on the bathroom floor. You
can still see the tile marks on my face.

Niles: (SOTTO TO FRASIER) Gives you some idea about the ride over in the car.

FRASIER CLAPS HIS HANDS AND RUBS THEM TOGETHER, TRYING TO
LIGHTEN THE MOMENT.

Frasier: Well, here we are. Now, Dad, rest assured the refrigerator is stocked with your
favorite beer, Ballantines, and we've got plenty of hot links and coleslaw. I even rented a
Charles Bronson movie for later.

Martin: You can cut the "Welcome to Camp Crane" speech. We all know why I'm here.
Your old man can't be trusted to be alone for ten minutes without falling on his ass, and
Frasier got stuck with me. Isn't that right?

FRASIER AND NILES LOOK AT EACH OTHER.

Frasier/Niles: No, no, no.

Frasier (CONT'D): I want you here. It will give us an opportunity to get reacquainted.

Martin: That implies we were acquainted at one point.

Niles: Listen, why don't I take Dad's things into his new "bachelor quarters" so you two
scoundrels can plan some hijinx?

<u>NILES EXITS</u> WITH THE BAGS DOWN THE HALLWAY TO THE BEDROOM.

Martin: I think that wife of his is making him nutso.

Frasier: Yes, we Crane boys sure know how to marry, don't we? (THEN) Dad, let me
get you a beer.

FRASIER CROSSES TO THE KITCHEN. MARTIN LOOKS AROUND THE ROOM.

Frasier (CONT'D): So, do you like what I've done with the place? Every piece was
carefully chosen. The lamp, Corbu. The chair by Eames. This sofa is an exact replica of

the one Coco Chanel had in her Paris atelier.

Martin: Nothing matches.

Frasier: It's a style of decorating. It's called eclectic. The theory behind it is, if you have great pieces of furniture, it doesn't matter if they match. They'll go together.

Martin: It's your money.

MARTIN WALKS OVER TO THE WINDOW AND GAZES AT THE SKYLINE.

SFX: THE DOORBELL RINGS.

Frasier: Great view, isn't it? (INDICATING) That's the Space Needle over there.

Martin: Thank you for pointing that out. Being born and raised here, I never would have known that.

AS NILES RE-ENTERS FROM THE OTHER ROOM, FRASIER CROSSES TO THE DOOR AND OPENS IT. IT'S A DELIVERYMAN.

Deliveryman: Delivery for Martin Crane.

Martin: In here.

Deliveryman: Coming through.

FRASIER STEPS BACK. THE DELIVERYMAN BRINGS IN A BARCALOUNGER.

Frasier: Excuse me, excuse me. Wait a minute.

Deliveryman: Where do you want it?

Martin: Where's the TV?

Niles: (INDICATING) In that credenza.

Martin: Point it at that thing.

Deliveryman: What about this chair?

Niles: Here. Let me get it out of the way.

NILES PICKS UP THE CHAIR AND MOVES IT. THE DELIVERYMAN REPLACES IT WITH MARTIN'S BARCALOUNGER.

Frasier: Careful. That's a Wassily. (RE: LOUNGER) Dad, Dad, as dear as I'm sure this piece is to you. I don't think it quite goes with anything here.

Martin: I know. It's eclectic.

MARTIN PAYS THE DELIVERYMAN. <u>HE EXITS</u>.

Frasier: Niles, help me out here.

Niles: Sit in it, Frasier, it's really comfortable.

FRASIER GRABS NILES BY THE SHIRT AND PULLS HIM ASIDE.

Frasier: I see what you're doing. You're agreeing with the old man because you're afraid he might ask to live with you and Maris.

Niles: (RE: SHIRT) Please, Frasier, you're scrunching my Tommy Hilfiger.

Frasier: Listen, you little twit . . .

Martin: You're going to have to run an extension cord over here so I can plug in the vibrating part.

Frasier: (BEATEN) Yes, yes, that will be the crowning touch.

Niles: Now that you two are settled in, I've got to run. I'm late for my dysfunctional family seminar.

AS HE HEADS FOR THE DOOR:

Niles (CONT'D): Dad, have you mentioned Eddie yet?

FRASIER TURNS TO MARTIN.

Frasier: (PANICKED) Eddie?

Niles: Ta ta.

<u>NILES EXITS.</u>

Frasier: Oh, Dad, no. Not Eddie.

Martin: He's my best friend. Hand me my beer.

Frasier: But he's weird. He gives me the creeps. All he does is stare at me.

Martin: It's your imagination.

Frasier: No, Dad, no. I'm sorry, but I'm putting my foot down. Eddie's *not* moving in here.

CUT TO:

Scene E

A BLACK SCREEN. IN WHITE LETTERS APPEARS THE WORD, "EDDIE."

CROSS FADE TO:

<u>INT. FRASIER'S LIVING ROOM – NIGHT – NIGHT/2</u>
(Martin, Frasier, Eddie)

MARTIN IS SITTING IN HIS BARCALOUNGER WATCHING THE CHARLES BRONSON MOVIE. WE PAN OVER TO FRASIER ON HIS COCO COUCH. WE CONTINUE THE PAN. SITTING NEXT TO FRASIER IS <u>EDDIE</u>, A SMALL LONG-HAIRED JACK RUSSELL TERRIER. EDDIE STARES AT FRASIER.

FADE OUT.

<u>END OF ACT ONE</u>

ACT TWO

Scene H

FADE IN:

<u>INT. COFFEE HOUSE – DAY – DAY/3</u>
(Niles, Frasier, Extras)

NILES IS THERE, <u>FRASIER RUSHES IN.</u>

Frasier: Oh, Niles, there you are. Sorry I'm late. Just as I was leaving, Dad decided to fix lunch by the glow of a small kitchen fire. (BEAT) I tell you, this last week with Dad has been a living hell. When I'm there, I feel like my territory is being violated and when I'm away, I worry about what he's up to. My nerves are completely shot. I've got to do something to calm down. (TO WAITRESS) Double espresso, please. (TO NILES) You don't still have the brochures from those rest homes, do you?

Niles: Of course I do. You're forgetting Maris is five years older than I am. But do you really think that's necessary?

Frasier: I don't have a life anymore. Tuesday I gave up my tickets to the theater. Wednesday, it was the symphony.

Niles: That reminds me, weren't you going to the opera on Friday?

FRASIER TAKES TWO TICKETS OUT OF HIS POCKET.

Frasier: Yes. Here.

Niles: Thank you. (LOOKING AT TICKETS) *Die Fledermaus.* Oh, well, they're free.

Frasier: Isn't there any way you and Maris . . .?

Niles: Funny you should mention that. Maris and I were just discussing this. We think we should do more to share the responsibility.

Frasier: You mean you'd take him?

Niles: Oh, dear God, no. But we'd be willing to help you pay for a home care worker.

Frasier: A what?

Niles: You know, someone who cooks, and cleans, and can help Dad with his physical therapy.

Frasier: Look, the last thing I need is someone else under foot.

Niles: No, no, someone part-time. That's the beauty of it. They'll only be there when you're not.

Frasier: These angels exist?

Niles: I know of an agency. Let me arrange to have them send a few over to meet you.

Frasier: Niles, I don't know how to thank you. I feel the overwhelming urge to hug you.

Niles: Remember what Mom always said. A handshake is as good as a hug.

Frasier: Wise woman.

THEY SHAKE HANDS.

CUT TO:

Scene J

A BLACK SCREEN. IN WHITE LETTERS APPEARS "THE HEALTH CARE WORKER."

FADE IN:

MONTAGE

INT. HALLWAY OF FRASIER'S BUILDING – DAY – DAY/4
(Frasier, Extras)

A QUICK SEQUENCE OF FRASIER BIDDING FAREWELL TO A NUMBER OF APPLICANTS WITH PLEASANTRIES SUCH AS "THANK YOU VERY MUCH," "YOU'LL BE HEARING FROM US," "IT'S BEEN A PLEASURE."

RESET TO:

INT. HALLWAY – MOMENTS LATER – DAY/4
(Frasier, Extras)

ANOTHER APPLICANT. SHE APPEARS ROBUST, KIND, NEATLY DRESSED: THE EPITOME OF COMPETENCE.

Frasier: I've never been more impressed with any human being in my entire life. It has truly been an honor to meet you.

FRASIER CLOSES THE DOOR.

Frasier (CONT'D) (O.S.): (BLOWING UP) Now what was wrong with that one?!!

THE WOMAN REACTS AND WALKS AWAY.

RESET TO:

INT. FRASIER'S LIVING ROOM – DAY – DAY/4
(Frasier, Martin, Eddie, Daphne)

Martin: She was casing the joint.

Frasier: Casing the joint? She spent two years with Mother Teresa.

Martin: Well, if I were Mother Teresa, I'd check my jewelry box.

SFX: THE DOORBELL RINGS.

Frasier: This is the last one. Can you at least try to keep an open mind?

Martin: I hate this whole stinking idea.

Frasier: There, was that so difficult?

FRASIER OPENS THE DOOR TO REVEAL DAPHNE MOON, AN ENGLISH WORKING CLASS WOMAN IN HER MID TO LATE TWENTIES. AT THIS MOMENT, SHE IS REACHING INTO HER BLOUSE AND ADJUSTING HER BRA.

Daphne: Oh hello. Caught me with my hand in the biscuit tin. (EXTENDING HER HAND) I'm Daphne. Daphne Moon.

Frasier: (THEY SHAKE) Frasier Crane. Won't you come in?

Daphne: Thank you.

SHE ENTERS.

Frasier: This is my father, Martin Crane. Dad, this is Daphne Moon.

THEY EXCHANGE GREETINGS.

Daphne: (RE: EDDIE) And who would this be?

Frasier: That is Eddie.

Martin: I call him Eddie Spaghetti.

Daphne: Oh, he likes pasta?

Martin: No, he has worms.

Frasier: Uh, have a seat, Miss Moon.

Daphne: Daphne. Thank you. (RE: BARCALOUNGER) Oh, will you look at that. What a comfy chair. Like I always say, start with a good piece and replace the rest (INDICATING FRASIER'S FURNITURE) when you can afford it.

SHE SMILES AT FRASIER. SO DOES MARTIN.

Frasier: Uh, yes, well, um, Miss Moon, tell us a little about yourself.

Daphne: Well, I'm originally from Manchester, England.

Frasier: Oh really. Did you hear that, Dad?

Martin: I'm three feet away. There's nothing wrong with my hearing.

Daphne: I've only been in the U.S. for a few months but I have quite an extensive background in home care and physical therapy, as you can see from my résumé. I also . . .

SHE LOOKS AT MARTIN.

Daphne (CONT'D): You were a policeman, weren't you?

Martin: Yeah. How did you know?

Daphne: I must confess, I'm a bit psychic. Nothing big. Just little things I sense about people. It's not like I can pick the lottery. If I could, I wouldn't be talking to the likes of you two, now would I?

SHE LAUGHS. MARTIN FINDS THAT AMUSING.

Frasier: Perhaps I should describe the duties around here. You would be responsible for . . .

Daphne: (TO FRASIER) Wait a minute, I'm getting something on you. You're a florist.

Frasier: No, I'm a psychiatrist.

Daphne: Well, it comes and goes. Usually it's strongest during my time of the month. Oh, I guess I let out a little secret there, didn't I?

Frasier: It's safe with us. (CHECKING WATCH) Well, I think we've learned everything we need to know about you. And a dash extra. Thank you very much. We'll be in touch.

Daphne: (TO MARTIN) You must be very proud of your son the psychiatrist.

Martin: Sons. Two sons. Two shrinks. They took after their mother, rest her soul. She was one too. It was quite a ho⋯⋯ ⋯ldn't scratch myself without being analyzed.

Daphne: We Brits don't believe much in psychiatry. I mean, isn't that what friends are for?

Frasier: That's very quaint.

Daphne: (TO EDDIE) You're a dog, aren't you?

Frasier: Well, we'll be calling you, Miss Moon.

Martin: Why wait? You're hired.

Daphne: Oh wonderful!

Frasier: Excuse me. Aren't we getting ahead of ourselves, here? I think we should discuss this. Privately.

Daphne: Oh, of course you should. I completely understand. I'll just pop into the loo. You do have one, don't you?

Frasier: (INDICATING) Yes.

Daphne: I love America.

DAPHNE EXITS.

Frasier: Dad, what do you think you're doing?

Martin: You wanted me to pick one . . . I picked one.

Frasier: But she's a kook. I don't like her.

Martin: What does it matter? She's only going to be here when you're not.

Frasier: Then what's my problem? (CALLING) Daphne.

DAPHNE RE-ENTERS.

Frasier (CONT'D): You've been retained.

Daphne: Oh, wonderful. I had a premonition I would.

Frasier: *Quelle Surprise.*

Daphne: I'll move my things in tomorrow.

Frasier: Wait a minute. Move in? There must be some misunderstanding. This isn't a live-in position.

Daphne: Oh dear. The lady at the agency said . . .

Frasier: Well, the lady at the agency was wrong. This is a part-time position. I'm afraid this just won't work out.

FRASIER STARTS TO USHER HER OUT.

Martin: Wait a minute, Frasier. I want to talk about this.

Frasier: Dad, there's nothing to discuss.

Daphne: You two need to talk. I'll pop back in here and enjoy some more of your African erotic art.

DAPHNE HEADS FOR THE BATHROOM.

Martin: Check out the one over the towel rack. You gotta be young to try that.

Frasier: Perhaps it's best if you leave.

Daphne: Well, all right.

Frasier: We'll contact you. If not by telephone, then through the toaster.

SHE EXITS.

Frasier: I'm not having another person living in this house.

Martin: Give me one good reason why.

Frasier: Well, for one thing there's no room for her.

Martin: What about the room across the hall from mine?

Frasier: My study?! You expect me to give up my study? Where I read, where I do my most profound thinking?

Martin: Use the can like the rest of the world. (THEN) You'll adjust.

Frasier: I don't want to adjust. I've done enough adjusting. I'm in a new city, I have a new job, I'm freshly divorced, I'm separated from my little boy, which by itself would make me nuts, and now my father and his dog are living with me. I think that's enough on my plate. The whole idea of getting someone in here was to help ease my burden, not to add to it.

Martin: Did you hear that, Eddie? We're a burden.

Frasier: Dad, you're twisting my words. I meant burden in its most positive sense.

Martin: Oh, as in "Gee what a lovely burden?"

Frasier: Something like that, yes.

Martin: Hey, you're not the only one getting screwed here. Two years ago I'm sailing toward retirement and some punk robbing a convenience store puts a bullet in my hip. Next thing you know, I'm trading my golf clubs in for one of these. (HE HOLDS UP THE WALKER) I had a lot of plans too, you know, and this may come as a shock, Sonny Boy, but one of them wasn't living with you.

Frasier: I'm just trying to do the right thing here, trying to be the good son.

Martin: Oh, don't worry, after I'm gone, you can live guilt-free knowing that you've done right by your papa.

Frasier: That's what you think this is all about, guilt?

Martin: Isn't it?

Frasier: Of course it is! But the point is, I did it. I took you in. And I've got news for you . . . I wanted to do it. Because you're my father. And you know how you repay me? Ever since you moved in here, it's been a snide comment about this or a smart little put-down about that. Well, I've done my best to make a new home for you here and once, just once, would it have killed you to say thank you? One lousy thank you?

THERE'S A PAUSE.

Martin: C'mon, Eddie. It's past your dinner time.

HE AND EDDIE EXIT TO THE KITCHEN. FRASIER ANGRILY EXITS, SLAMMING THE DOOR BEHIND HIM.

CUT TO:

Scene K

A BLACK SCREEN. IN WHITE LETTERS APPEARS "LUPE VELEZ."

FADE IN:

INT. RADIO STUDIO – LATER THAT DAY – DAY/4
(Frasier, Roz, Martin [V.O.], Claire [V.O.])

FRASIER COMES BLASTING IN TO HIS BOOTH.

Frasier: They have *got* to move the bathroom closer to the studio!

HE FLINGS HIMSELF INTO THE CHAIR AND PUTS ON HIS HEADPHONES. ROZ POINTS TO HIM. HE SPEAKS INTO THE MICROPHONE.

Frasier (CONT'D): I'll be right back after these messages.

HE PUNCHES A BUTTON ON THE CONSOLE.

Frasier (CONT'D): (TO ROZ, IRRITATED) Can't I just put that on tape?

The Good Son

Roz: Who stole the seat off your bicycle?

Frasier: Oh, sorry, it's this thing with my father and this person he wants to hire . . . I thought I was starting my life over with a clean slate. I had this picture of the way things were going to be and then, I don't know . . .

Roz: Ever heard of Lupe Velez?

Frasier: Who?

Roz: Lupe Velez. The movie star in the thirties. The Mexican Spitfire. Her career hit the skids so she decided to take one final stab at immortality. She figured if she couldn't be remembered for her movies, she'd be remembered for the way she died. And all Lupe wanted was to be remembered. So she plans this lavish suicide. Flowers, candles, silk sheets, white satin gown, full hair and make-up, the works. She takes an overdose of pills, lays on the bed and imagines how beautiful she's going to look on the front page of tomorrow's newspaper. Unfortunately, the pills didn't set well with the enchilada combo plate she sadly chose as her last meal. She stumbles toward the bathroom, trips and falls head first into the toilet. And that's how they found her.

Frasier: Is there a reason you're telling me this?

Roz: Yeah. Even though things may not happen like we planned, they can work out anyway.

Frasier: Remind me again how it worked for Lupe, last seen with her head in the toilet?

Roz: All she wanted was to be remembered. (BEAT) Will you *ever* forget that story?

ROZ GOES BACK INTO HER BOOTH, LOOKS AT THE CLOCK AND POINTS AT FRASIER.

Frasier: Welcome back. Roz, who's our next caller?

Roz: We have Martin on line one. He's having a problem with his son.

Frasier: Hello, Martin. This is Dr. Frasier Crane. I'm listening.

Martin (V.O.): I'm a first-time caller.

FRASIER STIFFENS.

Frasier: Welcome to the program. How can I help you?

Martin (V.O.): I just moved in with my son and, uh, it ain't working. There's a lot of tension between us.

Frasier: I can imagine. Why do you think that's so?

Martin (V.O.): I guess maybe I didn't see he had a nice new life planned out for himself and I kind of got in the way.

Frasier: You know these things are a two way street. Perhaps your son wasn't sensitive enough to see how *your* life was changing.

Martin (V.O.): You got that right. I've been telling him that ever since I got there.

Frasier: I'm sure he appreciated your candor.

Martin (V.O.): But maybe sometimes I've got to learn to keep my trap shut.

Frasier: That's good advice for us all. Anything else?

Martin: (V.O.): I'm worried my son doesn't know that I really appreciate what he's done for me.

Frasier: Why don't you tell him?

Martin (V.O.): You know how it is with fathers and sons. We always have a hard time saying that stuff.

Frasier: Well, if it helps, I suspect your son already knows how you feel.

THERE IS A PAUSE.

Frasier (CONT'D): Is that all?

Martin (V.O.): I guess that's it. Thank you, Dr. Crane.

Frasier: My pleasure, Martin.

Martin (V.O.): Did you hear what I said? I said, thank you.

Frasier: Yes, I heard.

MARTIN HANGS UP. FRASIER JUST SITS THERE WITHOUT SAYING ANYTHING. ROZ INTERRUPTS.

Roz: Uh, Dr. Crane? We have Claire on line four. She's having trouble getting over a break up.

Frasier: Hello, Claire. I'm listening.

Claire (V.O.): I'm, uh, well, I'm a mess. Eight months ago, my boyfriend and I broke up and I can't get over it. The pain isn't going away. It's almost like I'm in mourning.

Frasier: Claire, you *are* in mourning. But you're not mourning the loss of your boyfriend . . .

AS FRASIER CONTINUES THE CALL, WE:

CROSS FADE TO:

Scene L

The Good Son

INT. FRASIER'S LIVING ROOM – LATER THAT NIGHT – NIGHT/4
(Frasier, Martin, Eddie, Daphne)

WE PAN ACROSS THE APARTMENT TO SEE FRASIER AND HIS NEW "FAMILY" WATCHING TV. MARTIN IS SITTING IN HIS BARCALOUNGER. EDDIE, FRASIER AND DAPHNE ARE SITTING ON THE COUCH.

Frasier (V.O.): You're mourning what you thought your life was going to be. Let it go. Things don't always happen how you plan. It's not necessarily bad. It doesn't mean things won't work out anyway.

EDDIE PUTS ONE PAW ON FRASIER'S LEG.

Frasier (CONT'D) (V.O.): Have you ever heard of Lupe Velez?

FADE OUT.

END OF ACT TWO

CALL ME IRRESPONSIBLE

#40571-006

Written by Anne Flett-Giordano & Chuck Ranberg
Created and Developed by David Angell, Peter Casey & David Lee
Directed by James Burrows

ACT ONE

Scene A

A BLACK SCREEN. IN WHITE LETTERS APPEAR "IF YOU SPEAK, THEY WILL LISTEN."

FADE IN:

INT. RADIO STUDIO – DAY – DAY/1
(Frasier, Roz, Hank [V.O.], Marco [V.O.])

FRASIER IS ON THE AIR.

Frasier: The time is four twenty-five and this is Dr. Frasier Cane. Roz, who's our next caller?

Roz: We have Hank on line three. He's having trouble with his neighbor.

Frasier: Go ahead, Hank. I'm listening.

THERE'S A PAUSE.

Hank (V.O.): Am I on?

Frasier: Yes. I'm listening. (PAUSE) Hank, are you there?

Hank (V.O.): Am I on?

Frasier: Yes. Turn down your radio and just speak into the phone.

Hank (V.O.): Hello?

Frasier: Stop trying to hear yourself. We're on a seven second delay.

Hank (V.O.): Can you hear me?

Frasier: (DISCONNECTS CALL) Oh for crying out loud. People, would you please turn off your stupid radios?

Call Me Irresponsible

HE SEES <u>ROZ</u> SHAKING HER HEAD.

Frasier (CONT'D): I mean, just those of you calling in. Who else have we got, Roz?

Roz: On line two we have Marco. He's having relationship problems.

Frasier: Hello, Marco. I'm listening.

Marco (V.O.): Well I . . . I started seeing this woman two years ago. I think it was two years ago . . . It was right around Thanksgiving . . . Yeah, the leaves on the trees were changing . . .

Frasier: Close enough. What's your problem?

Marco (V.O.): It's not really my problem, it's more like her problem. Lately, she keeps pressing me for a commitment.

Frasier: Well, what's holding you back?

Marco (V.O.): I don't know. I just . . . I guess I just want to keep my options open. You know, in case somebody better comes along?

Frasier: Somebody better comes along? Somebody better comes along? Marco, Marco, Marco! Do you hear yourself?

Marco (V.O.): No, I turned my radio off after you blasted that other guy.

Frasier: I suggest you give your motives a thorough examination, and if you can't make a commitment, then you owe it to both of you to break it off.

Marco (V.O.): Yeah?

Frasier: *Yeah.* Thank you for your call. (DISCONNECTS THE CALL, CONTINUES) What's with guys like that anyway? Roz, you've been around the block a few times. You ever meet anyone like Marco?

Roz: They're all Marcos. You can't swing a dead cat without hitting a Marco.

Frasier: Come on now, if they were all Marcos no one would be having a relationship.

Roz: Well I'm not, my sister's not, none of my friends are. I think we may have entered the Marco Decade.

Frasier: What do you think, Seattle? Are there any non-Marcos out there? Or is Roz just destined to live a life of hopeless, loveless spinsterhood? Back after this.

FRASIER HITS A BUTTON ON HIS PANEL. ROZ TAKES OFF HER HEADPHONES.

Roz: (SARCASTIC) Gee, and to think I was this close to calling in sick today.

AS WE:

FADE OUT.

Scene B

A BLACK SCREEN. IN WHITE LETTERS APPEARS " 'TWAS TWO MONTHS BEFORE CHRISTMAS . . ."

FADE IN:

<u>INT. FRASIER'S LIVING ROOM – THAT NIGHT – NIGHT/1</u>
(Martin, Daphne, Frasier, Eddie)

<u>SPFX: FIRE IN FIREPLACE</u>

DAPHNE IS ADJUSTING A CAMERA ON A TRIPOD, AIMING IT TOWARD THE FIREPLACE. THERE ARE THREE HUMAN-SIZED STOCKINGS AND ONE LITTLE EDDIE STOCKING HUNG ABOVE THE FIREPLACE. MARTIN IS PUTTING THE FINISHING TOUCHES ON AN ARTIFICIAL CHRISTMAS TREE.

Martin: This feels weird. It isn't even Halloween yet. Do we really have to do this?

Daphne: If we're going to have a picture for the Christmas card, we've got to make it look like Christmas.

Martin: I don't see why we can't do what my wife and I used to do: Put Frasier and Niles in matching sweaters and sit them on the hood of the car.

Daphne: Well, this year we're going to be a little more artistic, all right?

Martin: Where the hell is Frasier anyway? I could use a little help.

Daphne: He's still napping. It's good for him. You know, my grandfather used to nap every afternoon. He lived to be ninety-three.

Martin: Really?

Daphne: He'd lie there on the sofa and you couldn't wake him for the world. Grammy would say, "He might as well be a dead man." Then of course one day we couldn't wake him because he really was a dead man. Poor Grammy. For weeks she kept insisting, "He's napping, he's napping."

MARTIN PUTS THE LAST ORNAMENT ON THE TREE.

Martin: Okay, I'm going to plug her in.

MARTIN PLUGS THE TREE IN AND IT LIGHTS UP. THEY BOTH STAND BACK AND ADMIRE THEIR WORK.

Daphne: Oh, that's lovely. (SINGING) "Deck the halls with boughs of holly . . ."

MARTIN JOINS IN.

Martin/Daphne: ". . . Fa la la la la la la la la. 'Tis the season to be jolly. Fa la la la la la la la la . . ."

AS DAPHNE AND MARTIN CONTINUE SINGING, <u>FRASIER ENTERS</u>, TAKING IN THE SCENE. DISORIENTED, HE LOOKS AT HIS WATCH, THEN FEELS HIS FACE.

Frasier: Exactly how long have I been asleep?

Martin: Oh good, you're up. Now we can get this picture taken.

Frasier: What picture?

Daphne: Our Christmas card picture. We told you about it last week, remember?

Frasier: Well, can we at least wait a few minutes? I'm still kind of puffy.

Daphne: Oh, you look fine. Now, the theme this year is "Santa's Workshop." Everybody put on your little elf hats.

DAPHNE AND MARTIN PUT THEIR ELF HATS ON.

Frasier: I am not putting that on my head. I am a respected professional.

Martin: But if you don't, it'll look stupid.

Frasier: Oh, I think that ship has already sailed.

Martin: Put the hat on, Frasier.

Frasier: Don't tell me what to do.

Martin: I am telling you. Put the hat on.

Frasier: No! You can't make me.

Daphne: Boys, boys, please don't fight. Are you forgetting what day it is?

Frasier: It's October twenty-first.

Martin: Could we just get the picture taken, please?

DAPHNE FINISHES SETTING UP THE CAMERA.

Daphne: All right, I've got it all set. Thirty seconds, gents.

MARTIN AND FRASIER START TO POSE. DAPHNE JOINS THEM.

Daphne (CONT'D): Wait, something's missing. Where's Eddie?

Martin: He's in the bathroom having a drink. (CALLING) Eddie!

EDDIE TROTS IN. HE'S WEARING REINDEER ANTLERS AND BELLS AROUND HIS NECK. HE GETS INTO THE PICTURE JUST AS THE CAMERA FLASHES.

SPFX: CAMERA FLASH

Frasier: I can always hope there's a postal strike.

AS WE:

FADE OUT.

Scene C

A BLACK SCREEN. IN WHITE LETTERS APPEARS "M & M'S AND SYMPATHY."

FADE IN:

INT. RADIO STUDIO - NEXT DAY - DAY/2
(Frasier, Roz, Catherine)

FRASIER IS ON THE AIR.

Frasier: Well, that's it for today's show. This is Dr. Frasier Crane. Now go out there and make it a great day, Seattle.

FRASIER TAKES OFF HIS HEADSET. ROZ ENTERS HIS BOOTH, CARRYING AN 8 X 10 GLOSSY.

Roz: There's a fan in the hall who wants your autograph.

Frasier: All right, give it here. I'll sign it.

ROZ HANDS FRASIER THE PICTURE. HE LOOKS THROUGH THE GLASS AND SEES CATHERINE, A VERY ATTRACTIVE WOMAN. SHE SEES HIM LOOKING AND SMILES SWEETLY.

Frasier (CONT'D): Is that her?

Roz: Uh-huh.

Frasier: Well, maybe I better handle this in person.

FRASIER TAKES AN 8 X 10 GLOSSY AND EXITS TO THE HALL.

RESET TO:

INT. STUDIO HALLWAY - CONTINUOUS - DAY/2
(Frasier, Catherine)

Frasier (CONT'D): Hello. My producer said you'd like my autograph. How should I make this out?

Catherine: You disgust me! You parasitic fraud!

Frasier: Well, that's different from the usual "best regards."

FRASIER STARTS TO WALK AWAY. CATHERINE PULLS HIM BACK BY HIS ARM.

Catherine: Oh, no, Mister. You're going to listen to me. For once you're going to face the consequences of what happens after you hang up on your callers.

Frasier: What consequences? What are you talking about?

Catherine: I'm Marco's girlfriend. Or should I say ex-girlfriend, thanks to you.

Frasier: Marco? You mean "Marco-who-didn't-want-to-commit" Marco?

Catherine: You damn radio shrinks. You couldn't just tell him to take a little more time. That kind of advice doesn't get big ratings. "Break up with her, get on with your life and ruin hers." Now that's entertainment!

Frasier: Now hold on one minute. I don't hand out advice lightly. Marco clearly stated he wanted to keep his options open.

Catherine: Oh, bull. Marco would never say that.

Frasier: You're right. To be exact he said he was only staying with you until someone better came along.

Catherine: He told you that?

Frasier: He told most of Seattle that.

THIS HITS CATHERINE HARD.

Frasier (CONT'D): I'm sorry I had to tell you, but at least now you know the truth.

CATHERINE TURNS HER BACK TO FRASIER. FRASIER HEADS BACK TO THE STUDIO. HE HEARS HER START TO CRY SOFTLY.

Frasier (CONT'D): Oh no, no. Please don't cry.

CATHERINE CRIES HARDER. FRASIER PUTS A FOLDER OVER HIS MIC.

Frasier (CONT'D): You're in a place of business.

Catherine: Boy, I can really pick 'em, can't I?

Frasier: Hey, don't go there. This is not your fault. You're an attractive woman. A tad over-emotional perhaps.

CATHERINE STARTS TO CRY EVEN HARDER. SHE TURNS HER BACK TO HIM.

Frasier (CONT'D): But some men like that.

FRASIER AWKWARDLY TRIES TO COMFORT HER, NOT KNOWING WHETHER TO OFFER HIS HANDKERCHIEF, PUT HIS ARM AROUND HER OR PAT HER ON THE SHOULDER.

Frasier (CONT'D): Ssh . . . It's okay . . . It's okay . . .

A TECHNICIAN ENTERS THE BOOTH.

Frasier (CONT'D): Hey, Stan. How're you doing? Nice job on the promos.

CATHERINE IS STILL SOBBING.

Frasier (CONT'D): (TO CATHERINE) Would you like to maybe sit down?

SHE SHAKES HER HEAD.

Frasier (CONT'D): How about a glass of water?

SHE SHAKES HER HEAD AGAIN. FRASIER LOOKS AROUND DESPERATELY AND SPOTS THE CANDY MACHINE.

Frasier (CONT'D): M & M's?

CATHERINE LOOKS UP AND DABS HER EYES.

Catherine: Plain or peanut?

Frasier: Whichever you like?

Catherine: (SNIFFLES) Peanut.

FRASIER EXITS TO THE CANDY MACHINE. SHE FOLLOWS HIM OUT. DURING THE FOLLOWING, FRASIER PUTS SOME CHANGE INTO THE MACHINE AND GETS THE M&M'S.

Catherine (CONT'D): I guess I should've seen this coming. Marco practically had a coronary when I brought over a toothbrush to keep at his apartment.

HE HANDS HER THE M & M'S AND THEY SIT DOWN ON CHAIRS NEXT TO THE CANDY MACHINE.

Catherine: Thanks. (OFFERING CANDY) You want one?

Frasier: No, thanks. (THEN) If he was that resistant, why did you stay with him?

Catherine: I just wanted it to work. I had so much invested in it.

Frasier: But that's no reason to settle for someone who isn't madly in love with you.

Catherine: Right now, I'm not sure if there are any men out there who are actually capable of falling madly in love.

Frasier: Of course there are. On the most basic level, men and women are the same. We both need to love and be loved, to have someone we feel we matter to, and who matters to us. To make a commitment to another human being is the ultimate expression of our humanity.

Catherine: (TOUCHED) Wow. Your wife is really lucky.

Frasier: I'm sure she'd agree with you, especially now that our marriage is over.

Catherine: Oh God, I'm sorry.

Frasier: It practically destroyed me. Even now . . . To this day . . . Well . . . Maybe I will have one of those M & M's.

FRASIER HELPS HIMSELF FROM HER BAG.

Catherine: Hey, you like the yellow ones too.

Frasier: Yeah, people try to tell you they're all the same.

Catherine: Why are relationships always so hard? And so fattening?

Frasier: They aren't always. In med school, I heard of a documented case of a couple that met, got along and lived happily ever after.

AMUSED, CATHERINE CHUCKLES.

Catherine: I don't mind the happily ever after part. It's the dating part. If I have to tell one more stranger the story of my life over northern Italian cuisine, I'm going to choke on a breadstick.

Frasier: I know. I've often felt it would save a lot of energy if we could just exchange résumés over appetizers.

Catherine: Half the time I'm ready to exchange goodbyes over appetizers.

Frasier: At least you don't get stuck with the bill.

Catherine: You haven't dated much lately, have you?

Frasier: No. I've grown quite used to eating alone.

Catherine: I always turn on the TV so it at least feels like there's someone else in the room.

Frasier: Is that what you'll be doing tonight?

Catherine: Unless I just keep eating M & M's, which is a distinct possibility.

Frasier: Look . . . I know this is a little unusual, but we seem to be having a rather nice conversation and, well . . . There's a little place around the corner that has pretty good food, not a breadstick in sight . . . (QUICKLY) Forgive me, that was terribly presumptuous. I don't even know your name and here I am . . .

Catherine: It's Catherine. And I'd love to. Just give me a minute to fix my make-up.

Frasier: Oh, sure, sure.

HE WATCHES HER EXIT DOWN THE HALLWAY, THEN:

Frasier (CONT'D): Yes!

HE HITS THE CANDY MACHINE. CANDY COMES OUT.

Frasier (CONT'D): All right! Milk Duds!

AS WE:

FADE OUT.

END OF ACT ONE

ACT TWO

Scene D

FADE IN:

INT. CAFE NERVOSA – DAY – DAY/3
(Frasier, Catherine, Niles)

IT'S SEVERAL DAYS LATER. FRASIER IS AT A TABLE WITH CATHERINE. THEY ARE HOLDING HANDS, EXAMINING EACH OTHER'S FINGERS.

Frasier: Soft and supple, yet strong, right down to the beautiful almond shaped nails.

FRASIER PULLS HIS HAND AWAY AND ADMIRES IT.

Frasier (CONT'D): You really like the way my hand looks?

Catherine: Uh-huh. What do you see in my hands?

Frasier: My future and my last chance at happiness.

CATHERINE SNORTS AND CAN'T HELP BUT LAUGH.

Frasier (CONT'D): That was a bit much, wasn't it?

Catherine: Yeah, a bit. It looked like the people at the next table were about to stone us with bran muffins.

CATHERINE GETS UP TO LEAVE.

Catherine (CONT'D): I've got to go. I'm late for work.

Frasier: Wait, wait. We haven't decided what we're doing tonight. Shall we dine at Antonio's? Le Cigare Volant?

Catherine: We've gone out the last three nights. Why don't we just stay in?

Frasier: What a wonderful idea. I'll send Dad and Daphne to a movie and I'll cook for you. Be at my house, eight o'clock.

Catherine: I won't be able to get there till eight-thirty. I have to stop off and change.

Frasier: No, no don't ever change. I like you just the way you are.

THE PEOPLE AT THE TABLES NEXT TO THEM GROAN.

Frasier (CONT'D): (TURNING) I know, I know. I'm a little out of practice, okay?

Catherine: See you tonight.

CATHERINE GIVES FRASIER A KISS AND STARTS OUT. NILES ENTERS AND PASSES CATHERINE, WHO EXITS. HE CROSSES OVER TO FRASIER'S TABLE SIGNALLING THE WAITER FOR A COFFEE.

Niles: I'll dispense with the usual adolescent teasing and come straight to the point. Who was that babe-o-rama?

Frasier: Niles, don't try to be hip. You remind me of Bob Hope when he dresses up as the Fonz. Her name is Catherine.

Niles: She's very fetching.

Frasier: She's more than that. She's smart, funny, she's a successful architect, and she has no idea how beautiful she really is.

Niles: So how long have you known her?

Frasier: Three days.

Niles: Have you two . . .?

Frasier: No, as if it's any of your business.

A BEAT.

Niles: But you . . .?

Frasier: Yes, soon.

ANOTHER BEAT.

Niles: We are talking about . . .

Frasier: Of course we are!

A BEAT.

Niles: Sex, right?

Frasier: Yes!

Niles: So, how did you two meet?

THE <u>WAITER APPROACHES</u> AND SETS DOWN A COFFEE FOR NILES.

Frasier: It was just one of those crazy things. She came to the station to chew me out.

Niles: You're kidding.

Frasier: No, a couple of days earlier, her boyfriend called in to my show and I told him to break up with her.

NILES STOPS SIPPING HIS COFFEE AND INHALES SHARPLY.

Frasier (CONT'D): I hope that sound means you burned your tongue.

Niles: Frasier, where are your ethics? You can't date someone who's involved with one of your patients.

Frasier: I'm not. Marco's not a patient. He's a caller. There's a big difference. Besides, I spoke to him before I even met Catherine.

Niles: Ah, rationalization. The last refuge of an unsound argument.

Frasier: Damn it, Niles! I'm not rationalizing. There's no problem here.

Niles: Well, as long as your conscience is clear. I'm not sure if mine would be.

Frasier: Frankly, I don't care about your conscience. I don't need your approval. I don't need you to like it. I don't need you for anything.

FRASIER STARTS TO EXIT.

Frasier (CONT'D): (AN AFTERTHOUGHT) Oh, by the way, my car is in the shop and I need you to give me a ride home from work.

Niles: No problem.

AS FRASIER EXITS, WE:

FADE OUT.

Scene E

A BLACK SCREEN. IN WHITE LETTERS APPEARS "HE'S BAAACK."

FADE IN:

INT. RADIO STUDIO – NIGHT – NIGHT/3
(Roz, Frasier, Marco [V.O.])

ROZ IS IN HER BOOTH. FRASIER ENTERS HIS BOOTH, TAKES HIS SEAT AND PUTS ON HIS HEADSET.

Roz: Ten seconds and I have news for you. Marco's on line two.

Frasier: Marco?

Roz: You know, the guy you got out of the way so you could get his girlfriend for yourself? And I thought this was going to be a dull day. Five seconds.

Frasier: I don't want to talk to him. I'm not talking to him. There's no way I'm talking to him.

Roz: . . . Three . . . two . . .

ROZ GIVES FRASIER THE "YOU'RE ON" SIGN.

Frasier: And we're back. Roz, who do we have on the line?

Roz: Marco.

Frasier: Hello, Marco.

Marco (V.O.): Hi, Dr. Crane. I spoke to you the other day and I took your advice and broke up with my girlfriend.

CUT TO:

INT. NILES' CAR – NIGHT – NIGHT/3
(Niles)

WHILE HE'S DRIVING, NILES IS PUNCHING VARIOUS BUTTONS ON HIS RADIO. WHEN HE HEARS FRASIER'S VOICE, HE TURNS UP THE VOLUME. (DURING THE FOLLOWING, WE'LL INTERCUT BETWEEN NILES' CAR AND THE RADIO STATION.)

Frasier: Well, what can I say but, "Bravo, Marco." Roz, who's our next caller?

Marco (V.O.): Wait, wait, wait. The problem is she's already dating someone else. It really makes me nuts, the thought of her with another guy. It makes me want to pound him.

Frasier: What makes you think she's dating someone else?

Marco (V.O.): Well, the other night I couldn't get her on the phone, so I drove by her place and saw her parked outside talking to some guy in a black BMW.

Frasier: Did you, uh, get a good look at the guy?

Marco (V.O.): No, it was too dark.

Frasier: Oh, thank God.

Marco (V.O.): Why?

Frasier: Well, I'd hate to see you do something rash.

Marco (V.O.): I think I made a big mistake, Doc. Do you think I should ask her to take me back?

Frasier: No! What I mean is . . . no! You don't want your ex-girlfriend, you just don't want anyone else to have her. Isn't that true?

Marco (V.O.): I don't know.

Frasier: Marco, you're not thinking straight now. I am. So let me do your thinking for you. Stop spying on your ex-girlfriend and get on with your life. In fact, you might even think about moving to a new city and starting over.

FRASIER HITS A BUTTON ON HIS CONSOLE.

Frasier (CONT'D): We'll be right back after this commercial break.

FRASIER TAKES OFF HIS HEADPHONES AND PUSHES BACK FROM THE CONSOLE, SPENT. ROZ IS STARING AT HIM THROUGH THE GLASS.

Frasier (CONT'D): *What*?!

AS WE:

FADE OUT.

Scene H

A BLACK SCREEN. IN WHITE LETTERS APPEARS "STOP! IN THE NAME OF LOVE."

FADE IN:

INT. NILES' CAR – NIGHT – NIGHT/3
(Frasier, Niles)

NILES IS PARKED AT THE CURB. THE CAR DOOR OPENS AND FRASIER GETS IN.

Frasier: Thanks for picking me up.

NILES STARTS THE CAR AND PULLS OUT INTO TRAFFIC.

Niles: No problem, Frasier. It's only a few miles out of my way . . . At rush hour. But I don't mind, really. It gave me a chance to listen to your show.

Frasier: I see.

Niles: I just have one question for you. Can you honestly tell me that the advice you gave Marco was based on his best interest and not on yours?

Frasier: No, I can't, Niles. And you know what else? I don't care. I'm in love and I don't care. Catherine's mine now. I'm in and Marco's out!

Niles: You're insane.

Frasier: Perhaps. But you just went through a stop sign.

NILES HITS THE BRAKES. THEY LUNGE FORWARD IN THEIR SEATS.

Frasier (CONT'D): Not now . . . we're in the middle of the intersection.

NILES GIVES IT THE GAS.

Frasier (CONT'D): I haven't felt this way in ages. There's an excitement about this. I feel tingly, Niles.

Niles: Tingly?

Frasier: That's right . . . tingly. I'm tingling all over. My senses are alive.

HE ROLLS DOWN THE CAR WINDOW.

Frasier (CONT'D): (YELLING OUT) Do you hear that, Seattle? I'm tingly! (A BEAT, REACTING) Hey, same to you buddy!

Niles: This goes against everything you stand for. This is not you.

Frasier: I know. That's what makes it so remarkable. Through my entire career as a psychiatrist, if I would so much as approach a breach in ethics it would make me queasy. I would actually get a sick feeling in the pit of my stomach, but this time . . .

Niles: Tingly?

Frasier: Bingo. Hey Niles, I've got an idea.

Niles: What?

Frasier: Next stop light, Chinese fire drill.

Niles: I'm warning you, Frasier. I'll mace you if I have to.

AS WE:

FADE OUT.

Scene J

FADE IN:

INT. FRASIER'S LIVING ROOM – LATER THAT NIGHT – NIGHT/3
(Catherine, Frasier, Eddie)

FRASIER AND CATHERINE ARE SEATED AT THE DINING ROOM TABLE. THEY HAVE JUST FINISHED THEIR MEAL. FRASIER POURS THE LAST BIT OF WINE INTO CATHERINE'S GLASS. THE LIGHTS ARE LOW AND SOFT MUSIC IS PLAYING IN THE BACKGROUND.

Catherine: That was the most delicious Salmon Marseilles I ever tasted.

Frasier: Then you should try my "salmon chanted evening."

Catherine: Tell me you didn't say that.

Frasier: It was the Lafitte talking. "Lafitte don't fail me now."

Catherine: Stop, stop.

FRASIER RISES, TAKES HIS AND CATHERINE'S DISHES AND SILVERWARE AND EXITS TO THE KITCHEN. CATHERINE FOLLOWS HIM AND LEANS AGAINST THE ISLAND.

Catherine (CONT'D): Have you ever made love in the kitchen?

FRASIER DROPS THE PLATES INTO THE SINK.

Frasier: Well, the dishes are done.

FRASIER QUICKLY MOVES TO CATHERINE AND THEY GO INTO A

PASSIONATE EMBRACE. WHILE KISSING, THEIR BODIES INTERTWINE, HE
BENDS HER BACK ONTO THE ISLAND AND HER LEG WRAPS AROUND HIS
FLANK. THIS GOES ON FOR A FEW BEATS UNTIL FRASIER'S PASSIONATE
MOANING SOUNDS BECOME QUEASY MOANING SOUNDS. HE PUSHES
CATHERINE AWAY.

Catherine: What's the matter?

Frasier: I'm sorry. I'm feeling a little queasy. Maybe I'm just not a kitchen person.

FRASIER EXITS INTO THE LIVING ROOM. CATHERINE FOLLOWS. FRASIER
TAKES A FEW DEEP BREATHS.

Catherine: Maybe you're just too warm.

SHE UNBUTTONS FRASIER'S SHIRT.

Frasier: Yeah, yeah, that's it. You look much too warm too.

FRASIER STARTS UNBUTTONING CATHERINE'S SHIRT. THEY CONTINUE TO
UNBUTTON, EMBRACE AND KISS, MOVING ACROSS THE ROOM UNTIL THEY
FALL ONTO THE SOFA. ONCE AGAIN, FRASIER STARTS MAKING
"QUEASING" NOISES.

Catherine: I'm sorry. Was I kneeling on you?

FRASIER CROSSES TO THE BALCONY.

Frasier: No, I think I just need a little fresh air. Are you feeling okay?

Catherine: I'm fine.

Frasier: Damn. It wasn't the fish.

Catherine: Well, there is a bug going around.

Frasier: No, it's not a bug.

Catherine: Then what is it?

A LONG BEAT, THEN:

Frasier: It's us. It's when we kiss and touch. I get queasy. It used to be tingly, now it's
queasy.

Catherine: Are you saying that the thought of making love to me makes you sick to your
stomach?

Frasier: Yes. But don't take it personally.

Catherine: Gee, why would I do that?

SHE RISES.

Frasier: It's not you. It's me. Every time I come close to breaching my ethics, I get sick.

Catherine: When did you breach your ethics?

Frasier: Marco called my show today. He wanted to get back together with you. I told him not to.

Catherine: So?

Frasier: So I have a feeling I told him that not because it was best for him, but because it was best for me.

Catherine: Who cares?

Frasier: Any psychiatrist worth his salt cares. That's why we don't get personally involved with our patients, or their girlfriends.

Catherine: Are you saying you want to break up with me?

Frasier: I don't want to. I have to. If I don't I'll throw up on your shoes.

Catherine: I don't believe this is happening. How can this be so easy for you?

Frasier: Easy? This is killing me. Don't you think I'd like to pick you up right now, carry you over to that Eames Classic and show you why it's the best engineered chair in the world?

Catherine: Then why don't you?

Frasier: I told you. I can't.

Catherine: And nothing will change your mind?

Frasier: I'm sorry.

Catherine: Well thanks a lot, Dr. Crane.

SHE CROSSES TO GET HER COAT.

Catherine (CONT'D): First, you screw up things with Marco and now you're dumping me. And to think, I was going to have sex with you. (TWISTING THE KNIFE) And it was going to be hot, like you've never had before. I'm talking steamy, sweat dripping down your back, neighbors pounding on the walls kind of sex. But hey, you won't be alone tonight. You've got your ethics.

CATHERINE CROSSES TO THE DOOR, THEN TURNS TO FRASIER.

Catherine (CONT'D): By the way, the fish was dry.

SHE EXITS.

Frasier: (CALLING AFTER HER) That was a cheap shot!

FRASIER CROSSES TO THE WINDOW AND SITS IN THE EAMES CLASSIC, LOOKING OUT AT THE SEATTLE SKYLINE. EDDIE ENTERS AND JUMPS UP ON THE FOOTSTOOL. HE STARES AT FRASIER.

Frasier (CONT'D): I envy you, Eddie. The biggest questions you ever face are "Who's going to feed me?" and "Who's going to walk me?" I won't have that kind of joy for another forty years . . .

AS FRASIER CONTINUES TO STARE AT THE SKYLINE, WE:

FADE OUT.

END OF ACT TWO

Scene K

FADE IN:

INT. FRASIER'S LIVING ROOM – NIGHT – NIGHT/1
(Frasier, Martin, Daphne, Eddie)

OVER THE END CREDITS WE SEE A SERIES OF REJECTED PHOTOS FROM THE CHRISTMAS CARD SHOOT.

FADE OUT.

END OF SHOW

A MIDWINTER NIGHT'S DREAM

#40571-015

Written by Anne Flett-Giordano & Chuck Ranberg
Created and Developed by David Angell, Peter Casey & David Lee
Directed by David Lee

ACT ONE

Scene A

FADE IN:

INT. CAFE NERVOSA – DAY – DAY/1
(Niles, Frasier, Eric, Daphne)

FRASIER AND NILES ARE AT A TABLE GIVING THEIR ORDER TO THE LONG-HAIRED WAITER, ERIC.

Niles: Double cappuccino, half-caf, nonfat milk, with enough foam to be aesthetically pleasing, but not so much that it would leave a mustache.

Eric: Cinnamon or chocolate on that?

Niles: (TO FRASIER) They always make this so complicated. (THEN, TO ERIC) Cinnamon.

Eric: (TO FRASIER) And you?

Frasier: Let's see, I think I'm in the mood for . . .

DAPHNE ENTERS THE CAFE. NILES INSTANTLY PERKS.

Niles: Oh look, it's Daphne. Daphne!

UPON HER APPROACH, FRASIER AND NILES START TO RISE.

Daphne: Hello, I thought I might run into you here. Sit, sit. I just stopped in for a bag of beans. We're running low at home.

Frasier: I'll have . . .

Eric: (TO DAPHNE) Can I get you something?

Daphne: Two pounds of . . .

Eric/Daphne: . . . the Kenya blend.

40

Daphne: You remembered.

Eric: Hard to forget.

Frasier: Excuse me. You never got my order.

Eric: (IGNORING FRASIER) Most people find that blend too intense.

Daphne: Not me. I like something that holds its body on my tongue.

NILES KNOCKS OVER THE SUGAR.

Frasier: (TO ERIC) Uh, we seem to have spilled something here.

ERIC TOSSES FRASIER A TOWEL.

Eric: (TO DAPHNE) I don't suppose you'd be interested in something robust, if it didn't come on too strong?

Daphne: If it was a little bit sweet I might take a liking to it.

AS FRASIER CLEANS OFF THE TABLE, NILES GRABS THE TOWEL FROM HIM AND WIPES HIS BROW.

Eric: Would you like to step over to the counter and try my special blend?

Daphne: I'd love to.

THEY CROSS TO THE COUNTER.

Frasier: (CALLING OUT AFTER THEM) Nothing for me, thanks.

Niles: Frasier, that man is hitting on our Daphne. I don't know how she stands it.

AT THE COUNTER, DAPHNE AND ERIC LAUGH.

Frasier: Yes, she's a brave little soul.

Niles: Look at him, he's running his dirty little eyes all over her.

Frasier: Apropos of nothing, Niles, how are things with you and Maris?

Niles: You're not implying that my concern for Daphne's welfare is anything less than pure, are you?

Frasier: I don't know. You tell me.

Niles: You know, that's your great shortcoming. You're always distrustful. You're always suspicious. Sometimes you just have to have faith that people are . . . (NOTICING ERIC AND DAPHNE) What the hell is he doing now?!

Frasier: I believe he's bagging her beans.

Niles: (ALARMED) What?! (THEN, REALIZING) Oh, yes. Well, of course.

DAPHNE CROSSES BY THEIR TABLE ON THE WAY OUT. SHE'S ALL AGLOW.

Daphne: Eric over there is taking me to a club to hear his band tonight. I realize it's not my regular night off but I'll switch it with Saturday, if it's all right with you. Isn't he cute? I already have a nickname for him: Eric the Red. It fancies him, doesn't it? He looks a bit like a Viking. Ta.

DAPHNE STARTS TO EXIT, THEN STOPS.

Daphne (CONT'D): Oh, look at me. I almost forgot my beans. Earth to Daphne.

DAPHNE TAKES HER BAG OF COFFEE AND EXITS, GIGGLING MERRILY.

Frasier: (CALLING AFTER HER) Why don't you just take the night off.

NILES IS BESIDE HIMSELF.

Niles: How could she like him? The man has community college written all over him.

Frasier: Niles, what is going on here? This infatuation with Daphne is getting way out of hand.

Niles: You mean it's noticeable?

Frasier: Painfully. Speaking as your older brother, I have to tell you it's getting embarrassing. I didn't think much about it when it was a simple flirtation, but now I'm wondering if it isn't symptomatic of something going on with you and Maris.

NILES IS SILENT.

Frasier (CONT'D): Well is it?

Niles: Oh, I can't lie to you, Frasier. Truth is, Maris and I are in a bit of a rut. We seem to have lapsed into this gray, numbing blandness.

Frasier: But that's nothing to be worried about. That's a fairly common thing after, what, fifteen years of marriage?

Niles: Nine.

Frasier: (ASTONISHED) Really. (THEN) Maybe you just need to find a way to spice things up.

Niles: You mean boudoir-wise?

Frasier: Well, for starters.

Niles: Like how?

Frasier: Well, I'm sure you and Maris could . . . you could . . . Well, it's you and Maris, so . . . I'm stumped.

AS WE:

FADE OUT.

Scene B

FADE IN:

INT. RADIO STUDIO – DAY – DAY/1
(Roz, Frasier)

ROZ IS IN HER BOOTH AS FRASIER ARRIVES FOR WORK.

Frasier: Hey Roz, how are you?

Roz: Do you really want to know how I am or are you just making conversation? Because if you really want to know how I am, I'll tell you.

Frasier: I was just making conversation. Actually, I need your advice.

Roz: On what?

Frasier: A subject in which you're quite well versed: sex.

Roz: How can I help you?

Frasier: This isn't about me. This is advice for a friend.

Roz: Uh-huh.

Frasier: No really. What do *you* do when the romance starts to go out of a relationship?

Roz: I get dressed and go home.

Frasier: Let's pretend you were actually capable of a long-term relationship. What would you do to keep things cooking?

Roz: Well, once I had a boyfriend take me out to a bar and we pretended we were strangers picking each other up. That was kind of hot.

Frasier: So you used fantasy and role playing.

Roz: Yeah, it was so much fun we tried it again. Only that time he got so into it he went home with someone else.

Frasier: Sorry.

Roz: Oh hell, she was gorgeous. One more drink and I would've gone home with her. My point is, women need to see the men they make love to as exciting, romantic figures. If you want to keep this woman interested, try creating a fantasy for an evening. Personally, I think you'd make a wonderful fireman.

Frasier: I told you we're not talking about me.

Roz: Yeah, right. Trust me. You'd look adorable with a big red hat and an axe. Almost showtime, Sparky.

FRASIER CROSSES INTO HIS BOOTH.

Frasier: Roz, I'm telling you it's not me. But if it were, I'll have you know that Frasier Crane would not have to rely on costumes and props to keep a woman trembling on the threshold of ecstasy. Although I do recall one steamy night when my ex-wife and I played a rousing little game of escaped convict and the warden's daughter.

ROZ POINTS TO THE ON-AIR SIGN. IT'S LIT UP. FRASIER REACTS.

Frasier (CONT'D): (OVER INTERCOM) How long have I been on?

Roz: Long enough.

Frasier: Celebrity voice of Dr. Frasier Crane impersonated.

AS WE:

FADE OUT.

Scene C

A BLACK SCREEN. IN WHITE LETTERS APPEARS "AHOY MATEY!"

FADE IN:

INT. FRASIER'S LIVING ROOM – NIGHT – NIGHT/2
(Frasier, Niles, Martin, Daphne, Eric)

IT'S THE MIDDLE OF THE NIGHT. THE ROOM IS DARK AND EMPTY.

SFX: DOORBELL. MORE DOORBELL. FRANTIC DOORBELL.

FRASIER ENTERS, TYING HIS ROBE. HE FLICKS ON THE LIGHTS AS HE CROSSES TO THE DOOR AND CHECKS THROUGH THE PEEPHOLE.

Frasier: Niles?!

HE OPENS THE DOOR TO NILES, WHO ENTERS WEARING A RAINCOAT. HE IS VERY AGITATED.

Niles: I'm sorry, Frasier, but the most horrible thing has happened. Maris kicked me out.

Frasier: Why? What for?

NILES TAKES OFF HIS RAINCOAT TO REVEAL A PIRATE COSTUME –
RUFFLED SHIRT, STRIPED PANTALOONS, AND A PLASTIC SWORD TIED ON
HIS SASH.

Frasier (CONT'D): Oh dear.

MARTIN ENTERS IN HIS ROBE.

Martin: What's going on out here? Niles?

Niles: Hello, Dad.

MARTIN LOOKS AT HIM FOR A LONG BEAT, THEN TURNS BACK.

Martin: Never mind, I don't want to know.

Niles: Dad, wait, there's a perfectly reasonable explanation for the way I'm dressed. I
was trying to create a romantic fantasy for Maris by dressing up as the dashing pirate,
Jean Lafitte.

Martin: (TO FRASIER) Why is he telling me? I said I don't want to know.

Niles: I'm just trying to explain.

Frasier: Fine, but keep in mind I reserve the right to yell "stop" at any time.

Niles: My plan was to leave a treasure map downstairs for Maris, with clues that would
lead her to my whereabouts, then hide in the linen closet and wait for her to find me.

Martin: Dressed like that?

NILES TAKES THE EYEPATCH OUT OF HIS POCKET.

Niles: Actually, at the time I was only wearing my eyepatch. Though, technically, is it still
an eyepatch when you're wearing it on your . . .

Frasier: Stop!

Martin: Go on, Niles. (TO FRASIER) Sorry. I'm hooked.

Niles: There I was, lying in wait, with my little plastic sword clenched in my teeth, when
suddenly the closet door was thrown open and I found myself face to face with the
upstairs maid. She began screaming what I gather were some very unflattering things in
idiomatic Guatemalan, when Maris stumbled upon the scene and completely
misconstrued it. The next thing I knew she ordered me out of the house. I barely had
time to grab my pantaloons and buckle my swash.

A BEAT, THEN MARTIN BURSTS INTO LAUGHTER.

Niles (CONT'D): Dad . . . Dad, it's not funny.

A BEAT. THEN MARTIN TRIES TO SUPPRESS HIS LAUGHTER.

Martin: Where'd you come up with this stupid idea?

Niles: Frasier.

Frasier: All I suggested was some sexual role-playing. You're the one who came up with the Pirates of the Caribbean.

Niles: (COLLAPSING ON SOFA) Oh, I've really bungled this one, haven't I?

Martin: Ah, come on. These things happen. You can stay with us tonight. Tomorrow morning you and Maris will sort things out.

Niles: What if we don't? What will I do then?

Frasier: Well I'm sure they can always use an extra busboy at the Jolly Roger. (LAUGHS, THEN) Sorry, just trying to lighten the mood. I'll go get you a robe and some blankets.

FRASIER EXITS DOWN THE HALLWAY.

Niles: I'll never be able to face the maid again.

Martin: I don't think it's your face she'll remember. (LAUGHS AGAIN) Sorry. Aw, come on, Niles. Everybody has embarrassing stories to tell. Did I ever tell you about the time I got locked out in the backyard in my underwear?

Niles: Only every Thanksgiving.

Martin: Well, don't worry. I won't be telling that story this year.

FRASIER RE-ENTERS WITH PILLOWS AND BLANKETS.

Frasier: Here we go. Canadian goose down pillows, Egyptian cotton sheets and a vicuna throw, in case you get chilly during the night.

Niles: How perfect.

Martin: I still say a couple of years in the service would have done you two a world of good. Goodnight.

MARTIN EXITS DOWN THE HALLWAY.

Niles: You know, Maris and I have had our disagreements, but it's never been this serious. I feel terrible having her mad at me. It's times like this when I kind of wish I could cry.

Frasier: Don't be embarrassed on my account.

Niles: No, it's not that. I'm just not someone who cries. It's not in my nature. When Maris' Uncle Lyle died, I had to shut my hand in the car door just to make a decent showing at the funeral.

Frasier: You're a complex little pirate, aren't you? Well, goodnight.

FRASIER TURNS OFF THE LIGHT AS HE EXITS. NILES CRAWLS UNDER THE BLANKET AND TRIES TO GET COMFORTABLE. HE CAN'T. AFTER A BEAT, HE PULLS A PLASTIC HOOK OUT FROM UNDER THE COVERS AND DROPS IT ON THE FLOOR. SUDDENLY THE DOOR OPENS, REVEALING DAPHNE AND ERIC. THEY LINGER IN THE DOORWAY, BACKLIT FROM OUTSIDE. NILES SCRUNCHES UP SO AS NOT TO BE SEEN.

Daphne: Thank you again, Eric. I had a wonderful time.

Eric: Me too.

THEY KISS. NILES TRIES TO PEEK OVER THE BACK OF THE SOFA.

Daphne: Well, goodnight.

Eric: Goodnight.

THEY KISS AGAIN. NILES IS DYING.

Daphne: I'd say goodnight again, but I'm starting to get a bit weak in the knees.

Eric: I'll call you.

THEY KISS AGAIN. ERIC EXITS. DAPHNE SHUTS THE DOOR, SIGHS, AND EXITS TO HER ROOM. NILES BEGINS TO CRY LIKE A BABY, AS WE:

FADE OUT.

Scene D

FADE IN:

INT. FRASIER'S LIVING ROOM – DAY – DAY/3
(Daphne, Martin, Frasier, Niles)

FRASIER, MARTIN AND DAPHNE ARE FINISHING BREAKFAST.

Daphne: . . . And he actually composed a song for me. Oh, I don't want to put a curse on it by talking about it too much. I know we've only had a few dates, but already I'm exhibiting the three signs of a woman in love: I can't stop thinking about him, I can't eat, and I bought myself all new underwear.

DAPHNE EXITS TO THE KITCHEN.

Martin: We've got to get her a girlfriend to talk to.

NILES ENTERS FROM THE HALLWAY IN A BATHROBE.

Niles: Well, I just got off the phone with Maris. She went to Arizona for the weekend.

Frasier: Why?

Niles: She said she was so shattered by the experience she had to fly to her favorite spa and contemplate the future of our marriage from a mud bath.

Daphne: It'll probably be good for Mrs. Crane. Eric thinks the earth is very grounding.

Niles: Eric, Eric, Eric! Must everything be about Eric?! (CATCHES HIMSELF) I'm sorry. I'm so upset I don't know what I'm saying.

Frasier: I suggest when Maris returns you two should invest some time in some intensive couples therapy. There's a Reichien workshop that I can . . .

Martin: Blah, blah, blah, blah. Look, all Maris needs is to know that you love her. Buy her some flowers, fix her a romantic dinner when she comes home. That's guaranteed to make any woman forgive you.

Niles: You really think that will work?

Martin: If it didn't, you wouldn't be here.

Niles: Well, I'd be willing to give it a try, but it's impossible. Our cook walked out in sympathy with Maris.

Daphne: I could help you prepare something. I have a late date with Eric . . . (OFF NILES' LOOK) . . . a. My elderly aunt, Erica. But I could come over early and have everything ready by the time Mrs. Crane arrives.

Niles: You would do that for me?

Daphne: Of course.

Niles: Well, thank you, Daphne.

Daphne: What do you think Mrs. Crane would like for dinner?

Niles: Well, you have free rein. Just bear in mind that she can't have shellfish, poultry, red meat, saturated fats, nitrates, wheat, starch, sulfites, MSG or dairy. (BEAT) Did I say nuts?

Frasier: Oh, I think that's implied.

AS WE:

FADE OUT.

Scene E

A BLACK SCREEN. IN WHITE LETTERS APPEARS "IT WAS A DARK AND
STORMY NIGHT." BEAT. THEN: "NO, REALLY."

SFX: THUNDER

FADE IN:

INT. NILES' CONSERVATORY – NIGHT – NIGHT/4
(Niles, Daphne)

SPFX: RAIN AND TREES BLOWING IN THE WIND

IT IS A TALL, VICTORIAN-STYLE ROOM WITH HUGE CONSERVATORY
WINDOWS OVERLOOKING THE WOODS. THINK TOAD HALL. A STONE WALL
FEATURES A ROARING FIREPLACE, IN FRONT OF WHICH IS A SMALL SOFA
AND A COFFEE TABLE SET FOR A ROMANTIC DINNER. THERE IS A GRAND
PIANO, AND TALL PALMS AND LEAFY INDOOR PLANTS ARE EVERYWHERE.
RAIN FALLS HARD AGAINST THE WINDOWS AND THE TREES OUTSIDE
BLOW IN THE WIND. NILES, IN A SMOKING JACKET, ENTERS WITH A DAMP
AND SHIVERING DAPHNE.

Niles: Here Daphne, come warm yourself by the fire. How did you get so wet?

Daphne: One of your trees blew down in your driveway. I had to walk the last hundred
yards. (A BEAT) I must say, you have a beautiful home.

Niles: Thank you. Actually, it was Maris' family home. When I was a mere intern I used
to drive through these hills dreaming of the life I would someday lead, and then one
afternoon there was Maris, looking so helpless, banging at the electric gates with her
little fists and a tire iron.

Daphne: They'd locked her in?

Niles: No, no, that was much later. This time she was coming home from the antique
mart with a rare bell jar once owned by Sylvia Plath, when the gates failed to open.
Naturally I stopped to offer my assistance, and as our hands touched there was a sudden
spark of electricity. Then as if by magic, the gates parted before us, and we took it as a
sign.

Daphne: You knew you were meant to be together.

Niles: Yes. We were married just three short years later.

DAPHNE PICKS UP AN ORNATE CLOCK.

Daphne: Oh, look at this. It's beautiful.

Niles: It's a glockenspiel. We bought it on our honeymoon in Zurich. I brought it down
from the attic to remind Maris of better times. It used to play beautiful music, but it

doesn't anymore. How's that for irony? (THEN) Well, why don't we get you some dry clothes so you can get dinner started and we can get you home in time for your date?

NILES STARTS TO EXIT. DAPHNE BEGINS SOFTLY WEEPING.

Niles (CONT'D): Daphne, what is it?

Daphne: Nothing.

Niles: No, it's definitely something. I'm a psychiatrist, I can read the signs.

Daphne: I'm sorry. I didn't want to spoil your reunion with Mrs. Crane, but . . . (SOBS) Eric broke up with me.

Niles: He did?

Daphne: Yes. He said he couldn't commit to me and his music at the same time. He had to stay focused. I know it was an excuse. I've heard his music. He must have another girl.

SHE STARTS TO CRY. NILES TENTATIVELY PUTS A COMFORTING ARM AROUND DAPHNE. THIS IS PROBABLY AS CLOSE AS THEY'VE EVER BEEN, AND HE CAN'T BUT APPRECIATE IT.

Niles: He's a fool, Daphne. If you can't appreciate you, you're better off without him.

Daphne: Right now I'm not so sure, but thank you, Dr. Crane.

SHE RESTS HER HEAD ON HIS SHOULDER.

SFX: TELEPHONE RINGS

Niles: (PICKS IT UP; INTO PHONE) Niles Crane . . . Oh Maris!

NILES LEAPS TO HIS FEET.

Niles (CONT'D): Where are you? . . . What do you mean you can't come home? . . . Yes, I know it's a bad storm . . .

NILES LOOKS AT DAPHNE, ALL BACKLIT FROM THE FIRE AND GLISTENING FROM THE RAIN. HE DOUBTS HE'S STRONG ENOUGH TO RESIST.

Niles (CONT'D): (INTO PHONE) . . . but I really think you should come home, Maris.

SPFX: ANOTHER FLASH OF LIGHTNING

SFX: MORE THUNDER

Niles (CONT'D): (INTO PHONE) Of course I sound excited, I am excited! . . . (COVERING) To have you home again. No, of course I don't want you to come home if it's not safe. (RESIGNED) All right, I understand. See you tomorrow then. Yes, yes, ditto.

NILES HANGS UP AND TURNS TO DAPHNE.

Niles (CONT'D): (NERVOUSLY) Looks like it's just the two of us.

Daphne: You mean Mrs. Crane won't be coming?

SPFX: ANOTHER HUGE FLASH OF LIGHTNING

SFX: A BIG THUNDERCLAP

LIGHT CUE: LIGHTS GO OUT

THE ROOM IS LIT ONLY BY THE FIREPLACE.

Daphne (CONT'D): Oh my, there goes the electricity. What do we do now?

SPFX: FLASH OF LIGHTNING

WITH A FLASH OF LIGHTNING, WE SEE NILES' LOOK OF TREPIDATION, AS WE:

FADE OUT.

END OF ACT ONE

ACT TWO

Scene H

FADE IN:

INT. FRASIER'S LIVING ROOM – NIGHT – NIGHT/4
(Martin, Frasier)

SPFX: RAIN AND LIGHTNING

MARTIN IS ON THE PHONE IN MID-CONVERSATION.

Martin: (INTO PHONE) No, no the storm's really bad. You shouldn't be driving anyway. Just spend the night. Okay goodnight, Daphne.

HE HANGS UP THE PHONE.

Frasier: You told her to spend the night?

Martin: Yeah. What's the big deal?

Frasier: You know how Niles feels about her.

Martin: Oh, relax. It's just another one of Niles' little crushes. Don't you remember the thing he had for his dental hygienist, Jodi? He had his teeth cleaned so much his gums hemorrhaged.

Frasier: I suppose you're right. Niles is all talk and no action. Besides he'd never try anything with Maris in the house.

Martin: Maris never got home. She's stuck in Arizona.

Frasier: I've got to get Daphne out of there.

Martin: Why?

Frasier: Why?! This is a recipe for disaster. You've got a vulnerable woman and an unstable man in a Gothic mansion on a rainy night. All that's missing is someone shouting "Heathcliff" across the moors.

FRASIER GRABS HIS COAT AND HEADS FOR THE DOOR.

Martin: Wait for me.

MARTIN PICKS UP HIS COAT, TOO, AND FOLLOWS.

Frasier: You're not coming.

Martin: Yes, I'm coming along.

THEY EXIT, AD-LIBBING ARGUMENT.

MUSIC CUE: THE DRAMATIC, OPENING CHORDS OF BEETHOVEN, AS WE:

CUT TO:

Scene J

INT. NILES' CONSERVATORY – NIGHT – NIGHT/4
(Niles, Daphne)

THE MUSIC WE HEAR TURNS OUT TO BE NILES AT THE PIANO, PLAYING PASSIONATELY. THE ROOM IS LIT BY THE FIREPLACE AND BY SEVERAL CANDELABRA. DAPHNE ENTERS IN A SILK PEIGNOIR.

Daphne: Oh Dr. Crane, you play beautifully.

Niles: Thank you.

NILES LOOKS UP AT DAPHNE AND HE GOES COMPLETELY OFF-KEY. HE ATTEMPTS TO END THE SONG IN A SMALL FLOURISH.

Daphne: I found this upstairs in the guest room. I hope it's alright.

Niles: I thought you were going to put on some of Maris' clothes. You know, something bulky from her wool collection.

NILES SITS ON THE KEYS OF THE PIANO.

Daphne: I was, but she's quite a bit smaller than me. This was all I could find that fit. Should I go look for something else?

Niles: No. Yes. No, no, the important thing is that it's big enough and warm enough and silky enough and I have to make a phone call.

AS NILES STARTS TO EXIT, WE:

CUT TO:

Scene K

INT. FRASIER'S LIVING ROOM - NIGHT - NIGHT/4
(Frasier [V.O.], Niles [V.O.], Eddie)

SFX: TELEPHONE RINGS

CLOSE ON: THE PHONE MACHINE AS IT PICKS UP.

Frasier (V.O.): Hello, this is Dr. Frasier Crane. At the sound of the tone, I'm listening.

SFX: PHONE MACHINE BEEP

EDDIE COMES OVER TO LISTEN TO THE FOLLOWING:

Niles (V.O.): Frasier? Frasier, this is Niles. If you're there, please pick up . . . Frasier?
. . . I'll just keep stalling in case you're there . . . All right, I guess you're not there. When you get in, give me a call, okay? Bye.

EDDIE PONDERS THIS, AS WE:

CUT TO:

Scene L

INT. FRASIER'S CAR - NIGHT - NIGHT/4
(Frasier, Martin)

SPFX: RAIN

THE RAIN BEATS DOWN ON THE CAR AS FRASIER AND MARTIN SPEED THROUGH THE NIGHT.

Martin: This is stupid.

Frasier: It is not.

Martin: Look, nothing is gonna happen between them anyway.

Frasier: But what if it does? He's my brother and he loves his wife. Oh, I know, I know. Their marriage isn't everyone's cup of tea, but on some twisted, bizarre level it works for them. And if he did anything stupid to hurt his marriage, he'd be the one to suffer. And I don't want to see my brother suffer.

Martin: Well, I just don't see where you get off telling a grown man what to do. (THEN) Hey, slow down. You're going to miss the turn on to Roosevelt.

Frasier: Dad, I let you come along specifically on the condition that you wouldn't give directions.

Martin: I'm not giving you directions, I'm telling you which way is faster.

Frasier: But if we take Roosevelt it'll add ten minutes.

Martin: Only in sunshine. In rain it's faster.

Frasier: What, do the laws of spatial relationships suddenly change when it rains?

Martin: You get better traction on Roosevelt. Of course you wouldn't need it if you bought the all-weather tires like I told you to, but no, you have to get those fancy German ones . . .

THEY BEGIN TO AD-LIB BICKERING ABOUT GERMANS, RAIN AND TIRES, BOTH TALKING AT ONCE AND NEITHER HEARING THE OTHER, AS WE:

CUT TO:

Scene N

A BLACK SCREEN. IN WHITE LETTERS APPEARS "COLONEL MUSTARD AND MISS SCARLET IN THE CONSERVATORY . . ."

FADE IN:

INT. NILES' CONSERVATORY - NIGHT - NIGHT/4
(Niles, Daphne)

DAPHNE IS SITTING BY THE FIRE DRINKING HER WINE AND DABBING HER EYES WITH A KLEENEX AS NILES ENTERS FROM OUTSIDE WITH AN ARMFUL OF FIREWOOD.

Niles: We'll have to make this last. It's all that's left of the firewood.

DAPHNE LETS OUT A WHIMPER. NILES SITS DOWN BESIDE HER.

Niles (CONT'D): Oh no, don't worry. If this runs out there's an antique sideboard in the drawing room that I suspect is a reproduction. (REALIZES) Oh, it's Eric, isn't it?

Daphne: (NODS) I don't know why I'm being so silly. We weren't together long enough for anything to really happen.

Niles: Sometimes the most powerful feelings come from the promise of what *might* happen . . . (LOOKS AT HER LONGINGLY) Just the anticipation can make all the little hairs on your neck stand on end.

DAPHNE STARES INTO THE FIRE, AS NILES QUICKLY SMOOTHS DOWN HIS NECK HAIRS.

Daphne: Dr. Crane . . .

Niles: Yes, Daphne.

Daphne: We're losing the fire.

Niles: No, we're not. It's burning with the heat of a thousand suns!

Daphne: (INDICATES FIREPLACE) But it's down to its last embers.

Niles: Oh, I'll put some wood on it.

AS NILES CROSSES TO THE FIREPLACE TO RESTOKE THE FIRE, WE:

CUT TO:

Scene P

<u>INT. FRASIER'S CAR – NIGHT – NIGHT/4</u>
(Martin, Frasier)

THE CAR HAS STALLED. FRASIER TRIES THE KEY, BUT THE ENGINE WON'T TURN OVER.

Martin: You flooded it, you flooded it. You had to keep pumping the gas and you flooded it.

Frasier: You can't flood a fuel injected engine.

Martin: Then it must be the rain.

Frasier: It's not the rain. It has nothing to do with the rain. I don't believe this. We're so close to the house. I can see the gargoyles.

Martin: If we'd taken Roosevelt . . .

Frasier: Then we'd be stuck on Roosevelt!

Martin: Never could admit it when you made a mistake.

Frasier: Call the auto club. I'm gonna make a run for it.

FRASIER GIRDS HIMSELF AGAINST THE STORM AND JUMPS OUT. HE SLAMS THE DOOR SHUT. MARTIN ROLLS DOWN THE WINDOW.

Martin: (YELLING) You'll make better time if you take the shortcut around the fountain. (BEAT, THEN) Well same to you.

AS WE:

CUT TO:

Scene R

INT. NILES' CONSERVATORY - NIGHT - NIGHT/4
(Daphne, Niles, Frasier)

NILES AND DAPHNE ARE ON THE FLOOR, RECLINED ON PILLOWS IN FRONT OF THE FIRE.

Daphne: It's always been my problem. I guess I fall in love too fast. The minute I feel that spark, I give my heart away.

Niles: Daphne, you must stop being so hard on yourself. What you see as a fault is also your greatest gift. To be so open and warm and loving . . .

Daphne: And foolish.

Niles: No, you're not foolish. You're perfect.

Daphne: But it was wonderful to be wrapped up in a man's arms.

Niles: Well, it feels equally wonderful to wrap your arms around a woman. If it's the right woman, under the right set of circumstances . . .

THEY ARE VERY CLOSE TO A KISS. IF NILES MADE HIS MOVE RIGHT NOW, SHE'D PROBABLY BE HIS.

SPFX: FLASH OF LIGHTNING AND CLAP OF THUNDER

SFX: MARIS' ANTIQUE CLOCK BEGINS PLAYING MUSIC

Daphne: Dr. Crane, your glockenspiel has sprung to life.

Niles: Oh. (REALIZES) Oh, the clock. My God, it hasn't run like that in years. Maris will be so delighted. Maris . . .

Daphne: You really love her don't you?

Niles: You know, I do. Love's a funny thing, isn't it? I mean, sometimes it's exciting and passionate, and sometimes it's something else. Something comfortable and familiar. That newly exfoliated little face staring up at you across the breakfast table, or sharing a little laugh together when you see someone wearing white after Labor Day . . .

Daphne: I hope someday someone will feel that way about me.

Niles: Don't worry, Daphne. You're a very special person. And someday a man worthy of you will come along, just as soon as the gods create him.

Daphne: That's one of the loveliest things anyone has ever said to me. Thank you, Dr. Crane. You're a good friend.

SHE KISSES HIM ON THE CHEEK. AT THIS MOMENT FRASIER APPEARS LIKE A SPECTER AT THE WINDOW, OR LIKE DUSTIN HOFFMAN IN "THE GRADUATE."

SPFX: LIGHTNING FLASHES

Frasier: (PRIMAL SCREAM) STO-OOOOOOP!

NILES AND DAPHNE REACT. FRASIER RUNS AROUND THE SIDE AND IN A SECOND COMES BURSTING THROUGH THE DOOR. HE IS SOAKED.

Frasier (CONT'D): Have you two gone mad? You'll regret this for the rest of your lives.

Niles: Frasier . . .

Frasier: Look at you two, here, alone, the fire, the candlelight, the nightie.

Daphne: Dr. Crane, you didn't think that Dr. Crane and I were . . . (APPALLED) *Dr. Crane!* You have some nerve to imply that your brother would do anything so deplorable. Why just moments ago he made a beautiful speech about how much he loves his wife. How he cherishes her excruciating little face and how they laugh at white people. (THEN, TO NILES) That didn't sound right.

Niles: Close enough.

Frasier: Well, I certainly didn't mean to suggest . . . Of course, I didn't think you were . . .

Daphne: Then just exactly what was it that you wanted us to stop?

Frasier: Well I wanted you to stop . . . standing here in silence. This is a night for music. Niles, come join me at the piano. Daphne, pour us all some wine.

FRASIER AND NILES CROSS TO THE PIANO AND SIT. DAPHNE POURS SOME WINE.

Frasier (CONT'D): Are you sure everything's alright?

Niles: Yes, and thank you for coming over. Everything is going to be fine. You see, my glockenspiel is working again.

AS FRASIER REVIEWS HIS GRAY'S ANATOMY, WE:

FADE OUT.

END OF ACT TWO

Scene S

(END CREDITS)

FADE IN:

<u>INT. NILES' CONSERVATORY – NIGHT – NIGHT/4</u>
(Frasier, Niles, Daphne, Martin)

<u>SPFX: RAIN</u>

FRASIER, NILES AND DAPHNE SIT AROUND THE PIANO, DRINKING WINE AND SINGING MERRILY. OUTSIDE A WET AND FRAZZLED MARTIN APPEARS. HE PEERS THROUGH THE WINDOW ANGRILY. AS HE STARTS TO LIMP QUICKLY AROUND THE SIDE TO THE DOOR WE:

FADE OUT.

<u>END OF SHOW</u>

SEASON TWO

SLOW TANGO IN SOUTH SEATTLE

#40572-026

Written by Martin Weiss
Created and Developed by David Angell, Peter Casey & David Lee
Directed by James Burrows

ACT ONE

Scene A

A BLACK SCREEN. IN WHITE LETTERS APPEARS, "SLOW TANGO IN SOUTH SEATTLE."

Frasier (V.O.): Hello, Steven. I'm listening.

FADE IN:

INT. RADIO STUDIO - DAY - DAY/1
(Frasier, Roz, Steven [V.O.])

FRASIER IS ON THE AIR.

Steven (V.O.): Well you see, Dr. Crane, my wife Tracy and I are having a baby. I know we're getting a little ahead of ourselves, but there seems to be a lot of different advice about whether it's okay to let your kid climb into bed with you in the mornings and . . .

Frasier: Stop right there, Steven. It's okay. I know I'll always cherish the times my son crawled in with my wife and me - finally there was someone for us to cuddle. *All* relationships need that kind of close and undivided attention. Isn't that so, Roz?

WE SEE ROZ IS READING A BOOK, NOT LISTENING.

Roz: Uh-huh.

Steven (V.O.): But what if you and your wife enjoy, you know, making love in the mornings.

Frasier: Trust me. Once the baby's born that won't be an issue any more. This is Dr. Frasier Crane on KACL. We'll be back after these messages.

FRASIER TAKES OFF HIS HEADSET AND WALKS INTO ROZ'S BOOTH.

Frasier (CONT'D): Roz, how can you be reading now?

Roz: I don't know. It's something I picked up in elementary school and it just stuck.

Frasier: What is it that's so captivating?

ROZ SHOWS HIM WHAT SHE'S READING.

Frasier (CONT'D): (SEES TITLE) *Slow Tango in South Seattle.* Oh, not you too. Why is it every woman I see is carrying that book?

Roz: Because it's impossible to put down. Here, read the first paragraph. I guarantee you'll be hooked.

Frasier: (READING) "There are tangos that come flowing from the wine-colored sea, from the rust of a hundred sunken ships. This is one of those dances."

Roz: Well . . .?

Frasier: There are books that make your stomach rumble and lurch and force your lunch ever upward. This is one of those books.

Roz: Men have no soul. (RE: BOOK JACKET) Except for this one. The future Mr. Roz Doyle, Thomas Jay Fallow.

Frasier: (AMAZED) Thomas Jay Fallow?

Roz: Do you know him?

Frasier: Yes. He used to drop into a neighborhood bar I frequented in Boston. He was a little pretentious. He stuck out like a sore thumb.

Roz: God, you used to drink with Thomas Jay Fallow?

Frasier: Actually, I spent most of my time helping him get through his writer's block. In the future I'll remember to use my powers for good and not evil.

HE DISDAINFULLY CASTS THE BOOK DOWN.

Roz: Well, I don't care what you think about him. He's going to be a guest tomorrow on Amber Edwards' "Book Chat." I want to meet him and you're going to introduce us.

Frasier: Oh, but if I see him, I'm going to have to read his book and tell him how much I liked it. You know how hard it is to lie to someone's face.

Roz: Oh it's easy for someone as sophisticated, charming and articulate as you.

Frasier: Maybe you're right.

Roz: See how easy it is?

AS WE:

FADE OUT.

Scene B

A BLACK SCREEN. IN WHITE LETTERS APPEARS, "HE WAS NOT YET A MAN, YET OH SO MUCH MORE THAN A BOY."

FADE IN:

INT. FRASIER'S LIVING ROOM – THE NEXT MORNING – DAY/2
(Daphne, Niles, Martin, Frasier, Eddie)

DAPHNE AND MARTIN ARE ON THE FLOOR TRYING TO DO LEG EXTENSIONS. EDDIE IS PLAYFULLY INTERFERING, BARKING AND GETTING IN THE WAY.

Daphne: Eight, nine . . . Stop that Eddie.

Martin: He just wants to play. Huh, boy?

Daphne: Well therapy is not a game. (TO EDDIE) Stop, I said. (EDDIE DOESN'T) He's completely ignoring me.

SFX: DOORBELL

DAPHNE GETS UP TO ANSWER IT.

Martin: He doesn't like taking orders.

Daphne: (POINTEDLY) I can't imagine who he gets that from.

SHE OPENS THE DOOR TO NILES, CARRYING A FRAMED PHOTO.

Daphne (CONT'D): Oh, hello, Dr. Crane.

Niles: Hello, Daphne.

Martin: (FROM FLOOR) Hey, Niles.

Niles: Ah. I see you're doing your exercises.

Daphne: That's right, and if someone doesn't let us get on with them he's going to get a little spank on his fanny.

NILES REACTS.

Martin: (GETTING UP) Oh, leave Eddie alone.

Niles: Oh, Eddie.

Martin: (TO NILES) What's up?

Niles: Well, when I brought you a beer in your room the other day, I couldn't help but notice you had photos of Frasier and Frederick and an autographed one from someone named Ken Griffey, Jr., but none of Maris and me. So, I brought you this.

HE HANDS MARTIN THE FRAMED PHOTO.

Martin: Gee, thanks (A BEAT) Uh, why is Maris wearing jodhpurs? She didn't start horseback riding did she?

Niles: No. She wanted to take it up but unfortunately her little quadriceps are so tight she's incapable of straddling anything larger than a border collie. Still, the wardrobe suits her.

Daphne: Yes, not everyone looks so natural carrying a riding crop.

BEFORE NILES CAN RESPOND, AN AGITATED <u>FRASIER ENTERS</u> FROM THE HALLWAY, CARRYING A BOOK.

Frasier: I simply do not believe this. This is outrageous!

Martin: What are you yapping about?

Frasier: I'm yapping about this. (RE: BOOK) This book! It's written by someone I knew. He's taken an incident from my own life. Something very personal that I told him one night in confidence and he's turned it into this trash.

Martin: You must be making a mistake.

Frasier: Why? Because no one would be so low as to steal another man's life?

Martin: (OPENS BOOKS FLYLEAF) No, because I've heard your stories. Nothing that's happened to you is worth $14.95.

Frasier: Oh, he stole my story all right, but does he thank me? No . . . He doesn't even list my name in his acknowledgments.

Martin: What's it about, anyway?

Frasier: That isn't important.

Daphne: It's about his first time.

Frasier: Thank you, Daphne.

Daphne: I just started the book, but I rather like it.

Niles: Your first time doing what?

Frasier: Changing a flat tire – what do you think?

Niles: Ohhh.

Martin: So this whole book is about the night you conceived Frederick?

Frasier: Very amusing, Dad. You'll be happy to know that wasn't my first time.

Martin: Hey, I'm happy to know it wasn't your only time.

Niles: So just who was this charitable lass?

FRASIER HESITATES A BEAT.

Daphne: His piano teacher.

Martin: What?! Your piano teacher?!

Frasier: Thank you again, Daphne.

Daphne: Well it's not like it's a secret. It's all right here in black and white . . . about your awkward, teenage lunging. And how you used to call your chest hair your "rug of love."

MARTIN AND NILES BURST OUT LAUGHING.

Frasier: Well not all of it's true. He did take some literary license.

Daphne: Then you're not really able to bring a woman to hidden realms of ecstasy with your panther-like prowess?

Frasier: Well, that part he got right.

Martin: Boy, this really fries me, knowing that woman was taking advantage of my kid. Plus I was shelling out ten bucks a week for piano lessons so you could get your hedge trimmed.

Niles: Wait a minute. We're not talking about Miss Warner, are we?

Martin: (TO NILES) Don't tell me this was going on during your lessons, too?

Niles: No. You'll be relieved to know that I was actually studying music, while Frasier was getting his Rachmaninoffs.

Frasier: Look, this wasn't some tawdry, older woman lusting after young flesh. We cared about each other. Clarice introduce me to a world I'd never known . . . and wouldn't know again for six and a half years.

Daphne: It's true. As Mr. Fallow put it, she saw your sensitive, poetic side. And you couldn't help noticing the way her ripe, heaving bosom would brush your cheek whenever she reached for the metronome.

Frasier: The heaving bosom, the metronome – how could someone who drank so heavily remember so much?

Niles: Yet still conveniently forget who told him the story.

Frasier: Well, he's going to get a little reminder today.

HE CROSSES OFF. MARTIN AND NILES STARE AFTER HIM FOR A BEAT, THEN BOTH GRAB FOR THE BOOK, AS WE:

FADE OUT.

Scene C

FADE IN:

INT. RADIO STUDIO - DAY - DAY/2
(Roz, Frasier, Thomas Jay Fallow, Bulldog, Gil Chesterton, Amber Edwards)

THOMAS JAY FALLOW IS ON THE AIR WITH AMBER EDWARDS. HE IS READING FROM HIS BOOK. AMBER LISTENS WITH RAPT ATTENTION.

Thomas: "I budded when you kissed me. I withered when you left me. I bloomed a few months while you loved me."

THROUGH THE WINDOW WE SEE ROZ IN THE HALL, HOLDING A COPY OF THE BOOK AND STARING AT THOMAS ADORINGLY. BEHIND HER FRASIER GESTICULATES ANGRILY. WE SEE BUT DO NOT HEAR HIM RANTING.

Amber: What was *The New York Times* book reviewer thinking? That's beautiful.

ANGLE ON THE HALLWAY, WHERE FRASIER HAS BEEN RANTING TO ROZ. NOW WE SEE THOMAS AND AMBER IN THE BOOTH BUT WE DO NOT HEAR THEM.

Roz: Would you calm down?

Frasier: Not until I have exacted my pound of flesh.

Roz: Could you at least wait until I've had my book signed?

Frasier: Why not let me sign it? It's my story. By the way, Roz, you haven't let anyone around here know that, have you? They'd have a field day with me.

Roz: Hey, give me credit for a little discretion, will ya?

BULLDOG COMES DOWN THE HALL AND IMMEDIATELY SPOTS FRASIER.

Bulldog: Hey, Piano Boy! Way to pound those keys!

Roz: I knew I couldn't trust Father Mike to keep his trap shut.

Frasier: Bulldog, please, I don't want it commonly known.

Bulldog: Hey, it's no big deal, Doc. It just so happens that when I was sixteen I had a similar experience with an older woman who introduced me to the mysteries of love. Of course, she was a pro . . .

Roz: Oh yuck.

Bulldog: Hey, it was a birthday present from my dad, okay?

Frasier: Thank you for that Norman Rockwell moment, but aren't you due in some smelly locker room somewhere?

Bulldog: Want to know the ironic thing, Doc? All I wanted was a bike.

BULLDOG EXITS. FRASIER GLARES AT ROZ.

Roz: Oh, come on. How'd you expect me not to tell? You can't keep something that juicy bottled up. I only told one person.

GIL CHESTERTON COMES DOWN THE HALL AND SEES FRASIER.

Gil: Hello, Frasier, Roz.

Roz: Hi, Gil.

Gil: I was just jotting down my latest restaurant review when I came up with the perfect sandwich to name after you at Rosenthal's Deli.

Frasier: Please don't keep us in suspense.

Gil: "Frasier Crane's Double Decker." It consists of aged pheasant, spring chicken, and of course plenty of tongue.

Frasier: (TO ROZ) I'll get you for this.

Roz: You already have. I won't be able to fantasize about teenage boys any more without seeing your face.

BULLDOG COMES BACK THROUGH, SEES GIL AND STARTS TO GOOF ON FRASIER BY QUOTING LINES FROM THE BOOK.

Bulldog: (TO GIL) "Ravish me, my young maestro."

Gil: "I'm your rhapsody, play me."

Bulldog: "I long to tickle the ivories of your loins."

Gil: My vessel yearns to dock in the magnificence of your harbor.

BULLDOG LAUGHS, THEN REALIZES.

Bulldog: Hey, that's not from the book.

<u>THEY TURN THE CORNER AND EXIT</u>.

Frasier: Doesn't that woman ever have to break for a commercial?

<u>THEY GO INTO</u> ROZ'S BOOTH, WHICH IS NOW OCCUPIED BY AMBER'S ENGINEER. FROM IN HERE WE CAN HEAR AMBER AND THOMAS.

Amber: One thing I must ask you – what was your inspiration for this wonderful love story?

Frasier: Don't make a sound. This is his last chance.

Thomas: Well Amber, it was actually given to me . . . by God.

Frasier: "By God"?! Can you believe this guy's grandiosity? *I'm* God and he knows it!

Amber: We'll be right back with the divinely inspired Thomas Jay Fallow after this station break.

THE "ON AIR" LIGHT GOES OFF.

Amber (CONT'D): (TO THOMAS) Will you excuse me? I want to call my ex-husband and say, "Okay, let's try again."

<u>SHE EXITS</u>, LEAVING HIM ALONE IN THE BOOTH. <u>FRASIER ENTERS</u>.

Frasier: Thomas Jay Fallow?

Thomas: (SURPRISED) Frasier . . . Frasier Crane. What are you doing here?

Frasier: So my name hasn't entirely escaped your sieve-like memory.

Thomas: Why would it?

Frasier: Well, it didn't seem to make it into your acknowledgments, you egomaniacal thief!

Thomas: (EXCITED) You read my book?

Frasier: I didn't have to read it. I lived it. Not that anyone would know that from reading your three pages of acknowledgments, in which you thank everyone from your kindergarten teacher to the man who designed the type-face. But no mention of me. Of course, why should you? All I did was provide you with the very story which you've ruthlessly merchandised into a multi-million dollar treacle machine.

A BEAT.

Thomas: Is there more?

Frasier: It figures a hack like you wouldn't recognize a forceful climax.

THOMAS LOOKS AT HIM FOR A LONG BEAT, THEN BEGINS TO BLINK. TEARS COME TO HIS EYES AND HE SNIFFLES.

Thomas: I don't know what to say . . . You're right.

Frasier: Well, that's a start.

Thomas: No, you're right. (HE STARTS CRYING) I'm so sorry . . . How could I be so thoughtless? I owe you everything.

THOMAS BURIES HIS FACE IN THE LAPELS OF FRASIER'S JACKET.

Frasier: I don't know about everything.

THOMAS IS WEEPING AS ROZ ENTERS.

Roz: God, Frasier, what did you say to the poor man?

AMBER ENTERS.

Amber: Thomas, what happened?

Roz: Frasier made him cry.

THOMAS LETS OUT ANOTHER SOB. SEVERAL MORE WOMEN STREAM IN FROM THE HALLWAY, COMING TO THOMAS' AID AND CASTING ACCUSING GLANCES AT FRASIER. AS THE WOMEN HUDDLE AND FUSS OVER THOMAS, AND ROZ PRESENTS HER BOOK FOR HIS SIGNATURE, WE:

FADE OUT.

END OF ACT ONE

ACT TWO

Scene D

A BLACK SCREEN. IN WHITE LETTERS APPEARS, "THE TEARS IT TAKES A SUMMER WIND TO DRY . . ."
Niles (V.O.): Maris is reading *Slow Tango in South Seattle.*

FADE IN:

INT. FRASIER'S LIVING ROOM - THAT EVENING - NIGHT/2
(Niles, Martin, Frasier, Daphne, Eddie)

NILES IS TALKING TO MARTIN.

Niles (CONT'D): I think it's put thoughts in her head. This morning I found her cooing over the college student who skims the koi pond.

Martin: I wouldn't concern myself.

Niles: So you think it's just innocent flirting?

Martin: No, I just wouldn't concern myself.

FRASIER ENTERS FROM OUTSIDE. HE'S A BIT DOWN.

Frasier: Hi Dad, Niles.

Niles: Congratulations, Frasier. Maris was listening to "Book Chat" today during her seaweed wrap and heard Thomas Jay Fallow acknowledge his enormous debt to you.

Frasier: Yes, I had a little talk with him at the station.

Niles: Did he seem properly contrite?

Frasier: I made him cry.

Martin: That's my boy. You must be feeling pretty good.

Frasier: Actually, Dad, the whole thing has left me strangely unsatisfied.

Martin: Why? You told him off, didn't you?

Frasier: Yeah?

Martin: So?

Frasier: I still feel sort of empty. I don't know why. I've been twisting it around in my mind all day.

Martin: You kill me, you know that. You get exactly what you want and you're still not happy. Life is not hard. You make it hard. You don't just let things happen and enjoy them. You analyze everything to death. You could learn a big lesson from this dog. You know what makes him happy? A sock. Come on, Eddie.

MARTIN AND EDDIE EXIT.

Niles: Ignore him. Obviously what's troubling you goes deeper than your usual malaise.

DAPHNE ENTERS CARRYING THE BOOK.

Daphne: (TO FRASIER) Shame on you!

Frasier: What for?

Daphne: What for? You just ran out on her, leaving her bed as empty as a swallow's nest after fall's first frost, and you ask me what for?

Niles: Is this true?

Frasier: I'd been accepted at Harvard, what else was I going to do?

Daphne: So you make off in the middle of the night without so much as a kiss on the forehead.

Niles: You never said goodbye?

Frasier: I promised I'd call her at Christmas.

<u>DAPHNE</u> "HMMPHS!" DISAPPROVINGLY AND <u>EXITS</u> TO THE KITCHEN.

Frasier (CONT'D): (CALLS AFTER HER) Well I didn't say what year.

Niles: Aha.

Frasier: Aha, what?

Niles: Aha, this. I have a theory.

Frasier: Well why else would you say "aha"?

Niles: Just listen. You thought you were angry at Thomas Fallow for failing to thank you for the contribution you made to his life. But perhaps the person you're really angry at is yourself. You never thanked Miss Warner for the contribution she made to your life.

Frasier: No, but I'm sure she understood. I was seventeen years old.

Niles: Well, perhaps she didn't. She was a vulnerable, lonely, middle-aged woman. It could be that her feelings for you were genuine. Feelings that you crushed when you disappeared without so much as a thank you or a goodbye.

Frasier: Yes, well, thank you and goodbye.

Niles: Fine, then. I'll just leave you with this thought. Your encounter with Thomas Jay Fallow was unsatisfactory because it didn't provide you the closure you were seeking. For that, you would have to make amends with Miss Warner.

<u>NILES EXITS. EDDIE ENTERS</u> WITH A SOCK IN HIS MOUTH AND DROPS IT ON FRASIER'S FOOT.

Frasier: (CALLING OFF) Very funny, Dad!

AND WE:

FADE OUT.

Scene E

FADE IN:

INT. FRASIER'S LIVING ROOM – LATE THAT NIGHT – NIGHT/2
(Frasier, Daphne)

FRASIER IS SITTING IN HIS CHAIR IN THE DIMLY-LIT ROOM READING THE NOVEL.

Frasier (V.O.): "He had been a teenage Balboa, an explorer of the rising pinnacles and gently curving slopes of my body, and in one explosive burst of discovery he had staked claim to the Pacific Ocean that was my soul. But now he was leaving. Going. Vanishing like a solitary boat on the lonely horizon. Departing like a train, rolling ceaselessly through the night. Exiting swiftly, like –"

FRASIER SIGHS IN EXASPERATION AND TURNS A COUPLE PAGES THEN READS ON.

Frasier (V.O.) (CONT'D): "And so, he was gone. And now, in the cool of the evening I play my piano and his last words resonate through the notes. 'I'll come back to you, my cherished one. In a world of constant flux, my love will never change.'"

FRASIER LETS THE BOOK REST IN HIS LAP. DAPHNE CROSSES THROUGH AND SWATS HIM WITH HER BOOK. ON HIS LOOK WE:

FADE OUT.

Scene H

A BLACK SCREEN. IN WHITE LETTERS APPEARS, "I FEEL OLDER SINCE HIS SHADOWS LEFT MY DOOR."

FADE IN:

EXT. CLARICE WARNER'S FRONT PORCH – DAY – DAY/3
(Frasier, Mrs. Warner, Clarice, Man)

FRASIER APPROACHES A SCREEN DOOR. THROUGH THE SCREEN HE SEES AN OLDER WOMAN PLAYING THE PIANO. HE IS SOMEWHAT TAKEN ABACK.

Frasier: Time, the subtle thief of youth.

HE KNOCKS ON THE DOOR. MRS. WARNER LEAVES THE PIANO AND ANSWERS THE DOOR.

Mrs. Warner: Hello, may I help you?

Frasier: Ms. Warner?

Mrs. Warner: Yes?

Frasier: I, I'm Frasier Crane.

Mrs. Warner: I'm sorry. My memory isn't what it used to be. But, please come in.

FRASIER FOLLOWS MRS. WARNER INTO THE LIVING ROOM.

Frasier: Surely, you must have some recollection of me. A fair haired boy outside your door, at the piano, on the piano?

Mrs. Warner: I'd like to.

Frasier: Well before all the memories come flooding back to you, I should tell you we had a romance that didn't have the happiest ending. That's why I'm here. The night we walked in the summer storm and I kissed the raindrops off your nose, I promised we'd always be together. But I didn't keep that promise. You helped a shy adolescent take his first uncertain steps toward becoming a man, and how did I repay this kindness? By running off and leaving you with nothing but your memories.

Mrs. Warner: And not many of those either.

Frasier: (PAINED) Oh.

HE TAKES HER HAND AND BEGINS TO PAT IT.

Frasier (CONT'D): Can you ever forgive me?

Mrs. Warner: You're so sweet. Of course I can forgive you.

SHE HUGS FRASIER. AN ATTRACTIVE WOMAN IN HER VERY-SEXY EARLY SIXTIES, CLARICE WARNER, ENTERS THE ROOM.

Clarice: Mother, what's going on here?

Mrs. Warner: Oh, Clarice.

Frasier: (STUNNED) You're Clarice?!

Mrs. Warner: This is Frasier Crane. Apparently we were quite an item at one time.

Clarice: Frasier? What are you doing here?

Frasier: Making an enormous mistake.

Mrs. Warner: (RISING) Why don't I make us all some iced tea.

SHE HEADS OUT. ON HER WAY, SHE PASSES CLARICE.

Mrs. Warner (CONT'D): (TO CLARICE) Hands off. This one's mine.

MRS. WARNER EXITS.

Clarice: I can't believe you're here. I mean, look at you.

Frasier: Look at you. You look incredible.

Clarice: Well, sure, compared to my mother.

Frasier: No, no, I mean even if I hadn't seen her.

Clarice: You came because of that book, didn't you?

Frasier: Yes, and let me say right off I'm sorry. That story was told to Mr. Fallow in confidence. He had no right to put it in print.

Clarice: There's no need to apologize. I mean, it's not like you mentioned my name. You didn't, did you?

Frasier: No, I would never do that.

THERE IS AN AWKWARD BEAT OF SILENCE.

Clarice: So, are you married?

Frasier: Divorced. You?

Clarice: No, I never married.

FRASIER DOES A SLIGHT GRIMACE.

Frasier: I actually came here to apologize about more than just the book. You see, I never felt quite right about the way I left things. I always felt as if I had abandoned you. It was selfish and cowardly.

Clarice: Frasier relax. I always felt guilty for short-changing you on your music lessons. Do you still keep it up?

Frasier: What? Oh, the piano – yes, yes. Look, it's very kind of you to let me off the hook . . .

Clarice: Oh, I could never be mad at you, Frasier.

Frasier: It's funny, I was so nervous about coming here but now it feels just like old times.

SHE SMILES. FRASIER TAKES A SEAT AT THE PIANO BENCH AND ACCIDENTALLY HITS THE METRONOME. IT BEGINS TO GO BACK AND FORTH.

Clarice: Oh, let me get that.

SHE REACHES ACROSS FRASIER FOR THE METRONOME, AND BRUSHES AGAINST HIM.

Frasier: At the risk of sounding forward, would you like to go out and get a cup of coffee with me?

Clarice: Thanks, but I'll have to say no.

Frasier: If you think I'm uncomfortable about the age difference, please rest assured that's no longer an issue.

A MAN IN HIS LATE-TWENTIES APPEARS AT THE DOOR, KNOCKS AND ENTERS.

Man: Hi honey, ready to go?

HE GIVES HER A KISS.

Clarice: Yeah sweetie, I'll be right out.

THE MAN EXITS. FRASIER LOOKS CRESTFALLEN.

Frasier: Are you and he . . .?

CLARICE SHRUGS.

Clarice: I wasn't interested in forty-year-old men then, and I guess I'm still not. Great to see you again though. (CALLING OFF) Bye, Mom.

CLARICE EXITS, LEAVING FRASIER IN SHOCK. MRS. WARNER ENTERS WITH THE ICED TEA.

Mrs. Warner: Good, we're alone now.

SHE SETS DOWN THE TEA, DIPS A FINGER INTO THE PITCHER AND DABS HER NOSE.

Mrs. Warner (CONT'D): Did you see what I did? I put a raindrop on my nose.

SHE SITS DOWN ON THE COUCH AND INVITINGLY PATS THE PLACE NEXT TO HER. AS ALL THE COLOR DRAINS FROM FRASIER'S FACE [A REALLY GOOD ACTOR COULD DO THIS], WE:

FADE OUT.

END OF ACT TWO

Scene J

(END CREDITS)

INT. CLARICE WARNER'S LIVING ROOM – LATER THAT DAY – DAY/3
(Frasier, Mrs. Warner)

FRASIER AND MRS. WARNER ARE SIDE-BY-SIDE AT THE PIANO PLAYING A DUET. FRASIER DOES NOT LOOK PARTICULARLY HAPPY TO STILL BE HERE. MRS. WARNER SLIDES A LITTLE CLOSER TO HIM ON THE PIANO BENCH. FRASIER DISCREETLY SLIDES A LITTLE FURTHER AWAY. MRS. WARNER SLIDES TOWARD HIM. FRASIER SLIDES AWAY AGAIN, AND WE:

FADE OUT.

<u>END OF SHOW</u>

THE MATCHMAKER

#40572-028

Written by Joe Keenan
Created and Developed by David Angell, Peter Casey & David Lee
Directed by David Lee

ACT ONE

Scene A

A BLACK SCREEN. IN WHITE LETTERS APPEARS, "WHERE THERE'S SMOKE . . ."

FADE IN:

<u>INT. FRASIER'S LIVING ROOM – NIGHT – NIGHT/1</u>
(Frasier, Daphne, Martin, Eddie)

IT'S THE MIDDLE OF THE NIGHT AND THE <u>APARTMENT IS DARK</u>.

<u>SFX: SMOKE ALARM</u>

Frasier (O.S.): Oh my God! Fire! Fire!

<u>MARTIN RUSHES IN</u> FROM THE HALL, WEARING PAJAMA BOTTOMS AND A T-SHIRT.

Martin: Eddie! Eddie, where are you, boy?

Frasier (O.S.): (BANGING ON DOOR) Dad! Dad, wake up! Dad, are you in there?

<u>MARTIN CROSSES INTO</u> THE KITCHEN.

Martin: Eddie! Here, Eddie!

<u>FRASIER RUSHES IN</u>, DRESSED IN PAJAMAS. HE TURNS THE <u>LIGHTS ON</u>.

Frasier: Dad! Dad, where are you!?

MARTIN RE-ENTERS FROM THE KITCHEN.

Martin: You seen Eddie?

Frasier: No! What's burning? What's on fire?

Martin: (CALLING) Eddie!

77

SFX: THE ALARM STOPS

<u>DAPHNE</u>, VERY AGITATED, <u>ENTERS</u> IN HER NIGHTGOWN.

Daphne: It's all right! False alarm. The one over my bed went off.

Frasier: Oh, thank God!

Daphne: (TO MARTIN) And don't worry about Eddie. He's back in my room.
(THEN) The noise the bloody thing makes! It would be less upsetting to just wake up on fire.

Martin: What the hell triggered it?

AS DAPHNE SPEAKS <u>EDDIE TROTS IN</u>, A PACK OF CIGARETTES IN HIS MOUTH.

Daphne: Who knows? I was dozing quite peacefully when it started screaming away for no reason at all.

Frasier: I see. No reason at all . . .

HE MOVES TO EDDIE AND REMOVES THE PACK OF CIGARETTES FROM HIS MOUTH.

Frasier (CONT'D): And what have we here? Eddie, you've been smoking in Daphne's room.

Daphne: Bad dog.

Frasier: Daphne.

Daphne: Oh, I know, I know. You have a no smoking rule. I'm sorry. But every now and then I feel a bit tense and I find a ciggy can be very soothing.

Martin: Oh, it's been real soothing. It should only be about an hour till my heart stops fibrillating.

MARTIN HEADS FOR THE HALL.

Frasier: Wait a minute, Dad.

MARTIN TURNS.

Frasier (CONT'D): You really thought the apartment was on fire?

Martin: I think you have to assume that when the alarm goes off.

Frasier: And in that harrowing, possibly life-threatening instant, the very first thought to enter your mind was . . . "Where's Eddie?"

Martin: No, that was my second thought. My first thought was, "Where's my pajama bottoms?"

Frasier: Actually, my first thought was you finding your pajama bottoms too.

MARTIN GOES.

Frasier (CONT'D): God, three a.m. Of course, this would happen the night before I have an early meeting. (A HAND ON THE LIGHT SWITCH; TO DAPHNE) Aren't you going back to bed?

Daphne: No, I'll sit up a bit. I'm feeling a bit blue.

Frasier: Is it anything you'd like to discuss?

Daphne: No, you need your sleep. It's nothing important.

FRASIER NODS AND HEADS OFF DOWN THE HALL. DURING THE FOLLOWING, HE STOPS AND TURNS BACK.

Daphne (CONT'D): Just this feeling that my life's a gaping sinkhole and I'm just marking time while the flower of my youth rots on the vine.

Frasier: (EAGER TO GO) Well, if you're sure . . .

FRASIER STARTS DOWN THE HALL. DAPHNE EMITS AN ACHINGLY POIGNANT, OPHELIA-LIKE SIGH. FRASIER, DEFEATED, TURNS.

Frasier (CONT'D): I really do wish you'd tell me about it.

Daphne: Well, if you have to know, it's my love life.

Frasier: Really? Have you been seeing a man?

Daphne: Only when I close my eyes and concentrate.

Frasier: I see - going through a little drought.

Daphne: Small wonder. I'm cooped up here most of the time. And when I do get out it's usually with your father. People see us and assume I'm his daughter or else his wife - either way it's like having my own personal can of stud repellent.

DURING THE FOLLOWING, DAPHNE BEGINS SMOKING ANOTHER CIGARETTE.

Frasier: Listen, I know how bleak things can look when you're going through a dry spell, but they always end sooner or later. I remember once in Boston feeling exactly the way you do now - and the very next week I met a lovely, if somewhat loquacious barmaid, fell madly in love and got engaged . . . (REALIZING, SADLY) Of course, she left me standing at the altar - but the point is I didn't give up. I took my poor, battered heart and offered it to Lilith, (THINKS) who put it in her little cuisinart and hit the purée button. But I rebounded. And look how far I've come . . . Divorced, lonely, and living with my father – who cares less about me than he does about his foul-breathed flea resort of a dog.

FRASIER TAKES THE CIGARETTE FROM DAPHNE AND BEGINS SMOKING IT. AND WE:

FADE OUT.

Scene B

FADE IN:

INT. CAFE NERVOSA – DAY – DAY/2
(Frasier, Roz, Niles)

FRASIER SITS ALONE AT A TABLE. NILES IS AT THE COUNTER. ROZ ENTERS AND CROSSES TO FRASIER. SHE'S A LITTLE MIFFED.

Roz: I figured I'd find you here. You know, you missed the meeting with the new station manager.

Frasier: Oh God, I completely forgot. Was he insulted?

Roz: No, I covered for you. (PEERING AT HIM) God, you look like you've been ridden hard and put away wet.

Frasier: Thank you. I was up until all hours talking with Daphne, competing to see who had the more pathetic love life. On the bright side, I won.

Roz: Your problems I know about – what are Daphne's?

Frasier: She's just having trouble meeting men.

Roz: Say no more.

ROZ PULLS AN ADDRESS BOOK FROM HER BAG.

Frasier: (REALIZING HER INTENT; LEERY BUT DIPLOMATIC) Oh no, Roz, that's all right, really. You don't have to donate one of your boyfriends to Daphne.

Roz: Please. I'd be happy to.

Frasier: Still – one hates to break up a collection.

NILES, CARRYING TWO COFFEES, APPROACHES THE TABLE.

Niles: Here we are. One triple espresso and one mocha latte. (SHOWING FRASIER HIS MOCHA; ANNOYED) Do those chocolate shavings look any different to you?

Frasier: No.

Niles: Well, they do to me. I think they've switched to an inferior domestic brand.

NILES TAKES A SIP AND SCRUNCHES UP HIS NOSE.

Niles (CONT'D): Waxy.

HE TAKES HIS HANDKERCHIEF AND DABS HIS LIPS. FRASIER TAKES THE HANDKERCHIEF FROM HIM.

Frasier: I'll have this sent to the lab for analysis.

THEN GIVING THE HANDKERCHIEF BACK TO NILES.

Frasier (CONT'D): Put that thing away.

Roz: (SPOTTING A NAME) Sven Bachman. An aerobics instructor. You can bounce a quarter off of . . . Well, just about any part of him.

Frasier: (TO ROZ) I don't think so.

Niles: (TO FRASIER) This place is going to hell in a handbasket. What's next? Humorous napkins?

Roz: This one's perfect - Gunther Dietrich. Loads of fun and he's a runway model.

Frasier: A German narcissist - there's an appealing combination.

Roz: Okay, I'll keep looking.

Niles: Looking for what?

Roz: I'm helping Frasier find a man for Daphne.

Niles: What?

Roz: (OFF THE BOOK) Here we go. He's a tennis coach and his name's Paolo -

Niles: For God's sake, Frasier. Paolo, Gunther, Sven? Why not just lather Daphne up with baby oil and hurl her over the wall of a prison yard?

Roz: Excuse me, but I've dated all these guys.

Niles: Where do you think I came up with the imagery?

Roz: (TO NILES) Listen, you little titmouse . . .

Frasier: Niles, you're completely out of line. (TO ROZ) But he does have a point. We have to remember that you and Daphne are different types of women. Where Daphne is a bit shy and inexperienced, you're more . . . Well, a lot more . . . Actually, you'd be hard pressed to find anyone . . .

Roz: Oh, I get it. Not one man I've ever dated is good enough for Miss Daphne. Is that what you're trying to say?

Frasier: No. That's what I'm trying *not* to say - and you're not making it very easy.

Roz: (RISING) I'm outta here.

Frasier: Roz, please . . . Wait.

Roz: No, no, I can't stay. The fleet's in.

ROZ EXITS.

Niles: Don't feel bad, Frasier. You did the right thing. When I think of the cads she might have unleashed on that delicate, innocent -

Frasier: Oh, get a grip, Niles! I don't know what sort of twisted fantasy you've concocted for yourself about your future with Daphne. I suspect it involves a comet hitting the earth and the two of you having to rebuild the species, but trust me, it's not going to happen. She needs a man, Niles, one who's in a position to do more for her than just smell her hair - and if I can help her find one, I will. Good day.

FRASIER GOES. NILES SITS GLUMLY. AT THE NEXT TABLE A CIGARETTE BURNS IN AN ASHTRAY. NILES TAKES THE CIGARETTE, WIPES IT OFF WITH HIS HANDKERCHIEF, THEN TAKES A DRAG. AND WE:

FADE OUT.

Scene C

FADE IN:

INT. RADIO STUDIO - A FEW HOURS LATER - DAY/2
(Frasier, Roz, Tom)

FRASIER IS ON THE AIR. ROZ IS IN HER BOOTH.

SFX: THE HIGH-PITCHED MONOTONE OF THE EMERGENCY BROADCAST SYSTEM

FRASIER PASSES THE TIME BY THUMBING THROUGH A MAGAZINE AND YAWNING A COUPLE OF TIMES. FINALLY, THE TONE ENDS.

Frasier: And so ends our test of the emergency broadcast system. If this had been an actual emergency, your radio would be melting in your hands. We'll be back after this newsbreak.

FRASIER REMOVES HIS HEADSET. ROZ CROSSES IN AND THROWS A HALF-EATEN DONUT IN A NAPKIN ON HIS DESK.

Roz: In the future, please keep your disgusting, half-eaten food off my console. In fact, just stay out of my sight.

Frasier: You're still mad at me. I can tell.

Roz: There's that keen sensitivity that keeps you in such demand with the ladies.

ROZ SLAMS THE DOOR BETWEEN THEIR BOOTHS. FRASIER OPENS IT.

Frasier: Roz, I'm sorry, but I feel very protective about Daphne. The man I'm looking for has to be good-looking, smart, successful.

THERE IS A LIGHT KNOCK AT THE OTHER DOOR TO FRASIER'S BOOTH. FRASIER TURNS TO FIND TOM O'CONNOR AT THE DOORWAY. HE IS IN HIS LATE 30'S AND SEEMS TO GLOW WITH ALL THE VIRTUES FRASIER HAS JUST ENUMERATED.

Tom: Excuse me.

Frasier: Yes?

Tom: I'm Tom O'Connor, the new station manager.

Frasier: (SHAKING HIS HAND) It's a pleasure to meet you. I'm sorry about missing that meeting this morning. I'm sure Roz explained. I overslept.

Tom: Actually, she told me you had a doctor's appointment.

Frasier: Well, she knows best. She keeps my appointment book.

Tom: Say, that's a beautiful tie.

Frasier: Thank you. I got it in London at this little custom shop. What was the name of it? It's right off Sloane Square. (TRYING TO REMEMBER HE SHUTS HIS EYES) What's it called? It's got this stone facade . . . God, I can picture it.

TOM TURNS FRASIER'S TIE AROUND AND READS THE LABEL.

Tom: Smythe and Son?

Frasier: No, that's not it. (OPENS EYES, SEES TOM HOLDING HIS TIE) Of course, that could be it.

Tom: You know, I just came from London. I spent the last five years there working for the BBC.

Frasier: Really? I love London – the theater especially.

Tom: Me too. I'm a big theater buff. I hated to leave, but . . . well, I'd just gone through sort of a messy break-up. I thought I'd sleep better with a continent between us.

Frasier: I know the feeling. (THE IDEA STRIKES HIM) So . . . I take it you're unattached?

Tom: Yes, but I haven't given up hope.

Frasier: Well, you may have come to the right place. So, getting back to London, were you fond of the British?

Tom: Yes, very much. I guess I've always had a weakness for people who are just a little eccentric.

Frasier: (THE WHEELS TURNING) *Really?*

Roz: (INTO HER MIC) Fifteen seconds.

Tom: Well, nice meeting you –

Frasier: Same here.

FRASIER SITS AND DONS HIS HEADPHONES. TOM TURNS TO GO AGAIN.

Frasier (CONT'D): Say, Tom, I know this is short notice, but if you're not doing anything Saturday, why don't you come by my place for dinner? Nothing fancy.

Tom: Thanks. I'd like that.

TOM CROSSES INTO ROZ'S BOOTH. THE "ON AIR" LIGHT GOES ON.

Frasier: Welcome back, Seattle. So, whom do we have up next, Roz?

Roz: We have James from Tacoma on line one.

Frasier: Hello, James. I'm listening.

ANGLE ON ROZ'S BOOTH. TOM STANDS FACING ROZ WITH HIS BACK TO FRASIER. TOM AND ROZ AD-LIB HELLOS.

Tom: (TO ROZ) Boy, it's the same every job I take. Word spreads like wildfire.

Roz: What's that?

Tom: Oh, you know. You tell one or two people you're gay and before you can blink it's all over the station.

Roz: They don't call it broadcasting for nothing.

FRASIER NOTICES ROZ TALKING TO TOM AND ASSUMES SHE'S HITTING ON HIM. FRASIER WAGS A FINGER AT ROZ INDICATING "GET AWAY FROM HIM."

Tom: (RE: FRASIER) He seems like a nice guy.

Roz: He's okay.

Tom: I hope he's more than okay. He just asked me out on a date and I accepted.

Roz: Frasier? Asked you out on a date?

FRASIER BEGINS SCRIBBLING ON A PIECE OF PAPER.

Tom: Yeah, he asked me to come to his place for dinner. So I wanted to ask you is there any particular wine he likes?

Roz: Tom, there's something you should know about Frasier –

FROM HIS BOOTH, FRASIER HOLDS UP A SIGN. IT READS, "HANDS OFF! HE'S TAKEN!" ROZ READS IT.

Tom: What?

Roz: (TO TOM) He's nuts about Chardonnay.

Tom: Thanks.

TOM EXITS, AND AS ROZ SMILES AT FRASIER, WE:

FADE OUT.

END OF ACT ONE

ACT TWO

Scene D

A BLACK SCREEN. IN WHITE LETTERS APPEARS, "SOME ENCHANTED EVENING . . ."

FADE IN:

INT. FRASIER'S LIVING ROOM – EVENING – NIGHT/3
(Frasier, Daphne, Martin, Niles, Tom)

FRASIER IS ARRANGING A CENTERPIECE ON THE DINING ROOM TABLE.

Martin: (SCREAMING AT THE TV) You over-paid, lard ass bum. You couldn't catch a cold in a snowbank.

FRASIER REACTS AS IF TO SAY HIS PERFECT ATMOSPHERE HAS BEEN DECIMATED.

Frasier: Dad, must you scream at the television? They can't hear you.

Martin: Hey, c'mon, this is a nail-biter. It's the fourth quarter and they're using a rookie quarterback.

Frasier: I don't care if it's the tenth quarter and they're using guns. I am trying to host a civilized dinner.

Martin: Fine. I'll watch the end in my room while I'm putting on my ascot.

MARTIN EXITS DOWN THE HALLWAY, AS DAPHNE ENTERS FROM THE KITCHEN AND SETS THE TABLE.

Daphne: (MURMURING FURIOUSLY TO HERSELF) Does he ask permission first, no, he just barges in and says he's set me up with God knows who and I'm supposed to turn cartwheels like I'm bloody Cinderella . . .

Frasier: Will you relax? I told you it's not a set-up. I didn't even tell Tom you'd be here.

Daphne: Oh, an ambush, then? Much nicer. My girlfriends in Manchester used to set me up all the time. And it was always some gangly bounder with a boarding house reach. And he wasn't going for the Coleman's hot mustard, if you know what I mean.

Frasier: Well, I think you'll be pleasantly surprised. And remember, he's nothing more than a co-worker here for a nice dinner. If some spark should ignite, fine, but there's no pressure, none whatsoever. (BEAT) Is that what you're wearing?

Daphne: Why, what's wrong with it?

SFX: DOORBELL

Frasier: Oh, there he is.

AS HE CROSSES TO THE DOOR:

Frasier (CONT'D): Don't you have something with a little more oomph? What about that strapless thing you have?

Daphne: Do you have any idea how uncomfortable a strapless bra is?

Frasier: Thanks to my fraternity days, as a matter of fact, I do. Just put it on. Trust me. He's worth it.

Daphne: So glad there's no pressure.

DAPHNE EXITS TO HER ROOM. FRASIER OPENS THE DOOR. TOM IS THERE, DRESSED IN AN OVERCOAT AND NICE SUIT, CARRYING A BOTTLE OF WINE.

Frasier: Tom, come on in.

Tom: Hi, Frasier.

HE HANDS FRASIER THE BOTTLE OF WINE.

Tom (CONT'D): I don't know. Something told me you'd like Chardonnay.

The Cast

The cast at the beginning of season six: Dan Butler (Bulldog Brisco), Peri Gilpin (Roz Doyle), John Mahoney (Martin Crane), Kelsey Grammer (Frasier Crane) and Moose (Eddie), David Hyde Pierce (Niles Crane) and Jane Leeves (Daphne Moon).

The real star of the show.

Frasier in his new home, the KACL Radio Studio.

And Martin in his – his beloved Barcalounger in Frasier's flat.

Call Me Irresponsible

Daphne prepares Eddie for the Crane household Christmas photograph.

Frasier shares M&Ms and sympathy with Catherine (guest star Amanda Donohoe).

A Midwinter Night's Dream

Daphne meets 'Eric the Red'.

A dark and stormy night ...

Slow Tango In South Seattle

When Frasier finds a story from his past has been novelized, Roz tries to calm him down ...

And Bulldog does the reverse.

The Matchmaker

Frasier's new boss puts smiles on Daphne and Frasier's faces ...

But not for long.

A Room With A View

A harsh word from father to son.

Frasier the inadvertent peeping Tom desperately tries to apologize to Daphne.

An Affair To Forget

Larking around on set, David Hyde Pierce prepares to enter the sensory deprivation tank.

Niles is comforted by Frasier, Martin and Eddie after yet another fight with Maris.

Frasier: My favorite.

TOM TAKES IN THE APARTMENT AND ITS VIEW OF SEATTLE.

Frasier (CONT'D): So, what do you think?

Tom: It's a hell of a view.

Frasier: It's even better from the bedroom.

Tom: Why don't we just start with a drink? (NOTING FOUR PLACES SET) Oh, four places. Who's joining us?

Frasier: Just my little household. My father and his charming physical therapist, Daphne.

Tom: You live with your dad? God, I can't even imagine that. I mean, it's great that you get along so well, but . . . (CONFIDENTIALLY) doesn't having him here put a crimp in your love life?

Frasier: Not at all. That is, except when I bring my dates home and he tries to steal them.

Tom: You're kidding? He really does that?

DAPHNE ENTERS IN A SEXY, STRAPLESS DRESS.

Frasier: Oh, yes. He's quite the old rascal. (THEN) Well, look who's here. I'd like you to meet Daphne Moon. Daphne, this is Tom O'Connor.

Tom: (TO DAPHNE) Pleasure to meet you.

Daphne: Likewise. Dr. Crane, you didn't take his coat – may I?

TOM TURNS HIS BACK TO DAPHNE SO THAT SHE CAN HELP HIM REMOVE HIS COAT. DAPHNE LOOKS AT FRASIER AND ELABORATELY CONVEYS HER DELIGHT, MOUTHING, "HE'S GORGEOUS. THANK YOU, THANK YOU." FRASIER BEAMS AND SMILES A "WHAT'D I TELL YOU?" SMILE. DAPHNE FOLDS THE COAT OVER HER ARM.

Daphne (CONT'D): Ooh. This is strange. I'm getting a little flash.

Tom: A flash?

Frasier: Daphne feels she possesses some kind of psychic powers. You know these English eccentrics. Ha, ha.

Daphne: (TO TOM) You've just been through a very painful break-up, haven't you?

Tom: Yes. (THEN TO FRASIER) Wait a minute. You told her that, didn't you?

Daphne: There was a bitter dispute about ownership of opera recordings.

Tom: Whoa, now I am impressed.

Daphne: Well, don't get too impressed. It comes and it goes. Now if you'll excuse me, I'll nip into the kitchen. I have a bird to baste.

DAPHNE EXITS TO THE KITCHEN.

Frasier: That's our Daphne. Isn't she something?

Tom: She's great. And I love hearing that accent again.

AS MARTIN HEADS DOWN THE HALLWAY, HE CALLS FROM OFF-STAGE:

Martin (O.S.): Hey, Frasier, I don't need to put on a tie for this joker, do I?

MARTIN ENTERS THE ROOM.

Martin (CONT'D): (SPOTTING TOM) Oh.

Frasier: Tom, I'd like you to meet my father, Martin Crane.

Tom: (EXTENDING HAND) Tom O'Connor. Nice to meet you.

THEY SHAKE.

Martin: Sorry about that joker business. I call everybody joker, or jerk, pinhead, bozo.

Frasier: And yet amazingly, he's free for dinner on short notice. (EXITING) Well, why don't I open some of this wonderful wine.

FRASIER EXITS TO THE KITCHEN, JOINING DAPHNE WHO IS BASTING A CHICKEN.

Frasier (CONT'D): Well?

Daphne: Oh, he's a looker. I'm glad you made me put on my lucky bra. He's worth every wire digging into my ribcage.

Frasier: You made quite an impression on him too. He said you were great.

Daphne: Go on . . . My God, will you listen to me, getting carried away like a school girl when I just met the man. I'm not raising my hopes tonight . . . though I'm glad I raised my bosom.

ANGLE ON MARTIN AND TOM IN THE LIVING ROOM.

Martin: Let me tell you, you're gonna love Seattle. It's a real people place. Good food, great bars.

Tom: I've heard that. Any you'd recommend?

Martin: I usually go to a place called Duke's. Great crowd there. A lot of young cops.

Tom: That could be fun.

Martin: Say, you a football fan?

Tom: Yeah. I really missed it while I was living in London.

Martin: We should take in a Seahawks game sometime. Frasier hates it, so it'd just be us.

Tom: Hey, Frasier warned me about you.

Martin: Okay, so I yell at the players too much.

FRASIER RE-ENTERS WITH TWO GLASSES OF WINE AND A CAN OF BALLANTINES.

Frasier: Here you are, Tom (HANDING GLASS TO TOM) And Dad, I selected an amusing little vintage for you, too. (HANDING HIM A BEER) You'll forgive me for not bringing you the pull-tab to sniff.

Martin: Merci beaucoup.

SFX: DOORBELL

FRASIER CROSSES TO THE DOOR, CARRYING HIS WINE. HE OPENS THE DOOR AND NILES IS STANDING THERE HOLDING A BOOK.

Niles: Hello, Frasier. Oh, thank you.

HE TAKES FRASIER'S GLASS OF WINE AND ENTERS. DURING THE FOLLOWING, NILES KEEPS CRANING HIS NECK TO GET A LOOK AT TOM.

Niles (CONT'D): (PROFFERING THE BOOK) I just stopped by to return your book.

Frasier: This is your book.

Niles: So it is. You should borrow it, it's absorbing. (LEANING IN, SOTTO) And who would that remarkably ordinary-looking chap on the couch be?

Frasier: Niles, I know why you're here and you're completely out of line.

TOM RISES TO GREET NILES.

Tom: Hi, I'm Tom O'Connor.

THEY SHAKE.

Niles: How do you do? Dr. Niles Crane.

WE HEAR DAPHNE FROM THE KITCHEN:

Daphne (O.S.): The bird's all done. All I need is a pair of big, strong arms . . .

SHE ENTERS.

Daphne (CONT'D): . . . to haul it out of the oven.

Niles: Well, I don't need to be asked twice.

NILES HURRIES INTO THE KITCHEN PAST DAPHNE. DAPHNE SMILES WEAKLY, OBVIOUSLY FEELING THWARTED AND EXITS BACK INTO THE KITCHEN. TOM, FRASIER AND MARTIN STAND A MOMENT IN SLIGHTLY EMBARRASSED SILENCE.

Frasier: That's my brother Niles. He's a little . . . (LOST, TO MARTIN) How would you explain Niles, Dad?

Martin: I usually just change the subject.

AS MARTIN CROSSES TO THE TABLE AND SITS, WAITING FOR HIS DINNER, WE:

FADE OUT.

Scene E

FADE IN:

INT. FRASIER'S LIVING ROOM – LATER THAT EVENING – NIGHT/3
(Frasier, Martin, Daphne, Niles, Tom)

EVERYONE IS SEATED AT THE TABLE FINISHING COFFEE. EVERYONE'S LAUGHING AND ENJOYING THEMSELVES, EXCEPT, OF COURSE, FOR NILES. TOM IS IN MID-STORY.

Tom: . . . So halfway through the interview, her stomach starts rumbling and her body mic's picking it up. But I have to ignore it because what am I going to say? "Would Her Majesty like a bicarbonate?"

DAPHNE LAUGHS.

Daphne: I could listen to your stories all night. They're so funny.

Niles: And all involving bodily functions.

DAPHNE GETS UP AND STARTS GATHERING DISHES.

Tom: (RISES) Here, let me help with these.

Niles: Many hands make light the work!

NILES RISES. HE AND TOM CLEAR THE DISHES, AS DAPHNE AND FRASIER WATCH IN HELPLESS EXASPERATION. NILES AND TOM EXIT INTO THE KITCHEN. ANGLE ON THE KITCHEN AS THEY CROSS TO THE SINK.

Tom: Niles, could I speak with you a moment?

Niles: Yes.

Tom: I was just wondering. Did I say or do anything that offended you?

Niles: No.

Tom: Then maybe it's all in my head because I sensed that you had a problem with my dating Frasier.

Niles: Well, if you must know . . . (STOPS) I'm sorry, what was the question?

Tom: Do you have some problem with my dating your brother?

NILES STARTS TO OPEN HIS MOUTH TO SAY SOMETHING, THEN STOPS. HE THINKS SOME MORE, THEN:

Niles: No. No problem at all. I'm sorry if I gave you that impression.

FRASIER ENTERS THE KITCHEN WITH THE REMAINING DISHES.

Frasier: Now, Niles, I didn't ask Tom to join us for dinner tonight so he'd be stuck in the kitchen talking to you. There're others who might want to have a crack at him.

Niles: Forgive me, brother. He's all yours.

TOM AND FRASIER EXIT BACK INTO THE LIVING ROOM. MARTIN ENTERS THE KITCHEN CARRYING AN ARMLOAD OF DISHES.

Martin: That Tom's a great guy, huh? So, what do you think, maybe him and Daphne . . .?

NILES STARTS TO LAUGH.

Martin (CONT'D): What's so funny?

Niles: Oh, just a little predicament Frasier's gotten himself in.

Martin: What?

Niles: Put down those plates and I'll tell you.

ANGLE ON THE LIVING ROOM. FRASIER, DAPHNE AND TOM ARE BY THE BAR. FRASIER'S POURING PORT.

Tom: I can't remember the last time I had such a wonderful evening.

Daphne: We should be thanking you. I can't remember when I laughed so hard.

FROM THE KITCHEN <u>WE HEAR MARTIN LAUGHING</u> HIMSELF SILLY.

Daphne (CONT'D): You've still got Mr. Crane going.

Frasier: Daphne, how about a little after dinner music.

Daphne: Good idea.

DAPHNE CROSSES TO THE STEREO.

Frasier: Quite a woman, isn't she?

Tom: Yes, she's really something. (THEN, SHYLY) Frasier, I was wondering . . .

Frasier: Yes . . .

Tom: Do you think before the evening's over we could get a little one on one time?

Frasier: I think that can be arranged.

FRASIER CROSSES TO DAPHNE WHO'S JUST PUT ON SOME MUSIC.

<u>SFX: ROMANTIC MUSIC</u>

Frasier (CONT'D): (TO DAPHNE QUIETLY) He just asked if he could be alone with you.

Daphne: No. This really is my lucky bra. Keep the wine flowing while I go fix my lipstick.

<u>DAPHNE EXITS</u> TO HER BEDROOM, AS <u>MARTIN AND NILES ENTER</u> FROM THE KITCHEN, BARELY ABLE TO CONTAIN THEIR MIRTH.

Martin: Yeah, I guess I'd better be hitting the old sack. I don't want to stand in the way of young romance.

Frasier: And Niles, I'd appreciate it if you would be running along.

Niles: Certainly. I can see I'm a third wheel here.

Frasier: What? That was surprisingly easy after your attitude all evening toward Tom.

Niles: I was wrong about Tom. If I had to choose a man for Daphne, that's just who I'd pick. (THEN, TO TOM) Nice meeting you, Tom. Goodnight.

Tom: (SMILING, EMBARRASSED) Goodnight.

<u>MARTIN EXITS</u> TO HIS BEDROOM. FRASIER ESCORTS NILES TO THE FRONT DOOR.

The Matchmaker

Niles: Oh, Frasier, a word in your ear . . .

FRASIER AND NILES EXIT INTO THE HALLWAY.

Niles (CONT'D): I have something to tell you. Dad wanted to, but I won the coin toss.

Frasier: Well, what is it?

Niles: I talked to Tom in the kitchen and he's feeling romantic.

Frasier: That's why you're leaving.

Niles: But are you aware the object of his affection is not Daphne but you?

Frasier: Me? That's impossible. Tom is not gay.

Niles: He seems to be under that impression.

Frasier: There's obviously been some misunderstanding.

Niles: Well, there's a triumph of understatement. Good lord, Frasier, what did you say to the man to lead him on so?

Frasier: I did not lead him on. I just asked him if he was single, and then we chatted about theater and men's fashion and . . . Oh, my God!

Niles: Ah, the perils of refinement.

Frasier: Do you realize what this means?

Niles: Yes. You're dating your boss. You, of all people, should know the pitfalls of an office romance.

Frasier: (AT SEA, STAMMERING) But . . . But, he said . . . I mean . . .

Niles: I see you're prepared to face your dilemma with eloquence. I'll call you tomorrow. Though, not too early, of course.

NILES EXITS INTO THE ELEVATOR. FRASIER RE-ENTERS THE APARTMENT. THE LIGHTS ARE LOW, SOFT MUSIC IS PLAYING. TOM, SITTING ON THE COUCH, SMILES AN "ALONE AT LAST!" SMILE. FRASIER, AT WIT'S END, RETURNS A SMILE THAT COMBINES PANIC AND A DEMENTED COQUETTISHNESS.

Tom: So . . .

Frasier: So! . . . God, I hate this song!

FRASIER SCURRIES OVER TO THE STEREO AND TURNS THE MUSIC OFF.

Tom: I've broken my rule for you. I usually don't date guys I work with.

Frasier: And I've sort of relaxed my rule for you too.

Tom: Well, now that we're finally alone, I want you to tell me all about yourself.

Frasier: Yes, I think maybe I'd better.

FRASIER SITS ON THE CHAIR. TOM PATS THE COUCH NEXT TO HIM. FRASIER WEARILY CROSSES AND SITS NEXT TO HIM.

Tom: You're cute when you're nervous.

Frasier: Then right now I must be downright adorable. Tom, I'm incredibly sorry, but we seem to have gotten our signals crossed here. The truth of the matter is, I'm completely straight.

A BEAT.

Tom: Hey, if you're not interested just say so.

Frasier: No, no. It's true. I really am. I asked you here tonight because you seemed very nice and you were going on so much about liking English people that I thought, "What a perfect man for Daphne."

DAPHNE VAMPS IN FROM THE HALL JUST IN TIME TO HEAR:

Tom: I can't believe this. You really had no idea that I'm gay?

SHE STOPS, REACHES BEHIND HER BACK AND UNHOOKS HER BRA. SHE TURNS AND AS SHE HEADS OFF, SHE RIPS HER BRA OFF, FLINGS IT WITH DISGUST, AND STALKS BACK TO HER ROOM.

Frasier: Don't take this wrong, but it never even occurred to me you might be gay.

Tom: It never occurred to me you might be straight.

Frasier: (UNCERTAIN) Thank you. I just feel awful that I've managed to lead you on all night.

Tom: It's okay. Honest mistake.

Frasier: But still, pouring you drinks, raising your hopes, letting you think you'd finally found someone sophisticated and sensitive who could help you mend your shattered heart and . . .

Tom: Frasier, I'll learn to love again.

Frasier: Oh. Yes, of course.

THEY CROSS TO THE DOOR.

Tom: Will you apologize to Daphne?

Frasier: For the rest of my days.

Tom: Does this mean your dad's not gay either?

Frasier: No, Dad's not gay.

Tom: But Niles . . . C'mon!

Frasier: Nope. 'Fraid not.

Tom: So this Maris guy he kept mentioning is a woman?

Frasier: Well, the jury's still out on that one.

AND WE:

FADE OUT.

Scene H

FADE IN:

<u>INT. FRASIER'S LIVING ROOM – LATE THAT EVENING – NIGHT/3</u>
(Frasier, Daphne)

FRASIER SITS SMOKING AND SIPPING COGNAC IN THE DIMLY LIT ROOM.
<u>DAPHNE ENTERS</u> FROM THE HALLWAY AND SEES HIM SMOKING.

Daphne: (SCOLDING) What, not again?

Frasier: Don't worry, I disconnected the alarm.

Daphne: Pity. I have half a mind to set it off and hope the firemen are cute.

Frasier: Daphne, I want to say again . . .

Daphne: I know, I know. You can stop beating yourself up. I'm not mad anymore. To tell you the truth, I was touched that you made the effort.

Frasier: Thank you.

Daphne: You know, you and your father, you've been good friends to me.

Frasier: Well, when you come down to it, that's all that really counts, isn't it? People who look out for you and whom you look out for. The mutual respect and affection.

Daphne: Absolutely.

Frasier: Amen.

A MOMENT OF SILENCE.

Daphne: Of course, it's no substitute for having your bones jumped by an expert, is it?

Frasier: Not remotely, no.

DAPHNE PICKS UP A CIGARETTE. AS FRASIER LIGHTS IT FOR HER, WE:

FADE OUT.

END OF ACT TWO

A ROOM WITH A VIEW

#40570-041

Written by Linda Morris & Vic Rauseo
Created and Developed by David Angell, Peter Casey & David Lee
Directed by David Lee

ACT ONE

Scene A

FADE IN:

<u>INT. FRASIER'S LIVING ROOM – LATE MORNING – DAY/1</u>
(Frasier, Martin, Niles, Eddie)

<u>FRASIER WALKS DOWN THE HALL</u> FROM HIS ROOM. HE IS PREPARING TO
LEAVE FOR WORK, TYING HIS TIE. HE LOOKS FOR SOMETHING ON THE
COFFEE TABLE. WE FIND OUT LATER IT IS A BOOK. HE LIFTS A NEWSPAPER
ON MARTIN'S TABLE, IT'S NOT THERE. HE CALLS FOR HELP.

Frasier: Dad?

NO ANSWER.

Frasier (CONT'D): Daphne?

A BEAT.

Frasier (CONT'D): Anybody home?

THERE'S NO ANSWER. FRASIER OPENS THE LID OF THE PIANO BENCH,
HOPING TO FIND THE BOOK, NO LUCK. STANDING AT THE PIANO, HE
TAKES A MOMENT TO NOODLE A FEW NOTES OF A CLASSICAL PIECE. HE
HITS A PIANO KEY THAT SOUNDS FLAT. HE HITS IT A FEW MORE TIMES IN
SUCCESSION THEN SEGUES SMOOTHLY INTO A BLISTERING RENDITION OF
"GREAT BALLS OF FIRE." FULLY ENJOYING THIS RARE MOMENT OF HAVING
HIS HOME ALL TO HIMSELF, FRASIER PLAYS AND SINGS WITH JOYOUS
ABANDON.

Frasier (CONT'D): (SINGING) "YOU SHAKE MY NERVES AND YOU RATTLE MY
BRAIN. TOO MUCH LOVE DRIVES A MAN INSANE. YOU BROKE MY WILL, BUT
WHAT A THRILL. GOODNESS GRACIOUS, GREAT BALLS OF FIRE!"

HE SPINS AROUND ON THE PIANO STOOL. AS HE SPINS HE SEES THE FRONT

DOOR OPEN AND HEARS MARTIN AND NILES, HE EFFORTLESSLY SEGUES
BACK INTO THE CLASSICAL PIECE. <u>MARTIN, NILES AND EDDIE ENTER</u>.

Martin: I think you're making too big a deal out of this.

Niles: But I've never seen Maris this angry. Her eyes were as dead as a shark's.

Martin: When your mother got mad at me, I'd just grab her, bend her backwards and
give her a kiss that made her glad she was a woman.

Niles: I can't do that with Maris. She has abnormally rigid vertebrae. She'd snap like a
twig.

Frasier: Let me guess, Maris has moved into the East wing again?

Niles: Lock, stock and slumber mask. (SIGHS) Sunday was her fortieth birthday. She
said in no uncertain terms that she wanted no acknowledgment of it whatsoever. And in
a moment I live over and over in my dreams, I believed her.

Frasier: What? No party? No gifts? No nothing?

Niles: Say that while weeping into an ermine lap robe and you've got her down
perfectly.

Martin: Why don't you just buy her a nice bottle of perfume?

Niles: She gets hives.

Martin: How about candy?

Niles: Hypoglycemic.

Martin: Then just get her a dozen roses.

Niles: Allergic

Martin: (GIVING UP) Gum?

Frasier: Oh for God's sake, Niles, just talk to her. Tell her you made a mistake. She's
obviously a little touchy about her age, but it's not like this is the first time she's turned
forty.

Niles: I know. I'll throw her a great big party this weekend. It'll be a costume ball with a
Louis Quatorze theme, right down to the powdered wigs and crushed velvet pantaloons.
May I presume you're both coming down with colds?

FRASIER AND MARTIN COUGH AND NOD.

Niles (CONT'D): I thought so.

<u>NILES EXITS</u>. FRASIER AND MARTIN AD-LIB "GOODBYE AND GOOD LUCK."

FRASIER RESUMES LOOKING FOR HIS BOOK.

Frasier: Dad, I can't find a book the station manager lent me and I promised to return it today.

Martin: What's it called?

Frasier: *The Life and Times of Sir Herbert Beerbohm Tree.* It's a wonderfully witty history of the English Theater.

Martin: Oh, all right, you caught me. I've got it hidden under my pillow. I only let myself read one chapter every night.

Frasier: Fine, so you didn't pick it up.

Martin: Ask Daphne when she comes home. She was looking for something to put her to sleep last night. That book sounds like it could put her into a coma.

MARTIN EXITS TO HIS ROOM. FRASIER THINKS FOR A BEAT, THEN HEADS DOWN THE HALL TO DAPHNE'S ROOM. AND WE:

CUT TO:

Scene B

INT. DAPHNE'S ROOM - CONTINUOUS - DAY/1
(Frasier, Daphne)

THE ROOM REFLECTS THE FACT THAT IT WAS ORIGINALLY FRASIER'S STUDY. IMPOSED UPON THIS IS THE PERSONALITY OF DAPHNE MOON. INCLUDED AMONG HER THINGS IS A COLLECTION OF ENGLISH TEA POTS ON WALL SHELVES.

THE DOOR OPENS. FRASIER LETS HIMSELF IN. HIS BOOK IS IN PLAIN SIGHT ON THE NIGHT TABLE NEXT TO DAPHNE'S BED. HE CROSSES PURPOSEFULLY TO THE BOOK, PICKS IT UP AND IS HEADING DIRECTLY BACK TO THE DOOR WHEN HIS EYES DRIFT TO AN INTRIGUING PHOTOGRAPH TUCKED IN THE MIRROR FRAME ACROSS THE ROOM. FRASIER CAN'T RESIST THE TEMPTATION TO LOOK AT THE PHOTO. HE WALKS TO THE MIRROR, PICKS UP THE PHOTO AND LOOKS CLOSELY. IT IS DAPHNE WITH PRINCE CHARLES. THEY STAND ON A MOOR, CHARLES IS WEARING HIS KILT. THEY LOOK EXTREMELY HAPPY. FRASIER PONDERS THIS FOR A BEAT, THEN TUCKS IT BACK INTO THE MIRROR FRAME.

FRASIER LOOKS AROUND THE ROOM TAKING IN THE DETAILS. HE SEES A SMALL DECORATIVE BOX, OPENS THE LID TO PEEK IN BUT QUICKLY CLOSES IT WHEN MUSIC STARTS PLAYING. FRASIER PICKS UP A PRESCRIPTION PILL BOTTLE ON A DRESSER. HE IS READING THE LABEL, HIS BACK TO THE DOOR, WHEN DAPHNE APPEARS IN THE DOORWAY. FLUSTERED, FRASIER ABSENTMINDEDLY SLIPS THE PILLS INTO HIS POCKET.

Daphne: Dr. Crane. What are you doing in here?

Frasier: (GUILTY) Daphne! I thought you were out. Not that I come in here when you're out. I simply needed my book. Which I have. (DISPLAYS IT) See?

SHE WATCHES HIM COOLLY.

Frasier (CONT'D): So I'll be off now. Me and my book. See Frasier go.

FRASIER QUICKLY EXITS AS DAPHNE WATCHES IN COOL SILENCE. AND WE:

FADE OUT.

Scene C

FADE IN:

INT. FRASIER'S LIVING ROOM – THAT EVENING – NIGHT/1
(Frasier, Martin, Niles, Daphne)

MARTIN AND FRASIER SIT AT THE DINING ROOM TABLE, DAPHNE IS IN THE KITCHEN PREPARING DINNER. NILES IS ON THE PHONE.

Niles: (INTO PHONE) Nadia, tell Mrs. Crane I want to speak to her, and don't take no for an answer. (A BEAT AS HE WAITS FOR MARIS TO GET ON, THEN HE SPEAKS LOW SO AS NOT TO BE HEARD) Nadia, tell her please, please, please come to the phone.

NILES HANGS UP THE PHONE AND CROSSES TO THE DINING ROOM TABLE AND SITS.

Martin: Maris hung up on you, huh?

Niles: Oh no, now she's got Nadia doing her dirty work. She's Maris' hatchet maid.

Martin: What happened to that Louis the Fourteenth birthday party idea?

Niles: Disaster there too. She reminded me that an entire branch of her family tree was slaughtered by the Huguenots

Martin: Oh, yeah.

Frasier: Well for now forget about Maris and have a nice meal in a more convivial atmosphere.

DAPHNE ENTERS FROM THE KITCHEN CARRYING A LARGE ROAST AND A CARVING KNIFE ON A PLATTER. SHE SLAMS IT DOWN ON THE TABLE AND EXITS TO THE KITCHEN. NILES, MARTIN AND FRASIER EXCHANGE A LOOK.

Niles: (SOTTO) What's she mad about?

Martin: Beats me.

DAPHNE RE-ENTERS FROM THE KITCHEN CARRYING A BOWL OF CARROTS AND A BOWL OF CREAMED ONIONS. SHE PLEASANTLY PUTS THEM DOWN IN FRONT OF NILES AND MARTIN, HER WARM ATTITUDE IN CONTRAST TO A MOMENT AGO.

Daphne: Here's your favorite, Mr. Crane, creamed onions. And Dr. Crane, I made my special glazed carrots just for you.

SHE PICKS UP THE CARVING KNIFE.

Daphne (CONT'D): (TO FRASIER) You. Carve.

DAPHNE STICKS THE KNIFE INTO THE ROAST AND EXITS TO THE KITCHEN.

Martin: Well, we don't know what, but we sure as hell know who.

DAPHNE ENTERS CARRYING A PLATE OF DINNER FOR HERSELF.

Daphne: If anyone needs me, I'll be eating in my room. (POINTEDLY TO FRASIER) You know where that is.

SHE EXITS TO HER ROOM.

Martin: What'd you do?

Frasier: This morning I went into her bedroom.

Martin: What?

Niles: Frasier, how could you? No matter how irresistible the force pulling you down that hall, exciting every molecule of maleness in your body, it must be fought.

Frasier: Oh, Niles, I went in to retrieve a book. (BEAT) What's the big deal? She goes into my room all the time and it doesn't bother me.

Martin: It doesn't matter. Women are different.

Frasier: That's sexism talking.

Martin: That's thirty-five years of marriage talking. Women protect their privacy. You know how they are about their handbags. You never go in there. It's always, "Bring me my purse." A husband could say, "Honey, I'm being robbed. There's a man holding a gun to my head and I don't have any money." The wife would say, "Bring me my purse."

Niles: Dad, once again your simple, homespun wisdom has pricked the balloon of Frasier's pomposity.

Martin: Well, when you got a bum hip, you look for something to pass the time. (TO FRASIER) You were wrong. You owe her an apology. Go do it.

MARTIN BEGINS SERVING HIMSELF.

Frasier: All right. I will go to Daphne's room and apologize.

FRASIER GETS UP AND HEADS TOWARDS THE HALL TO DAPHNE'S ROOM.
NILES GETS UP AND STARTS TO FOLLOW HIM.

Frasier (CONT'D): (WITHOUT LOOKING BACK) Alone, Niles.

NILES CIRCLES BACK TO SIT AND WE:

CUT TO:

Scene D

INT. HALLWAY OUTSIDE DAPHNE'S ROOM – CONTINUOUS – NIGHT/1
(Frasier, Daphne)

FRASIER COMES DOWN THE HALL TO DAPHNE'S CLOSED DOOR. HE
COMPOSES HIMSELF AND KNOCKS.

Daphne (O.S.): Yes?

Frasier: (SWEETLY) Daphne, it's Dr. Crane.

Daphne (O.S.): (COLDLY) Yes.

Frasier: Could you open the door, please?

AFTER A BEAT, THE DOOR OPENS A CRACK. DAPHNE STARES OUT AT HIM.

Frasier (CONT'D): This morning I behaved quite insensitively. I did need the book.
Nonetheless, I was wrong to go into your room without your permission and I'm sorry.

SHE STARES AT HIM.

Frasier (CONT'D): And I'll never do it again.

SHE CONTINUES TO STARE AT HIM.

Frasier (CONT'D): Ever.

SHE CONTINUES TO STARE.

Frasier (CONT'D): I'm being very nice.

SHE SAYS NOTHING.

Frasier (CONT'D): Well, goodnight, Daphne.

HE TURNS AND HEADS DOWN THE HALL. DAPHNE OPENS THE DOOR.

Daphne: Oh, wait. I'm being much too hard on you. I'm just a little sensitive about my privacy.

Frasier: No need to explain. It was all my fault and it'll never be an issue again.

Daphne: Thank you for being so understanding. I suppose my problem goes back to growing up in a house full of boys. My brothers were all snoops. They never gave me a moment's peace. Oh, it was a filthy little rite of passage for the Moon boys – when they reached a certain age, they'd sneak into the bathroom and peek at me in the shower.

Frasier: All eight of them?

Daphne: Well, all except for my brother Billy, the ballroom dancer. He never peeked at me. Though he did peek at my brother, Nigel.

DAPHNE EXITS BACK INTO HER ROOM. AS FRASIER REACTS AND HEADS DOWN THE HALLWAY, AND WE:

CUT TO:

Scene E

FADE IN:

INT. FRASIER'S KITCHEN/LIVING ROOM – A SHORT TIME LATER – NIGHT/1
(Frasier, Martin, Niles, Daphne)

FRASIER, NILES AND MARTIN ARE CLEARING THE DINNER DISHES. MARTIN IS SCRAPING THEM INTO THE SINK. DAPHNE IS STILL IN HER ROOM. FRASIER IS ALSO MAKING COFFEE. DURING THE FOLLOWING, FRASIER GETS A BAG OF COFFEE BEANS AND POURS THEM INTO THE GRINDER.

Frasier: Coffee, Dad?

Martin: Why not? I'm up six times a night anyway. I might as well be alert.

DURING THE FOLLOWING, FRASIER EXITS BACK TO THE LIVING ROOM TO CLEAR THE REMAINING DISHES. MARTIN FLIPS ON THE DISPOSAL. WE HEAR A HUM. IT'S JAMMED.

Martin (CONT'D): Oh, geez. (TURNS IT OFF) The disposal's jammed. (TO NILES) You want to stick your hand down there and see what's stuck?

Niles: Dad, it's me. Niles.

Martin: (WEARY) Yeah, I know. I'm asking you because you got skinny little fingers.

Niles: Skinny little freshly-manicured fingers. (OFF MARTIN'S LOOK) Are you sure it's off?

Martin: Positive.

Niles: (AS THOUGH DIRECTING A CROWD THROUGH A BULL-HORN) *Move away from the switch.*

Martin: (SOTTO) Oh, geez.

MARTIN TAKES A STEP BACKWARDS. WITH A LOOK OF GREAT DISTASTE, NILES INCHES HIS HAND INTO THE GARBAGE DISPOSAL.

Niles: It's wet and slimy and God knows what. It's like sticking my hand into the mouth of Hell.

FRASIER RE-ENTERS, PUTS DOWN THE DISHES AND HITS THE BUTTON ON THE COFFEE GRINDER. NILES' HAND SHOOTS OUT OF THE GARBAGE DISPOSAL.

Niles (CONT'D): Yaaa! (COVERING EYES AND OFFERING HAND) Somebody count, somebody count!

Frasier: They're all there, Niles. Sorry.

Martin: Give me a call when the coffee's ready.

MARTIN EXITS. FRASIER GOES TO THE SINK TO UNJAM THE DISPOSAL. HE PULLS A SPOON OUT OF THE DISPOSAL.

Niles: Well, I better get home. Maris will be missing me.

Frasier: I thought she's not speaking to you.

Niles: She's not. But what fun is it not speaking to someone if they're not there to not speak to?

NILES EXITS TO THE LIVING ROOM AND HEADS FOR THE DOOR. FRASIER FOLLOWS.

Niles (CONT'D): Oh, by the way, I'm out of cash. I need something to tip your garage attendant.

Frasier: Oh, of course.

FRASIER REACHES INTO HIS POCKET AND PULLS OUT NOT ONLY A DOLLAR BILL, BUT ALSO DAPHNE'S PILL BOTTLE.

Frasier (CONT'D): Oh, perfect.

Niles: What?

Frasier: These pills.

Niles: I was thinking money, but you know him better than I do.

FRASIER HANDS NILES THE DOLLAR.

Frasier: No, it's Daphne's prescription. While I was in her room, I must have inadvertently . . . knocked it into my pocket.

Niles: An interesting phenomenon. I can't walk through a drugstore without aspirin and decongestants leaping into my trousers.

Frasier: Okay. I was curious, I looked around a little. (READING THE LABEL) "One before bedtime." Great. Daphne's sure to discover they're missing when she turns in tonight.

AT THIS POINT, <u>DAPHNE ENTERS</u>. SHE CARRIES A ROLLED UP EXERCISE MAT UNDER HER ARM AND HEADS TOWARDS MARTIN'S BEDROOM.

Daphne: Oh, you're heading off, Dr. Crane?

Niles: Yes. Yes, I am.

Daphne: Say hello to your wife.

Niles: I'll certainly try.

Daphne: (YELLING DOWN HALLWAY) Mr. Crane, time for your exercises.

<u>DAPHNE EXITS</u> DOWN THE HALLWAY.

Frasier: Okay, this is my chance. I've got to put them back.

<u>FRASIER DASHES INTO THE HALLWAY TO DAPHNE'S BEDROOM</u>. NILES HEADS AFTER HIM.

Frasier (O.S.) (CONT'D): Alone, Niles.

<u>NILES</u> SPINS ON HIS HEEL, CROSSES TO THE DOOR AND <u>EXITS</u>.

CUT TO:

Scene H

<u>INT. HALLWAY OUTSIDE DAPHNE'S ROOM/DAPHNE'S ROOM –
CONTINUOUS – NIGHT/1</u>
(Frasier, Daphne [O.S.], Martin [O.S.])

<u>FRASIER DASHES DOWN THE HALL</u> TOWARDS DAPHNE'S ROOM, PILL BOTTLE IN HAND. <u>HE</u> THROWS OPEN THE DOOR AND <u>ENTERS</u>. HE RUNS TOWARDS THE TABLE WHERE HE PICKED UP THE PILLS, PUTS THEM DOWN, PAUSES TO ADJUST THE BOTTLE JUST SO, AND RUNS BACK TO THE DOOR. HE OPENS THE DOOR AND STOPS DEAD WHEN <u>HE HEARS DAPHNE AND MARTIN</u> IN THE DINING ROOM.

Martin (O.S.): The Sonics game is on. I'll do my exercises tomorrow.

Daphne (O.S.): Fine. If you change your mind, I'll be in my room.

FRASIER GETS A PANICKED LOOK ON HIS FACE. HE SHUTS THE DOOR AND FRANTICALLY LOOKS AROUND FOR AN ESCAPE ROUTE. HE CHECKS THE WINDOW, IT'S SEVENTEEN STORIES DOWN. HE LOOKS UNDER HER BED TO HIDE, IT IS TOO SMALL. WE HEAR DAPHNE RIGHT OUTSIDE HER ROOM.

Daphne (O.S.) (CONT'D): (YELLING TO MARTIN) I just thought a man who spends half his life prattling on about sports might actually want to move a muscle of his own once in awhile.

Martin (O.S.): Ha, ha.

FRASIER LOOKS AROUND THE ROOM FOR A PLACE TO HIDE, HE FINALLY RUNS INTO THE CLOSET AND CLOSES THE DOOR AT EXACTLY THE SAME MOMENT DAPHNE ENTERS. DURING THE FOLLOWING, WE INTERCUT BETWEEN DAPHNE'S BEDROOM, DAPHNE'S CLOSET AND DAPHNE'S BATHROOM. DAPHNE GOES INTO THE BATHROOM. WE HEAR WATER RUNNING IN THE SINK.

AFTER A BEAT, THE CLOSET DOOR OPENS AND FRASIER PEEKS OUT. THE COAST APPEARS CLEAR. HE TAKES A FEW STEPS OUT OF THE CLOSET, HEADING FOR THE DOOR. HE HEARS THE WATER STOP RUNNING AND DAPHNE HUMMING, AS SHE HEADS BACK INTO THE BEDROOM. HE CAN'T MAKE IT TO THE DOOR AND RUNS BACK INTO THE CLOSET, CLOSING THE DOOR BEHIND HIM JUST AS DAPHNE ENTERS WITH A GLASS OF WATER. SHE GOES TO THE PRESCRIPTION BOTTLE AND TAKES HER MEDICATION. SHE THEN BEGINS TO UNDRESS.

CUT TO:

INT. DAPHNE'S CLOSET – CONTINUOUS – NIGHT/1
(Frasier)

FRASIER IS MORTIFIED SEEING DAPHNE THROUGH THE SLATS. HE TURNS HIS FACE AWAY.

THE CLOSET DOOR OPENS AND DAPHNE'S BRA AND PANTIES FLY PAST FRASIER INTO A HAMPER IN HER CLOSET. DAPHNE'S HAND REACHES IN TO GRAB HER ROBE. FRASIER SEES THAT SHE CANNOT REACH IT SO, TO ASSIST HER, HE PUTS THE ROBE WITHIN HER REACH BY HANGING IT OFF HIS INDEX FINGER. SHE TAKES IT.

CUT TO:

INT. DAPHNE'S ROOM – CONTINUOUS – NIGHT/1
(Daphne, Frasier, Eddie)

DAPHNE, NOW DRESSED IN HER ROBE, GOES BACK INTO THE BATHROOM.

AFTER A BEAT, <u>FRASIER</u> PEEKS OUT AGAIN, SEES THE COAST IS CLEAR AND MAKES ANOTHER <u>DASH FOR THE DOOR</u>. HE GETS FURTHER THIS TIME AND IS NEARLY TO THE DOOR AND SAFETY WHEN <u>DAPHNE</u>, STILL HUMMING, <u>RE-ENTERS</u> FROM THE BATHROOM. THIS TIME FRASIER IS FORCED TO HIDE ON THE SIDE OF THE BED. SHE STOPS AT A DRESSER TO BRUSH HER HAIR. AS SHE DOES, HE JUMPS OVER THE BED TO THE OTHER SIDE.

DAPHNE WALKS ACROSS THE ROOM TO HER CLOSET TO GET A NIGHTGOWN. <u>FRASIER</u> SEES HE'S EXPOSED AND HAS NO CHOICE, BUT TO <u>DUCK INTO THE BATHROOM</u>.

WE SEE <u>EDDIE</u> NUZZLE OPEN THE BEDROOM DOOR AND <u>ENTER</u>. NEITHER DAPHNE NOR FRASIER SEE HIM ENTER. <u>DAPHNE EXITS</u> TO THE BATHROOM.

CUT TO:

<u>INT. DAPHNE'S BATHROOM – CONTINUOUS – NIGHT/1</u>
(Frasier, Daphne, Eddie)

<u>DAPHNE ENTERS</u>. FRASIER IS HIDING BEHIND THE BATHROOM DOOR. DAPHNE PULLS BACK THE SHOWER CURTAIN, STEPS IN, THEN THROWS HER ROBE OUT. THE SHOWER CURTAIN IS CLEAR PLASTIC WITH AN OPAQUE DESIGN. WE CAN SEE DAPHNE'S FACE AND SHE CAN SEE INTO THE ROOM, BUT HER BODY IS MODESTLY COVERED. SHE SEES <u>EDDIE ENTER THE BATHROOM</u> AND START TO DRINK FROM THE TOILET. FRASIER DOES NOT SEE EDDIE AND ASSUMES DAPHNE IS TALKING TO HIM.

Daphne: What are you doing? That's disgusting, you filthy thing.

<u>ANGLE ON FRASIER</u> BEHIND THE DOOR. HE IS MORTIFIED.

Daphne (CONT'D): Get out of here right now! Get out!

FRASIER COMES OUT, SURPRISING DAPHNE.

Frasier: Daphne, I can explain . . .

DAPHNE SCREAMS. <u>FRASIER</u> SCREAMS TOO AND <u>RUNS OUT</u>. AND WE:

FADE OUT:

END OF ACT ONE

ACT TWO

Scene J

FADE IN:

<u>INT. CAFE NERVOSA – THE NEXT MORNING – DAY/2</u>
(Frasier, Niles, Roz)

FRASIER IS SEATED AT A TABLE. HE LOOKS GLUM. <u>NILES ENTERS</u> IN A VERY UP MOOD.

Niles: Good morning, Frasier.

FRASIER GRUNTS IN REPLY. A WAITRESS PASSES:

Niles (CONT'D): *Cara mia, prego uno mezzo latté decaffinato.* And a bran muffin. No, due bran muffins. Maris and I burned up a lot of energy last night . . . (SOTTO TO FRASIER) a lot of energy . . . And I have to replenish my body.

NILES COYLY WHISTLES A HAPPY TUNE WHILE HE SMOOTHS A NAPKIN ON HIS LAP. FRASIER WATCHES HIM CLOSELY.

Frasier: Is that a love bite on your neck?

Niles: Hang the euphemism, Frasier. It's a hickey.

Frasier: Hmm. Well, when one considers Maris's limited lung capacity, that's quite a feat. So, I take it you and Maris achieved détente.

Niles: Twice.

Frasier: What magic words did you use to melt your little glacier?

Niles: When I got home, I sat her down, stared deeply into her eyes and said, "Here are the keys to your new Mercedes."

Frasier: You bought her a Mercedes?

Niles: Yes. (THEN) The things that tiny woman can do when properly motivated . . .

Frasier: Niles . . .

Niles: My little vixen had to go for a B-12 shot this morning.

Frasier: Niles, if you're through marinating in your own testosterone, I have my own problem. Remember last night when I went to put Daphne's pills back in her room? Well, she caught me again.

Niles: You're joking.

Frasier: No. I was so embarrassed, I left the house before she got up this morning. I left a note trying to explain what I was doing, but . . . well, considering the circumstances, I honestly don't see how Daphne can forgive me this time.

Niles: Oh, come now. How bad could it be? It's not as if you . . . you . . . saw her naked or something.

FRASIER LOOKS AT NILES. NILES STARES FOR A BEAT, THEN REALIZES.

Niles (CONT'D): You did. (TAKES A DEEP BREATH) Well, there goes my afterglow.

NILES COMPOSES HIMSELF. ROZ APPROACHES THE TABLE AND SITS. THEY AD-LIB HELLOS. ROZ EYES NILES.

Roz: So, Niles, you got a little last night, didn't you?

NILES REACTS.

Roz (CONT'D): I can always tell. (PATTING FRASIER ON THE HAND) Don't worry. You'll meet somebody.

THE WAITRESS CROSSES OVER WITH NILES' COFFEE AND BRAN MUFFIN.

Roz (CONT'D): (TO WAITRESS) Non-fat cap please.

Niles: Roz, this was a private conversation. I was helping my brother with a problem of some delicacy.

Roz: Don't worry. Shower Boy told me all about it.

Frasier: I'm mortified about this and I can't think what I can possibly do to make it up to Daphne.

Niles: Nothing says "I'm sorry" quite like an in-dash CD player and a passenger-side airbag.

Frasier: (TO ROZ) Maris got angry at him so Niles bought her a Mercedes.

Roz: Woof.

Frasier: (TO NILES) But if you're suggesting I buy my way out of my problem, the answer's no. It's the coward's way out.

Niles: Just remember, this coward has a hickey.

Roz: (TO NILES) Buy me a Mercedes and I'll make your neck look like a relief map of the Andes.

Frasier: Don't encourage him. I happen to believe that bribery is an unhealthy way for a couple to deal with conflict.

Niles: And during which of your failed marriages did you hone this theory?

FRASIER AND NILES AD-LIB BICKERING, "YOU'RE BEING DEFENSIVE.", "I AM NOT. THAT'S MERELY A REBUTTAL." ETC. FINALLY:

Roz: Oh, knock it off! (TO FRASIER) I agree with your brother.

Niles: Roz, you agree with me?

Roz: Keep your voice down. I know people here.

Frasier: What do you mean you agree with him? You think any woman can be bought off? Don't you find that insulting?

Roz: A woman's only going to forgive you if she wants to. A gift just helps grease the wheels a little. Didn't you ever hear that story George Burns tells about Gracie Allen? (OFF THEIR LOOKS) Gracie has her eye on this sterling silver centerpiece. George says it's way too expensive. Case closed. A few months later, George is going through some mid-life crisis and cheats on Gracie with some starlet.

Niles: George cheated on Gracie?

Frasier: Yes, Niles. And Ward Cleaver got it on with Lumpy's mother. It's a tough world out there.

Roz: Anyway, George becomes overcome with guilt. It eats at him for months. Finally, the only thing he can do to make himself feel better is to go out and buy her the silver centerpiece. Fast forward to seven years later, George overhears Gracie talking to a girlfriend. She says, "I wish George would cheat again. I really need a new centerpiece."

ROZ LAUGHS.

Roz (CONT'D): I love that story. It's got it all: lust, passion, intrigue, silverware, a fur coat . . .

Frasier: Wait a minute. You didn't mention a fur coat.

Roz: You don't think the starlet walked away empty-handed, do you?

OFF FRASIER AND NILES' REACTION, WE:

SMASH CUT TO:

Scene K

<u>INT. FRASIER'S LIVING ROOM - LATER THAT EVENING - NIGHT/2</u>
(Frasier, Martin, Daphne, Niles, Eddie)

<u>FRASIER ENTERS</u> THE FRONT DOOR. <u>MARTIN COMES OUT</u> OF THE KITCHEN.

Martin: Oh, Dr. Crane, I'm glad you're here. I need your advice. I have a son who's a total numbnut.

Frasier: Hello, Dad. Love your icebreaker.

Martin: You better get her to stay, Frasier. She knows my moods, she knows how to handle me and I like her.

Frasier: She's talking about quitting?

Martin: Yeah. Now go in there and apologize.

FRASIER GATHERS HIMSELF AND STARTS FOR DAPHNE'S HALLWAY.

Frasier: I can't go in there.

MARTIN HEADS TO HIS ROOM.

Martin: Of course you can't. Because I *asked* you to go in there. Of course, when I said don't go in there, what'd you do? You went in there. Now I say go in there, so you *won't*. That's why I love Eddie. He does what I tell him to. Come on, Eddie.

MARTIN EXITS DOWN THE HALLWAY. FRASIER STOPS EDDIE FROM FOLLOWING MARTIN BY HOLDING HIM BY THE TAIL.

Frasier: He's defying you too, Dad!

DAPHNE ENTERS FROM THE HALLWAY AND SEES FRASIER HOLDING EDDIE. FRASIER TURNS TO SEE DAPHNE WATCHING HIM. FRASIER LOOKS GUILTY. DAPHNE ROLLS HER EYES AND STARTS TO MOVE OFF TO THE FRONT DOOR. FRASIER FINALLY LETS EDDIE GO. EDDIE RUNS TO MARTIN'S ROOM.

Frasier (CONT'D): Daphne, wait. We have to talk. I feel terrible.

Daphne: (SUCKERING HIM IN) Oh, now, Dr. Crane, your note explained everything, you've got nothing to feel bad about.

Frasier: Oh, well, I'm glad to hear that.

Daphne: A servant like me doesn't deserve privacy anyway. Matter of fact, why don't we just get everything out in the open. (SHE DUMPS THE CONTENTS OF HER PURSE ON THE DINING ROOM TABLE) Here's my personal telephone book, a couple of letters from friends I opened today. And my birth control pills. I haven't had much use for these lately, as I'm sure you know. And here's my driver's license. As you can see I'm a full two years older than I originally disclosed – also, four pounds heavier. But it's in a spot that doesn't show – to *most* people.

Frasier: Listen, I know how hard it must be living in someone else's home.

Daphne: Yes, it is hard. But I put up with it because I happen to love this job. All I ever asked for was one room. A little corner I could call my own. I never minded that it was a damn-sight too small and I was up to my eyeballs in your precious earth tones and your African knickknacks. But now I have to put up with you in there too. (PICKING UP AN AFRICAN STATUE OFF THE TABLE) And that's one leering love god too many.

Frasier: Daphne, you're absolutely right. You should have a place to call your own. If you agree to stay, I'll happily pay to have your room redecorated. Make it yours. Paint, wallpaper, new upholstery, whatever you need to feel comfortable.

Daphne: How about a dead bolt, an electrified fence and a German police dog?

SFX: DOORBELL

Frasier: Daphne, I assure you, as long as we live under the same roof, I will never ever set foot in your room again.

Daphne: All right, then, I'll give it another try.

DAPHNE OPENS THE DOOR, NILES IS THERE.

Niles: Evening all.

THEY AD-LIB HELLOS.

Daphne: (VERY HAPPY) Good evening, Dr. Crane.

Niles: You're awfully chipper, Daphne.

Daphne: I'm quite excited really. Your brother has just offered to pay to have my room redecorated.

Niles: Really?

Daphne: As a matter of fact I may just take a trip downtown and start looking at fabrics. I'm thinking of doing the whole thing in pinks and yellows.

SHE EXITS. FRASIER POURS HIMSELF A SHERRY.

Frasier: She really is determined to keep me out of there.

Niles: So, you're putting things right with Daphne by opening up your checkbook?

Frasier: Oh, Niles, I know what you're thinking. It's merely a gesture.

Niles: Oh, I see. When I do it, it's a bribe. When you do it, it's a gesture.

Frasier: Our situations are completely different. You paid Maris off because you're afraid of her.

Niles: Oh, and you're not the least bit intimidated by Daphne?

Frasier: No.

Niles: Then it wouldn't alarm you if I were to, say, do this?

NILES DARTS TOWARDS DAPHNE'S BEDROOM.

Frasier: Niles. Niles! Where are you going?

FRASIER RUNS AFTER HIM CARRYING HIS SHERRY. AND WE:

CUT TO:

Scene L

INT. HALLWAY OUTSIDE DAPHNE'S ROOM/DAPHNE'S ROOM –
CONTINUOUS – NIGHT/2
(Frasier, Niles, Martin, Daphne, Eddie)

FRASIER FINDS NILES STANDING OUTSIDE DAPHNE'S DOORWAY. HE
PUCKISHLY CHALLENGES FRASIER BY STICKING ONE FOOT INTO DAPHNE'S
ROOM.

Niles: Uh oh, my foot's in Daphne's room.

Frasier: Get out of there.

Niles: Why? You're not afraid of getting . . . (JUMPING ACROSS THE THRESHOLD)
. . . in trouble, are you?

Frasier: Niles.

NILES JUMPS BACK OUT.

Niles: Now we're safe.

Frasier: Stop it.

NILES JUMPS IN AND OUT AGAIN AND AGAIN.

Niles: Trouble. Safe. Trouble. Safe.

Frasier: (OVER NILES) You're acting like a child. Get out of there!

Niles: Trouble. Safe. Trouble . . .

THIS TIME NILES ACCIDENTALLY KNOCKS OVER AN EARRING TREE FULL
OF JEWELRY.

Frasier: Look what you've done now.

HE RUSHES INTO DAPHNE'S ROOM TO PICK IT UP.

Frasier (CONT'D): She's going to find out.

Niles: So you'll just write her a bigger fatter check.

Frasier: No, Niles, she'll quit.

Niles: What?! (SUDDENLY PANICKED) Why didn't you say so? Help me pick these
up.

FRASIER HAS PUT HIS GLASS OF SHERRY ON THE NIGHT TABLE TO PICK UP
THE JEWELRY. NILES KNOCKS IT OVER ONTO THE BED.

Frasier: Oh my God

NILES LOOKS FOR SOMETHING TO MOP UP THE SHERRY. HE GRABS A TOWEL FROM THE BOTTOM OF A PILE OF FOLDED LAUNDRY ON DAPHNE'S BED. THE LAUNDRY FALLS OVER AND SPILLS TO THE FLOOR. FRASIER AND NILES FRANTICALLY TRY TO MOP UP THE SHERRY AND REFOLD DAPHNE'S LAUNDRY.

Frasier (CONT'D): Pick it up. Pick it up.

MARTIN ENTERS WITH EDDIE, THEY TALK OVER ONE ANOTHER.

Martin: My God, what are you two doing?

Frasier: It's Niles' fault.

Niles: It is not.

Frasier: Never mind. Just help us clean up this mess.

THE THREE GUYS WORK LIKE CRAZY TO GET EVERYTHING PICKED UP AND BACK INTO ITS PLACE. MARTIN IS SPRAWLED ACROSS HER BED TRYING TO MOP UP THE SHERRY. FRASIER'S GOT HIS HEAD UNDER THE BED LOOKING FOR A STRAY PENCIL. NILES IS REFOLDING HER LINGERIE. HE'S GOT A TEDDY TUCKED UNDER HIS CHIN IN ORDER TO FOLD IT. EDDIE SITS ON THE BED WITH A BRA IN HIS MOUTH. DAPHNE ENTERS IN TIME TO SEE THIS VERY INCRIMINATING TABLEAU AS FRASIER PEEKS OUT FROM UNDER HER BED, WE:

Daphne: What in bloody hell?

CUT TO:

Scene N

EXT. CAR DEALERSHIP - DAY - DAY/3
(Daphne, Frasier, Martin, Niles, Eddie)

WE SEE DAPHNE IN THE DRIVER'S SEAT OF A SHINY NEW CONVERTIBLE. EDDIE IS IN THE PASSENGER SEAT. SHE HAPPILY PLAYS WITH THE STEERING WHEEL. SHE PRESSES A BUTTON AND TO HER DELIGHT THE ROOF STARTS TO COME UP.

Daphne: Oooo!

ANGLE ON FRASIER WHO STANDS WITH NILES AND MARTIN AND A SALESMAN.

Frasier: What about this sporty little sub-compact? Bet you could park that anywhere.

DAPHNE STOPS THE ROOF FROM RISING AND SITS UP TO PEER OUT THE

DEALERSHIP WINDOWS.

Daphne: Is that a Mercedes dealership across the street?

FRASIER PUSHES DAPHNE BACK DOWN ONTO THE SEAT AS WE:

FADE OUT.

END OF ACT TWO

Scene P

(END CREDITS)

FADE IN:

INT. DAPHNE'S ROOM – NIGHT – NIGHT/3
(Daphne, Eddie)

DAPHNE ENTERS HER ROOM AND STARTS TO GET READY FOR BED. BEFORE SHE UNDRESSES, SHE CHECKS THE CLOSET, THE BATHROOM, UNDER THE BED AND ANYPLACE ELSE HUMANLY POSSIBLE FOR A PERSON TO HIDE. ONCE POSITIVE THAT SHE'S ALONE, SHE BEGINS TO TAKE OFF HER BLOUSE. AT THAT POINT WE SEE EDDIE'S NOSE POKE OUT FROM UNDERNEATH A PILE OF LAUNDRY. HE STARTS TO WATCH HER. DAPHNE SPOTS HIM AND SHAKES HER FINGER AT HIM. SHE OPENS HER DOOR AND EDDIE SCURRIES OUT. AND WE:

AND WE:

FADE OUT.

END OF SHOW

AN AFFAIR TO FORGET

#40570-044

Written by Anne Flett-Giordano & Chuck Ranberg
Created and Developed by David Angell, Peter Casey & David Lee
Directed by Philip Charles MacKenzie

ACT ONE

Scene A

FADE IN:

<u>INT. RADIO STUDIO - DAY - DAY/1</u>
(Frasier, Roz, Gretchen [V.O.])

<u>FRASIER</u> IS ON THE AIR. <u>ROZ</u> IS IN HER BOOTH.

Frasier: You're on KACL with Dr. Frasier Crane. We have time for one last call. Go ahead, Gretchen, I'm listening.

Gretchen (V.O.): (GERMAN ACCENT) Well you see, Dr. Crane, my husband is a fencing instructor, and lately he spends all his time with his wealthy new student. He's with her day and night. I'm afraid there's some . . . bumsen going on.

Frasier: Is this merely a suspicion or do you have any evidence?

Gretchen (V.O.): No, it's just a feeling.

Frasier: Well, unfortunately in these matters, there's no simple way to know for sure.

Roz: Oh yes, there is.

Frasier: Well this is your lucky day, Gretchen. Sitting in with us today, we have one of the world's five leading "bumsen" experts.

Roz: If you want to know if a man's cheating, you offer him two choices for dinner: One that's really rich and fattening and one that's light and sensible. If he picks the one that's calorie packed, he doesn't mind turning into a bloated pig, which means he's happily married and you're in the clear.

Frasier: You know Roz, when I hear advice like that, I think there ought to be a law against two or more women gathering at a water cooler. Now Gretchen . . .

Gretchen (V.O.): Does it really work, Roz?

Roz: Trust me. If he chooses the diet plate, it means he's staying in shape for his new

116

squeeze, and you should get yourself a lawyer who can sue the sweat off a racehorse.

Gretchen (V.O.): I'm going to do it. Thank you for your help, Roz. You too, Dr. Crane.

Frasier: Don't mention it.

SHE HANGS UP.

Frasier (CONT'D): "Dr. Crane and Friends" will be back tomorrow with more advice and (POINTEDLY TO ROZ) fewer recipes. Thanks for listening, Seattle.

THEY SIGN OFF. ROZ ENTERS FRASIER'S BOOTH.

Roz: I know you hate it when I butt into your show.

Frasier: (BUT YOU STILL DO) And yet . . .

Roz: You'll forgive me when you find out the wonderful thing I'm doing for you. You see there's this great woman who lives in my building. She's bright and funny and . . .

Frasier: Stop right there. I do not go on blind dates. They're a hideous waste of time. No, thank you, no.

Roz: She's not for you, she's for your father.

Frasier: What time should he pick her up?

Roz: Oh this is great. She'll be so excited. (THEN) Wait a minute. So blind dates are okay for him, but not for you?

Frasier: Yes. That also goes for games with balls, domestic beer, and giant trucks that roll over smaller ones.

AS THEY HEAD OUT THE DOOR, WE:

FADE OUT.

Scene B

FADE IN:

INT. FRASIER'S LIVING ROOM - LATE AFTERNOON - DAY/1
(Niles, Martin, Daphne, Frasier, Eddie)

NILES, MARTIN AND EDDIE ARE SITTING AT THE TABLE. THEY HAVE A MODEL SHIP KIT. NILES READS THE INSTRUCTIONS.

Niles: (READING) "So you want to build a three-masted schooner . . . Step One - take inventory of all parts."

Martin: We don't need to read all the instructions.

Niles: Yes, we do. It says right here in bold face, "Read all instructions."

Martin: Just hand me the right side of the hull.

Niles: You'll get your hands on that piece at step sixteen and not a moment sooner.

Martin: Can we just get started here?

Niles: Okay, Dad. (READING INSTRUCTIONS) "So you want to build a three-masted schooner . . ."

MARTIN ROLLS HIS EYES. DAPHNE ENTERS FROM THE KITCHEN. AS SHE CROSSES BY, SHE LOOKS AT THE PICTURE ON THE BOX.

Daphne: Oh, look at that. What a beautiful ship. I bet you'll have fun building that.

Martin: Not half as much fun as we're having reading about it.

Daphne: Did I ever mention one of my ancestors was a mutineer on the HMS Bounty?

Martin: No kidding.

Daphne: From what we could gather he made it safely to Pitcairn Island where he was quite fruitful and multiplied. For all I know there's a girl who looks exactly like me running around the South Seas, frolicking in the surf, all brown skinned and bare breasted.

NILES SNAPS A MAST WHICH HE'S BEEN HOLDING IN HIS HAND. MARTIN AND DAPHNE BOTH LOOK AT HIM.

Niles: (READING INSTRUCTIONS) "So you want to build a two-masted schooner . . ."

Daphne: Schooner? I thought it was a frigate.

Niles: No, a frigate has a fore and aft main sail.

Daphne: No, that's a brigantine.

Niles: Oh yes, you're right. Then what's a frigate?

Martin: That's when you just don't give a damn anymore.

MARTIN EXITS TO THE KITCHEN FOR A BEER. FRASIER ENTERS FROM OUTSIDE, COMING HOME FROM WORK.

Frasier: Hello all.

DAPHNE AND NILES AD-LIB HELLOS.

Frasier (CONT'D): So, Niles, will you be spending the evening with us?

Niles: Yes. As much as my Maris misses me, she feels that family comes first. She insisted I come over and spend quality time with Dad.

Frasier: She wanted you out of the house, huh?

Niles: Like a Jehovah's Witness.

MARTIN RE-ENTERS FROM THE KITCHEN, BEER IN HAND, AND CROSSES BACK TO THE DINING ROOM TABLE.

Frasier: Dad, I have a proposal for you. There's a woman in Roz's building who's very interested in going out with you. Roz says she has a terrific personality.

Martin: So I guess that makes me the pretty one.

Frasier: Just hear me out. She likes sports, she likes beer . . .

Martin: Yeah, so does Duke.

Frasier: But Duke won't kiss you goodnight at the end of the evening.

Martin: He will if he's had a few. Tell Roz thanks, but no thanks.

Daphne: Well, I think you're making a mistake. Trying new things is what keeps us all young and vibrant.

Niles: You're right, Daphne. For weeks all Maris did for excitement was float in her sensory deprivation tank, now she's taken up fencing. I've never seen her more vital. She practices with her instructor late into the evening.

Frasier: Maris has a fencing instructor?

Niles: Yes. Gunnar was the Bavarian champion three years running.

Frasier: He's Bavarian?

Niles: You're full of questions I've already given the answers to.

Frasier: Oh, am I?

Niles: So recapping, he's Bavarian and he doesn't speak a word of English so Maris gets to brush up on her German while she parries and thrusts.

Martin: So Maris is learning German . . . (ASIDE TO FRASIER) Just when you thought she couldn't get any cuddlier.

NILES PICKS UP A MODEL PIECE. HE REACTS, THEN OPENS HIS HAND. A PIECE OF THE BOAT IS STUCK TO IT.

Niles: Dad, did you touch the spanking aft?

Martin: Yeah, I pre-glued it for you.

Niles: Well you might have said something. The instructions on the glue specifically say, "Avoid contact with skin." Though of course you wouldn't know that.

Daphne: Not to worry. This type of thing used to happen to my brothers all the time. I can get that off with some nail polish remover. Come with me.

NILES AND DAPHNE CROSS THROUGH THE LIVING ROOM TOWARD THE POWDER ROOM.

Niles: So your brothers used to build a lot of models?

Daphne: Actually, I suspect they just sniffed a lot of glue.

Niles: That can cause brain damage, you know.

Daphne: Well, that confirms it.

THEY EXIT INTO THE POWDER ROOM.

Frasier: Dad, we need to talk. It's about Niles.

Martin: Boy, I can't tell you how many times I heard that from your mother.

Frasier: I took a call today from a German woman who suspects her husband – a fencing instructor – is having an affair with his wealthy new client.

Martin: And . . .

Frasier: (DETERMINED) German fencing instructor . . . Wealthy new client . . .

Martin: (EQUALLY DETERMINED) And . . .

Frasier: Well, don't you find that incriminating?

Martin: No. I find that a coincidence. Seattle's a big city. There must be a bunch of German fencing instructors, each one of them with dozens of students.

Frasier: Yes, but are they wealthy students?

Martin: No, most of them are inner-city kids who are trying to work their way out of the ghetto with nothing but a foil and a dream.

Frasier: Yes, well, somewhere in that slag heap of sarcasm there may be a kernel of truth. Maybe I am letting my imagination get the best of me.

Martin: Just trust me. Forget it.

MARTIN GOES BACK TO MAKING THE MODEL.

Martin (CONT'D): C'mon. Help me put this model together.

FRASIER CROSSES TO THE TABLE.

Frasier: Boy, Niles has always loved these models. Remember that Christmas when Mom gave him "The Visible Man and Woman," and he had to glue all the internal organs in place?

Martin: All I remember is you two fighting over it.

DAPHNE RE-ENTERS FROM THE POWDER ROOM.

Frasier: Niles was getting on my nerves so I snuck into his bedroom and stole his ovaries.

Daphne: There's a story I'm glad I missed the beginning of.

DAPHNE CONTINUES ON INTO THE KITCHEN, AS WE:

FADE OUT.

Scene C

A BLACK SCREEN. IN WHITE LETTERS APPEARS, "BAVARIANS AT THE GATE."

FADE IN:

INT. RADIO STUDIO – NEXT DAY – DAY/2
(Frasier, Roz, Gretchen [V.O.])

ROZ IS IN FRASIER'S BOOTH SETTING UP FOR THE SHOW. FRASIER ENTERS.

Frasier: Sorry I'm late, Roz.

Roz: Hey, Frasier. Did you have a chance to ask your dad about the date?

Frasier: Yes, he said he'd love to go, if not for the problem with the horses.

Roz: What horses?

Frasier: The wild horses that aren't strong enough to drag him out of the apartment.

Roz: Darn it. I already got her hopes up. I don't suppose you'd consider going out with her?

Frasier: Sorry. I've been on my share of pity dates.

Roz: Yes, but this time you wouldn't be the one being pitied. (OFF HIS LOOK) Listen, we've got some great callers today. Get this. Line three is a guy who just found out his girlfriend is his long-lost sister.

ROZ STARTS OUT, THEN TURNS BACK:

Roz (CONT'D): Oh yeah, and that German woman is calling back about her husband's affair.

Frasier: Gretchen?!

Roz: Yeah.

ROZ EXITS INTO HER BOOTH.

Frasier: I want her first!

Roz: Are you kidding? What am I supposed to tell the guy dating his sister?

Frasier: Tell him to hang on and relax, we've all been there.

ROZ CUES HIM.

Frasier (CONT'D): Hello Seattle. You're listening to Dr. Frasier Crane on KACL 780. Let's get right to the phones. Roz?

Roz: We have Gretchen calling back about her husband's affair. She thinks she has more evidence.

FRASIER QUICKLY PUNCHES THE BUTTON.

Frasier: Hello, Gretchen, I'm listening.

Gretchen (V.O.): (CRYING) Oh, Dr. Crane, Gunnar picked the diet plate!

ROZ LOOKS KNOWINGLY AT FRASIER.

Frasier: Gunnar . . .? Still that's no proof. Proof is phone bills, credit card receipts, lipstick on the collar . . .

Gretchen (V.O.): I found a love letter he wrote to her.

Frasier: Well, how long were you going to keep that a secret? Work with me here, Gretchen. What does it say?

Gretchen (V.O.): *"Mein kleine leberknodel . . ."*

Frasier: I'm sorry, I don't speak German

Gretchen (V.O.): It means "my little liver dumpling."

Frasier: (HOPEFUL) Maybe he's writing to you.

Gretchen (V.O.): It can't be me. He says he loves her beautiful little body, as thin as his sword, and her skin as white as bratwurst, and that she's his *Nichteinmenschlichfrau.*

Frasier: What is that?

Gretchen (V.O.): I don't know if there's a word in English. The closest translation is "not quite human woman."

Frasier: Oh dear God, it is her!

Gretchen (V.O.): What?

Frasier: I mean, it's not you.

Gretchen (V.O.): What should I do?

Frasier: I don't know! I need time to think. Let's go to commercial.

AND ON FRASIER'S DESPERATION, WE GO TO COMMERCIAL.

FADE OUT.

END OF ACT ONE

ACT TWO

Scene D

FADE IN:

A BLACK SCREEN. IN WHITE LETTERS APPEARS, "AN AFFAIR TO FORGET."

INT. RADIO STUDIO - MOMENTS LATER - DAY/2
(Frasier, Roz, Gretchen [V.O.])

ROZ CUES FRASIER THAT THEY'RE OUT OF COMMERCIAL.

Frasier: We're back. Gretchen I've considered your problem and I think the only course of action is for you to immediately confront your husband and insist he end this affair.

Gretchen (V.O.): But what if he won't?

Frasier: He has to! Innocent people are being hurt. Remind him of how much he means to you, remind him of all your years together. Are there children?

Gretchen (V.O.): No.

Frasier: Damn. Still, it's got to be a clean break. He must never see this woman again, even accidentally.

Gretchen (V.O.): We never had these problems back home.

Frasier: Then maybe that's where you should return, to the stable influence of Bavaria.

Gretchen (V.O.): How did you know we were from Bavaria?

Frasier: Well . . . I'm a master of dialects and I noticed there was a glottal quality to the occlusion of your dipthongs. Your pronunciation screams Bavarian.

Gretchen (V.O.): I'm originally from Austria.

Frasier: Do you want to split hairs or do you want your husband back? I'm sorry Gretchen, it's time for another commercial.

Roz: Another commercial?

Frasier: (FIRMLY) Yes, Roz, another commercial!

ROZ PLUGS IN A CART AND THEY GO OFF THE AIR. SHE RUNS INTO FRASIER'S BOOTH.

Roz: What is going on?

Frasier: What makes you think something's going on?

Roz: Well, when the person giving advice sounds crazier than the person calling in, I've got to think something's going on.

Frasier: Nothing's going on.

Roz: Wait a minute. You know who it is, don't you?

Frasier: (CAUGHT) Who?

Roz: The leberknodel.

Frasier: All right. Yes, I do know. But the husband's a close friend of mine. No one you know. How can I tell him? He'll be crushed.

Roz: Don't they teach you anything at Harvard? You never tell the person who's being cheated *on*. You confront the person who's doing the cheating.

Frasier: Oh no, that's out of the question.

Roz: It's easy. Just tell her you know she's been mattress surfing with another guy and if she doesn't knock it off you'll tell her husband.

Frasier: You don't understand. This isn't an easy woman to talk to. She doesn't deal well with confrontation. I once questioned the political correctness of her serving veal. An hour later we found her locked in the garage with the engine running on her golf cart.

Roz: Whoa, it's Maris.

AND WE:

FADE OUT.

Scene E

A BLACK SCREEN. IN WHITE LETTERS APPEARS, "IT'S A SENSORY DEPRIVATION TANK."

INT. NILES' SPA – LATER THAT DAY – DAY/2
(Frasier, Marta, Niles)

WE'RE IN A CORNER OF A ROOM IN WHICH A SENSORY DEPRIVATION TANK SITS PROMINENTLY. OTHER DOORS SUGGEST A STEAM ROOM OR SAUNA, ETC. PEGS ON THE WALL HOLD WHITE TERRYCLOTH ROBES.

FRASIER IS ESCORTED INTO THE ROOM BY MARTA, A 78-YEAR-OLD GUATEMALAN MAID. SHE POINTS AT THE SENSORY DEPRIVATION TANK.

Marta: Missy Crane *esta en la caja.*

Frasier: Mrs. Crane is in the box?

Marta: *En la caja.*

MARTA EXITS. FRASIER KNOCKS ON THE TANK.

Frasier: Maris? This is Frasier. We've got to talk about Niles.

THERE'S NO ANSWER.

Frasier (CONT'D): Look I know you've been deceiving him. We have to talk about this, so will you please come out of there?

A BEAT.

Frasier (CONT'D): You are in there, aren't you?

THERE IS A KNOCK FROM INSIDE THE TANK.

Frasier (CONT'D): Look, you can't hide in this ridiculous deprivation tank forever. (SOFTENING) I know you're having an affair. I care about you and Niles and I want to help you do what's best for your marriage.

THE DOOR TO THE TANK SLOWLY OPENS . . . AND A SOPPING WET AND MISERABLE NILES EMERGES. FRASIER IS AGHAST. MARTA RE-ENTERS AND PUTS TOWELS ON THE TANK.

Frasier (CONT'D): Oh God, Niles, I'm so sorry. (TURNS TO MARTA) Marta, you said Mrs. Crane was in the box.

Marta: (RE: NILES) Si, Missy Crane.

Frasier: (INDICATES NILES) No, that's *Mister* Crane!

Marta: (REALIZES HER MISTAKE) Oh, *Mister* Crane!

SHE SHRUGS AND EXITS, PRACTICING SAYING "MISTER," "MISTER," AS SHE
GOES. FRASIER SEARCHES FOR SOMETHING TO SAY TO NILES, THEN:

Frasier: Towel?

HE OFFERS NILES A TOWEL, AND WE:

FADE OUT.

Scene H

A BLACK SCREEN. IN WHITE LETTERS APPEARS, "TO THE VICTOR GOES THE
SPOILED."

FADE IN:

INT. FRASIER'S LIVING ROOM – LATER – NIGHT/2
(Frasier, Martin, Niles, Daphne, Eddie)

FRASIER AND MARTIN ARE NERVOUSLY WAITING FOR NILES TO APPEAR.

Martin: So, he didn't say anything about what happened with Maris?

Frasier: Dad, he was on a car phone. He was breaking up – in both senses.

Martin: I'm worried about him. He's always been such a sensitive kid.

Frasier: Yes, but when he gets here, it's important not to let him know how worried we
are. We'll only fuel his anxieties.

Martin: You're right. If we coddle him, he'll think this is the end of the world.

SFX: THE DOORBELL RINGS

FRASIER AND MARTIN EXCHANGE A LOOK, THEN GO TO THE DOOR AND
OPEN IT. NILES IS THERE.

Frasier: Hello, Niles.

Martin: Hello, son.

THERE'S A BEAT, THEN NILES HOLDS OUT HIS ARMS IN A NEEDY GESTURE
AND THE TWO OF THEM STEP FORWARD AND ENVELOPE HIM IN THEIR
ARMS. THEY MOVE HIM TO THE COUCH WHILE AD-LIBBING CODDLING
WORDS SUCH AS, "IT'S OKAY," "IT HAPPENS, IT HAPPENS . . ." "IT'S NOT
OVER YET," "DON'T WORRY ABOUT THIS, IT'S GONNA BE FINE."

Martin (CONT'D): Sit down, son.

NILES SITS ON THE COUCH. EDDIE JUMPS UP NEXT TO HIM AND LICKS HIS FACE.

Martin (CONT'D): Frasier, pour him a brandy.

Frasier: Actually, I'm out of brandy, but I do have an excellent sherry, two types of port, oh, and a new twelve-year-old single-malt scotch. It's a little on the peaty side.

Martin: Just pour him a drink!

FRASIER POURS HIM A SCOTCH.

Martin (CONT'D): What happened?

Niles: Nothing.

Frasier: But when I left you were storming up to Maris's room to have it out with her.

Niles: Yes, and with each step I thought of another question to hurl at her, but when I reached the door, I froze.

Martin: That's okay, son. There's nothing wrong with taking your time figuring out the best way to handle this.

Niles: I turned around, walked out of the house, got in the car and started driving.

Frasier: Well I'm glad you ended up here.

FRASIER PUTS A DRINK DOWN IN FRONT OF HIM.

Niles: Actually I ended up at the Oregon border check, but I had some fruit in the car so I had to turn back. What am I going to do? She's my whole life.

Frasier: Look, I'm sure whatever Maris is feeling for Gunnar, it's just infatuation. (HINTING) You know how you can be in love with one person and still be infatuated with someone else?

Niles: No.

Frasier: Boy, you are upset.

Niles: Of course I'm upset. I've been vanquished by a dashing, young, "Uber-mann." First Poland and France, now me.

Frasier: Look, she may have succumbed to his Teutonic charms temporarily, but in the long run she's going to choose the man who's also smart and sensitive.

Niles: Oh Frasier, that's just something we used to tell ourselves in chess club. The truth is women don't want men like us. Men of intellect. They want men of action. Men like Gunnar.

Frasier: Well, the first course of action you should take is to talk to Maris.

Niles: But I'm not sure I should talk to her. Maybe if I just sit tight, this whole thing will blow over. Why open that wound?

Frasier: That wound has already been opened, and you're the one who's been hurt. Talk to her. Someone once told me: "To understand all is to forgive all."

Niles: That's the biggest load of drivel I've ever heard in my life. What simpleton's almanac did that come from.

Frasier: It came from a letter you wrote me when I was having my problems with Lilith. You urged me to reach out to her and find out why she did what she did.

Niles: (TRYING TO GET IT) "To understand all is to –"

Frasier: All right, that part was hackneyed but there was some good stuff in the letter. I still have it. Let me get it.

FRASIER EXITS.

Niles: Frasier's right, isn't he, Dad?

Martin: Eh . . .

Niles: You sound dubious.

Martin: Well, you know, something like this happened between your mother and me, too.

Niles: And you handled things differently?

Martin: Yeah. First, I took it up with the other man. I told him if he went near your mother again, he'd be the other woman. (BEAT) It took a whole lot more than that to keep our marriage together, but at least it showed her how much I cared.

Niles: So what would you have me do? Go grab the guy by the scruff of the neck and escort him out of my house?

Martin: Could ya do that?

Niles: Well, I have fantasized about it, and it does sound like a way to go, but I'm so confused. A minute ago what Frasier was saying sounded good, too.

Martin: Hey, suit yourself. Frasier's very smart, very sincere and very divorced.

Niles: Well, I do have to talk to Maris eventually. At least your way I'll be going at it from a position of strength. I'm going to do it, Dad. I'm going to stand up to him. Maris has fencing practice tonight but it's Gunnar who's going to be taught a lesson!

Martin: That's my boy. Are you gonna do it right now?

Niles: Yes, Dad.

HE THROWS BACK HIS SCOTCH.

Niles (CONT'D): I'm pumped, I'm psyched . . . and I'm fairly sure I just swallowed an entire twist of lemon.

NILES EXITS AS FRASIER ENTERS FROM THE HALLWAY WITH A LETTER.

Frasier: Where's Niles?

Martin: He just left.

Frasier: What? Has he gone to talk things through with Maris?

Martin: No, he's gone to have it out with this guy and set him straight.

Frasier: And you let him go? What if this guy doesn't want to talk? What if he wants to fight?

Martin: It's okay. He's still better off. He'll have found his manhood.

DAPHNE ENTERS.

Martin (CONT'D): I tell ya, I'd be proud if Niles traded a couple of teeth for his *cajones*.

Daphne: I've got to stop walking in on the middle of conversations.

SHE CROSSES INTO THE KITCHEN, AND WE:

FADE OUT.

Scene J

A BLACK SCREEN. IN WHITE LETTERS APPEARS, "GET OUT YOUR DICTIONARIES."

FADE IN:

INT. NILES' CONSERVATORY - LATER - NIGHT/2
(Niles, Frasier, Gunnar, Marta)

GUNNAR IS SEATED ON THE COUCH, WITH HIS FENCING EQUIPMENT, WAITING FOR MARIS. NILES ARRIVES AND STEPS INTO THE ROOM.

Niles: There you are. (GUNNAR LOOKS UP) Yes, I'm talking to you, strudel boy. No one seduces my wife and gets away with it!

FRASIER STEPS IN, WITH MARTA.

Niles (CONT'D): (TO GUNNAR) You probably thought because of my refined bearing and swimmer's build I wouldn't put up a fight for the woman I love, but you're dead wrong, because real men have a thing called honor. But you wouldn't know that, would you?

Frasier: Niles . . .

Niles: You wouldn't know how decent people behave.

Frasier: Niles . . .

Niles: You wouldn't know the meaning of the word "rectitude."

Frasier: Niles! He wouldn't know the meaning of anything you're saying. He doesn't speak English, remember?

A BEAT.

Niles: Damn.

Gunnar: (TO MARTA) *Worüber ist er so böse?*

Marta: (SHRUGS) *Ich weiss nicht.*

Niles: Marta, you speak German?

Marta: *Que?*

Frasier: Uh . . . *¿Habla alemán?*

Marta: *Sí. Trabajé para una familia alemána en Guatemala quien lleguen despues de la guerra.*

Frasier: (TO NILES) She worked for a German family who turned up in Guatemala right after the war.

Niles: Good, then she can translate for me. Tell her to tell him –

Frasier: Wait Niles.

Niles: Why?

Frasier: Look at him. If he knew you were calling him "strudel boy" he'd be wiping his feet on your face.

Niles: Oh hang that, Frasier. If there are going to be scuffs, they're going to be scuffs of honor. (TO GUNNAR) How dare you steal my wife! (TO FRASIER) Translate!

Frasier: Oh all right. (TO MARTA) *Señor Crane quiere que preguntas a Gunnar, "Como se atrevez a robar mis zapatos?"*

Marta: (TO GUNNAR) *Was fällt Dir ein meine Schuhe zu stehlen?*

FINALLY UNDERSTANDING, GUNNAR DRAWS HIS SWORD ON NILES.

Gunnar: *Schweinehund!*

NILES GRABS ONE OF GUNNAR'S OTHER FENCING SWORDS.

Niles: Fine. You challenge me. *En garde.*

Frasier: Oh, yes, that's just what we need, a fourth language. Niles, you can't fight him.

Niles: Are you forgetting I've been fencing since prep school?

Frasier: So what? The man was born with a sword in his hand. He probably performed his own Caesarean!

GUNNAR HAS BEGUN TO PARRY AND THRUST. NILES SCRAMBLES TO DEFEND HIMSELF.

Niles: Oh my God, he's gonna kill me.

FRASIER AD-LIBS, "DUCK! PARRY! THRUST! ETC." AS THE FIGHT QUICKLY TURNS INTO AN AMUSING, BRILLIANTLY CHOREOGRAPHED ROUT, ENDING WITH NILES FLAT ON THE FLOOR. GUNNAR STANDS OVER HIM, THE POINT OF HIS SWORD AGAINST THE SOFT FLESH OF NILES' NECK.

Gunnar: *Entschuldige Dich sofort! Ich habe nicht Deine Schuhe gestohlen!*

Niles: (STRAINED VOICE, TO FRASIER) Is he giving up?

Marta: (TO FRASIER) *¡Pideme perdon! ¡No robo sus zapatos!*

Frasier: (TO NILES) He says he wants you to apologize. He did not steal your shoes.

Niles: Shoes?? What does he mean he didn't steal my shoes?

Frasier: Oops, sorry. I guess I mistranslated.

Niles: How could you confuse "wife" with "shoes"?

THEY GO INTO ONE OF THEIR AD-LIB BICKERINGS, WITH FRASIER SAYING, "IT'S BEEN A LONG TIME SINCE HIGH SCHOOL. YOU'RE IN NO POSITION TO COMPLAIN" AND NILES SAYING, "YOU SHOULD HAVE STUDIED HARDER. MARIS IS NOT FOOTWEAR" ETC.

GUNNAR PRESSES HIS SWORD HARDER AGAINST NILES' NECK. NILES YELPS.

Frasier: (TO MARTA) Not shoes, wife! I mean, *no zapatos, esposa!*

Marta: (GIGGLES) Ohhh! (TO GUNNAR) *Nicht Schuhe, Frau!*

Gunnar: Frau?

SADLY HE TAKES THE SWORD FROM NILES' NECK AND CASTS IT ASIDE.

Gunnar (CONT'D): *Ja, ich probat. Maris ist unwiderstehlich.*

Marta: (TO FRASIER) *Si, yo probado. Maris es irresistible.*

Frasier: (TO NILES) He tried. Maris is irresistible. (THEN, TO MARTA, IN SPANISH) Irresistible?

Marta: (SHRUGS, THEN TO GUNNAR) *Unwiderstehlich?*

Gunnar: *Ja.*

Marta: *Si.*

Frasier: O-kayy.

Gunnar: *Aber sie hat mich abgewiesen.*

Marta: *Pero me desecha.*

Frasier: But she refused him.

Niles: Really?

Frasier: *¿Verdad?*

Marta: *Wirklich?*

GUNNAR NODS. MARTA NODS. FRASIER NODS.

Niles: What did Maris say?

Frasier: *Que decía?*

Marta: *Was hat sie gesagt?*

Gunnar: *Ich liebe Niles.*

Marta: *Me amo a Niles.*

Frasier: I love Niles.

Niles: She loves me! She loves me! My marriage is whole again.

NILES HUGS FRASIER, THEN MARTA.

Niles (CONT'D): Maris!

NILES EXITS UP THE STAIRS.

Frasier: Now if I can just do the same for Gunnar and Gretchen.

Gunnar: Gretchen?

Frasier: (TO MARTA) Tell Gunnar his wife loves him very much. I mean – *Diga a Gunnar que su esposa le ama mucho.*

Marta: (TO GUNNAR, POINTING AT FRASIER) *Deine Frau liebt ihn sehr.*

GUNNAR REACTS, DRAWS HIS SWORD ON FRASIER.

Gunnar: *Schweinehund!*

Frasier: (TO MARTA) Not me, she loves him! Marta, damn your pronoun problems!

FRASIER GRABS NILES' SWORD AND TRIES TO FEND OFF GUNNAR'S ADVANCES, AS WE:

FADE OUT.

END OF ACT TWO

SEASON THREE

Moon Dance

MOON DANCE

#40570-063

Written by Joe Keenan & Christopher Lloyd
and
Rob Greenberg & Jack Burditt
and
Anne Flett-Giordano & Chuck Ranberg
and
Linda Morris & Vic Rauseo
Created and Developed by David Angell, Peter Casey & David Lee
Directed by Kelsey Grammer

ACT ONE

Scene A

FADE IN:

INT. RADIO STUDIO - DAY - DAY/1
(Frasier, Roz, Marianne [V.O.])

FRASIER IS ON THE AIR. ROZ IS IN HER BOOTH.

Frasier: We have thirty seconds left. I think we have time for one quick call. (PUSHING A BUTTON) Hello, Marianne, I'm listening.

Marianne (V.O.): (VERY EXCITED) Oh my God, I'm really on?

Frasier: Yes, your problem please . . .

WE HEAR A DOG BARKING OVER THE LINE.

Marianne (V.O.): Lucky, Lucky, get down! George, get the dog.

Frasier: Fifteen seconds . . .

Marianne (V.O.): Oh my God, oh my God, this is so exciting.

WE NOW HEAR A BABY CRYING OVER THE LINE.

Marianne (V.O.) (CONT'D): (CALLING OFF) Honey, get the baby. George, get your son!

Frasier: Ten seconds . . .

Marianne (V.O.): Okay, okay, here it is, Dr. Crane. If my husband and I don't have sex in the next two days, I'm going to a department store and pick up a stranger.

IN THE BACKGROUND WE HEAR SOMEONE SAY, "HELLO!"

Marianne (V.O.) (CONT'D): (CALLING OFF) Oh, Timmy, look who's here, Nana and Pop Pop! (THEN) I'll call you back.

SHE HANGS UP.

Frasier: To all you Mariannes out there, sex with a stranger is never the answer. Better to pack the kids off with Nana and Pop Pop, lock Lucky in the basement, lead your husband to a sturdy kitchen table and let the postman ring twice. (THEN) That's all, listeners. I'll be on vacation next week, but on Monday be sure to tune in to my replacement, noted podiatrist, Dr. Garreth Wooten. He'll be discussing his newest book, (PICKING UP A COPY) *Bunions and Blisters and Corns.* Oh My!

FRASIER HITS A BUTTON. THEY'RE OFF THE AIR. ROZ ENTERS FRASIER'S BOOTH.

Roz: I hate it when that foot freak subs for you. He's always trying to feel my arches. Couldn't you just have Frederick visit you here?

Frasier: Sorry Roz, the taxi's waiting to take me to the airport.

Roz: I hope it goes well. I hated family trips. My father was always dragging me through a gazillion museums.

Frasier: The only museums my father ever brought me to had the word "wax" written over the door.

THEY SHARE A LAUGH.

Roz: Have a great time.

SHE GIVES FRASIER A HUG.

Roz (CONT'D): And don't forget to bring me a really great present.

Frasier: How'd you like me to bring you a nice T-shirt from Colonial Williamsburg?

Roz: How'd you like me to give your home phone number to a bunch of people with webbed toes?

Frasier: It happens to be a very nice vacation spot. Frederick and I are going to dip candles, tan leather, churn butter . . .

Roz: (IMITATING THE COMMERCIAL) "Frederick Crane, you just finished the first grade! What are you going to do now?" "I'm going to Butter World!"

FRASIER REACTS, THEN PICKS UP HIS GARMENT BAG AND EXITS. AND WE:

FADE OUT.

Scene B

FADE IN:

INT. FRASIER'S LIVING ROOM - DAY - DAY/1
(Martin, Daphne, Niles, Eddie)

MARTIN IS IN HIS CHAIR WITH THE NEWSPAPER. DAPHNE ENTERS WITH A
BASKET OF LAUNDRY.

Martin: Hey, Daph - Bring that laundry over here, will you?

Daphne: What for?

SHE CROSSES WITH THE LAUNDRY.

Martin: I was just reading about this intelligence test you can give your dog. You throw a
towel over his head, and see how long it takes him to shake it off. (CALLS) Eddie!

EDDIE TROTS IN WITH A SOFT TOY BANANA IN HIS MOUTH AND DROPS IT
ON THE FLOOR.

Daphne: And the faster he takes the towel off, the smarter he is?

Martin: No, the faster he folds it. (THEN, TO EDDIE) Sit down, boy. Good.

HE TAKES A TOWEL AND TOSSES IT OVER EDDIE'S HEAD.

Martin (CONT'D): They ranked all the dogs and the smartest is the border collie. He
did it in seven seconds. Come on, boy! Take it off! (LOOKS AT WATCH) Six, seven . . .
Okay, next smartest was the poodle. I *know* he's as smart as a poodle. (LOOKS AT
WATCH) Okay, so he's no poodle. (LOOKS AT WATCH) A dachshund . . . a German
shepherd . . . a labrador.

Daphne: If you ask me, he's refusing to do that trick because he knows if he does it
right, you'll have him doing it every time we have company.

Martin: Hey! I bet you're right. He's putting one over on me and that takes *real*
intelligence.

SFX: DOORBELL

Daphne: (UNDER HER BREATH) Not really.

MARTIN TAKES THE TOWEL OFF EDDIE'S HEAD AS DAPHNE CROSSES TO
ANSWER THE DOOR. NILES IS THERE WITH THE NEWSPAPER.

Daphne (CONT'D): Hello, Dr. Crane.

Niles: I appreciate the false cheer, Daphne, but surely you've read this. (RE: THE
PAPER) Today's society page.

Martin: (COVERS HIS EARS) Don't tell me, don't tell me, don't tell me! I'm saving it for after dinner!

Niles: (OPENS IT) Apparently Maris is going on a three week cruise. Her friends threw her a bon voyage party. Look at this photo – Maris on the arm of a new beau, Pierson Broadwater. How could she be ready to date so soon? Especially Pierson. The man is a first-class feeb. He once wore his yachting cap backward so he'd look "with it."

Daphne: (LOOKS AT PAPER) She's just standing there, barely touching him, with only the tiniest bit of a smile on her face.

Niles: You can practically hear the zing, zing, zing of her heartstrings.

Daphne: (SCOFFING) Oh, Dr. Crane.

DAPHNE EXITS DOWN THE HALLWAY WITH THE BASKET OF LAUNDRY.

Martin: I think you're over-reacting.

Niles: No, I'm not. Broadwater is just the latest in a parade of escorts. According to Marta, my ex-maid and current mole, the gigolos have been swarming around Maris like ants on a Snickers bar.

Martin: Son, you've got no reason to believe Maris is involved with anyone. She's probably just getting out of the house, having a little fun. You might consider it yourself. Ever since you two separated you've been holed up like a fugitive.

Niles: Dad, if you're suggesting I start dating again, save your breath. Women don't exactly find me irresistible.

Martin: You've had lots of girlfriends.

Niles: Oh, let's count them. There's Maris. Dora, my childhood pen pal from Costa Rica. And I seem to recall a little girl in the fourth grade who lured me to a stairwell to show me her underpants.

Martin: Oh come on, you're exaggerating.

Niles: All right, perhaps I am. But let's face it. I've never been God's gift to women.

Martin: Hey, Niles, I think your problem is you still think of yourself as that same geeky kid you were in high school. But you've come a long way since then. And you're not doing yourself any favors staying home every night. Just think about it.

MARTIN EXITS TO THE KITCHEN. NILES UNFOLDS THE PAPER AND LOOKS AT MARIS' PICTURE.

Niles: (WHINING) Pierson Broadwater . . .?!

DAPHNE RE-ENTERS.

Daphne: Wine, Dr. Crane?

Niles: Well, wouldn't you?

AND WE:

FADE OUT.

Scene C

FADE IN:

INT. ELEVATOR IN FRASIER'S BUILDING – EVENING – NIGHT/2
(Martin, Daphne, Eddie)

DAPHNE AND MARTIN ARE RETURNING FROM WALKING EDDIE.

Daphne: Oh, let it go. The man had a right to be proud of his dog.

Martin: I just don't like show-offs, okay? (AS THE SHOW-OFF) "Ginger, catch the Frisbee!" "Ginger, roll over!" "Ginger, do my taxes!"

Daphne: Just because Eddie's not clever at tricks –

Martin: The hell he isn't. He just likes the kind that give him a chance to use his brain. Eddie is a thinker.

RESET TO:

INT. HALLWAY OUTSIDE FRASIER'S APARTMENT – CONTINUOUS – NIGHT/2
(Martin, Daphne, Eddie)

THE ELEVATOR DOORS OPEN AND DAPHNE EXITS.

Martin (CONT'D): Just watch. Open the door for him.

DAPHNE OPENS THE APARTMENT DOOR. MARTIN STEPS OUT OF THE
ELEVATOR AND ADDRESSES EDDIE WHO'S STILL IN THE ELEVATOR.

Martin (CONT'D): I taught him the names of all of his chew toys. (TO EDDIE) Eddie, get your banana. (TO DAPHNE) Now he's thinking. You can see the little gears turnin'. "Which one's the banana?" . . . Now he's thinking, "Where the heck did I leave the banana?"

THE ELEVATOR DOORS CLOSE.

Daphne: Now he's thinking, "Wait, we passed a fruit stand on Oak Street."

MARTIN PUSHES THE ELEVATOR BUTTON AND THE DOORS OPEN. EDDIE
RUNS OUT.

RESET TO:

INT. FRASIER'S LIVING ROOM – CONTINUOUS – NIGHT/2
(Martin, Daphne, Niles, Eddie)

MARTIN, DAPHNE AND EDDIE ENTER. NILES IS THERE.

Daphne (CONT'D): Dr. Crane!

Niles: Hello. I hope it's all right I let myself in.

Martin: Fine. What's up?

Niles: I just came by to ask you a question. Are you free Saturday night?

Martin: Sure.

Niles: (BOASTING) Well, I'm not. (THEN, FOR EFFECT) I have a date.

Daphne: Bravo, Dr. Crane.

Martin: Hey, no kidding? Who is she?

Niles: Marjorie Nash – (PROUDLY) the "fruit at the bottom" yogurt heiress. I bumped into her at the Frye museum. Before I knew it, your advice was thundering in my ears and I found myself asking her out. We'll be attending our club's winter dance, the Snow Ball.

Martin: Good for you.

Daphne: What's she like?

Niles: She's terribly haughty and rumors persist about her husband's death, but heck, a date's a date.

Daphne: The Snow Ball . . . sounds very glamorous.

Martin: I didn't know you could dance.

Niles: Well, just because we're going to a dance doesn't mean . . . Oh dear, you don't suppose she'll actually want me to?

Martin: Well, let's see, what do you have at a ball? A dance floor, an orchestra . . . I think you should be prepared for anything.

Niles: That never occurred to me. I've taken Maris to dozens of these and she never once asked to dance. Maris dislikes public displays of rhythm. (PANICKING) This is terrible. My first date is a miserable failure before it even begins. I'll just have to cancel.

Daphne: Oh, Dr. Crane, all you need are a few dancing lessons. I'd be happy to give you some.

Niles: You would?

Daphne: Oh yes, growing up I used to practice all the time with my brother Billy, the ballroom dancer.

Niles: I could never prevail upon you that way. It's much too much trouble. (GRABBING A CHAIR) We'll need to move this, won't we?

Martin: I'll just get out of your way.

DAPHNE AND NILES MOVE THE COFFEE TABLE TO CLEAR A LITTLE DANCE FLOOR. DURING THE FOLLOWING, NILES WILL AWKWARDLY FOLLOW DAPHNE'S INSTRUCTIONS.

Daphne: We'll start with a box step. It's very simple. Here - take my hand like so and put your other one round my waist. Now . . . start with your left foot.

Niles: Which one?

Daphne: Oh, hush. Step toward me, then bring your right forward and over and slide the left over to meet it. Then the right goes back, the left back and over, the right slides next to it and that's it. Once again now. (REPEATING THE MOVES) One two three, one two three, one two three, one two three . . .

Niles: This is boring, yet difficult.

Martin: There's no trick to dancing. It's a matter of coordination. Hell, if you can ride a bike or skip rope or kick a ball you can certainly . . .

MARTIN AND NILES EXCHANGE A LOOK, THEN MARTIN EXITS TO HIS ROOM, AND WE:

DISSOLVE TO:

Scene D

WE HEAR THE FINAL STRAINS OF "ISN'T IT ROMANTIC?"

FADE IN:

INT. FRASIER'S LIVING ROOM - A FEW HOURS LATER - NIGHT/2
(Niles, Daphne, Martin, Eddie)

NILES AND DAPHNE ARE FINISHING A DANCE. WE CANNOT SEE NILES' FACE. HE'S STILL NO ASTAIRE BUT HIS DANCING HAS IMPROVED.

Daphne: You're really doing very well, Dr. Crane. Earlier you seemed a bit tense. You've really relaxed now, haven't you?

REVERSE ANGLE - OR THEY SPIN AROUND - TO REVEAL NILES' FACE OVER DAPHNE'S SHOULDER. HE APPEARS COMPLETELY INTOXICATED. MARTIN

ENTERS FROM THE KITCHEN.

Niles: Yes – two – three. Thanks – two – three.

THEY FINISH WITH A LITTLE FLOURISH.

Martin: Hey, you two are looking pretty sharp.

Daphne: I think we're ready to move on to the samba. (TO EDDIE; PLAYFULLY) Eddie, fetch me a samba tape . . . Xavier Cugat . . . (TO MARTIN) Now he's thinking "The later Hollywood stuff, or the early New York recordings?

Martin: Now guess what I'm thinking.

DAPHNE GIVES HIM A LOOK AND EXITS.

Martin (CONT'D): I'm hittin' the sack.

HE HEADS TOWARD HIS ROOM AS NILES CONTINUES TO MOVE ABOUT THE ROOM DOING A LITTLE DANCE.

Niles: One – two – three, 'nite – two – three . . .

SFX: HIS CELLULAR PHONE RINGS

Niles (CONT'D): One – two – three . . .

HE TAKES THE PHONE FROM HIS JACKET.

Niles (CONT'D): (INTO PHONE) Hello – two – three. Oh, Marjorie . . .

MARTIN STOPS.

Niles (CONT'D): (INTO PHONE) How are you? . . . Really? . . . Oh, that is a shame. Well, there will be other dances . . . No, no . . . I understand completely.

NILES HANGS UP AND EXCHANGES A LOOK WITH MARTIN.

Martin: Sorry, son. Well, I guess you won't be needing those dance lessons.

Niles: Guess not.

MARTIN CONTINUES OUT AS DAPHNE RE-ENTERS.

Daphne: Now in the samba, you have to hold me a little closer. Ready?

NILES CONSIDERS TELLING DAPHNE ABOUT THE CALL, THEN:

Niles: I'm a dancer. A dancer dances.

AS DAPHNE TURNS ON THE MUSIC AND THEY BEGIN TO SAMBA, WE:

FADE OUT.

END OF ACT ONE

ACT TWO

Scene E

FADE IN:

INT. CAFE NERVOSA - AFTERNOON - DAY/3
(Niles, Martin, Daphne, Waitress)

NILES IS SEATED. THE WAITRESS COMES BY TO TAKE HIS ORDER.

Niles: (TO WAITRESS) Nonfat, half-caf latte, with a sprinkle of cinnamon *and* chocolate. I'm feeling reckless today.

Waitress: Maybe instead of nonfat milk you should go for the two percent?

Niles: I said reckless, not self-destructive.

THE WAITRESS CROSSES OFF. MARTIN AND DAPHNE ENTER.

Daphne: Well, look who's here. My dancing partner. Hello, Fred.

Niles: Hello, Ginger.

Daphne: It's a little joke we have.

Martin: Oh. Well you'll have to say it again so I can get the words exactly right when I tell it to my friends at parties.

Niles: Look, Daphne, I got some new CDs. Tonight we master the Mambo and the Conga. I can feel myself growing a pencil-thin moustache just saying them.

Martin: You're having more lessons tonight?

Daphne: Oh, yes, I've never seen anyone quite so eager to learn. I'll just go get us some coffees.

SHE CROSSES TO THE COUNTER.

Martin: Why didn't you tell her your date cancelled and you don't need any more lessons?

Niles: I would've, but the dear thing is having so much fun.

Martin: I think you're the one having so much fun. You think I haven't noticed the way you look at Daphne?

Niles: What are you implying!

Martin: You know damn well what I'm implying. Take my word for it. You're sticking a fork in a toaster here.

Niles: Well my muffin's stuck. Besides, what's the harm in a few dance lessons?

Martin: It's nighttime, you're alone, there's music playing, you got your arms around her – you're gonna end up saying something you can't take back.

Niles: I will not.

Martin: You will. You're a man. Look, something happened when I was separated from your mother. There was this pretty coroner in the city morgue. I guess I always had a crush on her. Any time we found a dead body I'd say, "Okay, boys, I'll take it from here." So, one night I asked her down to the corner bar.

Niles: Coroners have their own bars?

Martin: No, corner, Niles. The bar on the corner. Anyway, we had a few drinks, the lights were low, Sinatra was on the juke box – suddenly it all started pouring out. I told her how I felt. I knew the second it was out of my mouth it was a mistake. She let me down easy, but we still had to go on seeing each other all the time and it was very uncomfortable. After that the morgue was a pretty chilly place.

DAPHNE RETURNS WITH CUPS OF COFFEE.

Daphne: The smell of freshly ground coffee always takes me back to Grammy Moon's kitchen – the hours we spent trying to sober that old woman up. What time are we going to start your lesson tonight, Dr. Crane?

MARTIN LOOKS AT NILES.

Niles: Actually, we don't have to worry about that anymore. I just got a call from Marjorie – something came up so I won't be going to the ball.

Daphne: Oh, I am sorry.

Niles: Quite all right. Thank you for all your help.

Daphne: It seems such a shame to waste all that hard work. I hope you don't think I'm being too forward, but what would you think of our going to the dance together?

Martin: He's already taken up enough of your time. He couldn't ask you to do that.

Daphne: But it would be as much fun for me as it would for him. I'd love a chance to put on a pretty gown and have an elegant evening out. What do you say, Dr. Crane?

Martin: Tell her what you say, Dr. Crane.

Niles: Pick you up at seven?

AS MARTIN ROLLS HIS EYES, WE:

FADE OUT.

Scene H

FADE IN:

INT. FRASIER'S LIVING ROOM – EVENING – NIGHT/3
(Frasier, Martin, Daphne, Niles, Eddie)

MARTIN IS IN HIS CHAIR, READING THE NEWSPAPER, EDDIE COMES UP TO
HIM WITH A LITTLE TOY PIG IN HIS MOUTH. HE PUTS HIS CHIN ON
MARTIN'S LEG. MARTIN TAKES THE PIG.

Martin: No, Eddie. That's not your banana, that's Mr. Pig. (SHOWING EDDIE
PICTURES IN A BOOK) Listen to the difference: banana, pig, banana, pig. (THEN
RUBBING EDDIE'S HEAD) I still love ya, ya little pinhead. Go sit down.

EDDIE SITS IN A CHAIR. FRASIER ENTERS.

Martin (CONT'D): Boy, am I glad you're back. Listen –

Frasier: Dad, stop. I am still officially on vacation until ten a.m. tomorrow.

Martin: It's about –

Frasier: (A LA JIMMY BURROWS) Bup, bup, bup, bup, bup . . . I don't want to hear
about how hard Daphne pushed you to exercise, or the boring foreign film Niles made
you sit through, or the progress of Eddie's on-again, off-again romance with the
ottoman.

Martin: But you don't understand.

Frasier: Dad, please, for all intents and purposes, I am not here.

SFX: DOORBELL

DAPHNE ENTERS FROM THE HALLWAY. SHE IS DRESSED IN A BEAUTIFUL
GOWN AND LOOKS ABSOLUTELY STUNNING. SHE CROSSES TO THE DOOR.

Daphne: I'll get it. I'm so excited. This is my first ball. I hope he likes the way I look.

SHE OPENS THE DOOR TO NILES.

Daphne (CONT'D): Hello.

NILES ENTERS. HE IS WEARING A TUX AND IS HOLDING A PERFECT SINGLE
ROSE. HE'S TAKEN BY HOW BEAUTIFUL SHE LOOKS.

Niles: I thought I'd found the most perfect English rose . . . until now.

HE HANDS THE FLOWER TO DAPHNE.

Daphne: Oh, you. Shall we go?

Niles: Our carriage awaits.

THEY HEAD OUT.

Martin: (WARNING) Niles, you get her home at a decent hour. I'm gonna be waiting up.

Daphne: Oh, Mr. Crane. (SHE LAUGHS)

THEY EXIT.

Martin: (CALLING AFTER THEM) And your carriage better have a full tank. I don't want to hear you ran out of gas.

WE HEAR DAPHNE'S OFF-SCREEN LAUGH. MARTIN SHUTS THE DOOR.

Frasier: What the hell was that?

MARTIN CROSSES TO THE KITCHEN.

Martin: Eddie, did you hear someone? It couldn't be Frasier, he's still on vacation.

Frasier: Was that a date? Dad?

MARTIN EXITS INTO THE KITCHEN. CLEARLY, HE'S NOT GOING TO ANSWER HIM. FRASIER CROSSES TO THE FRONT DOOR, OPENS IT, THEN SLAMS IT.

Frasier (CONT'D): Hi, everyone, I'm home.

FRASIER FOLLOWS MARTIN INTO THE KITCHEN, AND WE:

FADE OUT.

Scene J

FADE IN:

INT. COUNTRY CLUB BALLROOM – NIGHT – NIGHT/3
(Niles, Daphne, Lacey & Andrew Lloyd, Conductor)

IT IS A BEAUTIFUL ROOM, RICHLY APPOINTED. THROUGH THE WINDOWS WE SEE THE STARRY NIGHT SKY, PERHAPS A MOON. A CRYSTAL CHANDELIER HANGS ABOVE THE DANCE FLOOR. TABLES SET WITH CHINA, CRYSTAL, CANDLES, AND BEAUTIFUL FLORAL CENTERPIECES SURROUND THE DANCE FLOOR. THERE IS AN ORCHESTRA AND A BAR. WAITERS SERVE THE GUESTS. SOPHISTICATED COUPLES IN FORMAL ATTIRE DANCE AND MINGLE. THE ATMOSPHERE REEKS OF OLD MONEY. SINCE IT'S THE "SNOW

ALL" IT'S ELEGANTLY DECORATED WITH A WINTER THEME.

ILES ENTERS WITH DAPHNE ON HIS ARM. SHE IS IMPRESSED BY THE URROUNDINGS.

aphne: (RE: ROOM) Oh, Dr. Crane. It's so beautiful. It's like a dream.

iles: (LOOKING AT DAPHNE) Isn't it though? (BEAT) Just for tonight could you call e Niles?

aphne: When I was in school I knew a boy named Niles and I called him Niley.

iles: Just for tonight could you call me Niles?

HE SMILES. THEY CROSS THROUGH THE ROOM. AS THEY GO:

iles (CONT'D): You're a vision. Everyone's looking at you.

aphne: You look awfully handsome yourself . . . Niles.

ILES LAUGHS GIDDILY.

iles: Would you like some champagne?

aphne: That would be lovely.

iles: Back in a moment.

ILES WALKS A FEW STEPS AWAY TO THE BAR.

iles (CONT'D): (TO BARTENDER) Two champagnes, *tout de suite*.

ACEY AND ANDREW LLOYD APPROACH.

acey: (DRIPPING WITH PITY) Niles dear . . . (SHE AIR-KISSES HIM ON BOTH HEEKS) How are you?

iles: Fine. (HE AIR-KISSES HER ON BOTH CHEEKS) Thank you.

ndrew: Haven't seen you for ages. We feel terrible about you and Maris.

acey: Oh, yes. We were just devastated. Everyone's talking about it.

iles: Oh. How is everyone?

acey: Devastated.

APHNE APPROACHES FROM BEHIND NILES, TO OVERHEAR. NILES IS NOT WARE SHE'S THERE.

acey (CONT'D): We were just saying that to Maris when we ran into her and Barclay

Paxton at the Breeder's Cup.

Andrew: No, she was with Carlo Binaldi at the Breeder's Cup. She took Barclay to Billy and Binky's birthday bash.

AS ANDREW AND LACEY WALK OFF:

Lacey: But anyway, Niles, if there's anything we can do to cheer you up just let us know

Niles: (SOTTO) How about a murder-suicide pact?

NILES TURNS TO SEE DAPHNE. HE HANDS HER A GLASS OF CHAMPAGNE.

Daphne: Well, they weren't very nice.

Niles: Everyone in our set seems to have this idea that while Maris is living the high-life, I'm sitting home crushed and lonely.

Daphne: Oh, never mind those gossipy twits. Tonight, you're all mine. Now, take me in your arms, Niles, and let the music carry us away.

DAPHNE PUTS OUT HER ARMS. NILES MOVES TO HER. THEY START THE FIRST STEP OF A DANCE WHEN THE MUSIC STOPS.

Conductor: Thank you. We'll be back in ten minutes.

Niles: (FEIGNING EXHAUSTION) Whew!

AND WE:

DISSOLVE TO:

Scene K

INT. COUNTRY CLUB BALLROOM – AN HOUR LATER – NIGHT/3
(Niles, Daphne, Lacey & Andrew Lloyd, Claire Barnes)

NILES AND DAPHNE DANCE A WALTZ. HE IS MORE COMFORTABLE NOW, SMILING AND NODDING TO HIS SOCIAL ACQUAINTANCES AS THEY DANCE BY. THEY FINISH DANCING WITH A LITTLE FLOURISH. DAPHNE LAUGHS.

Daphne: (HEADING TOWARD TABLE) Oh, I can't remember when I've had a better time. I'm on cloud nine.

Niles: I'd have to look down to see cloud nine.

THEY MOVE TOWARD A TABLE.

Niles (CONT'D): You look ravishing. Daphne, that is the most exquisite gown.

Daphne: Thank you. It was way out of my price range, but did you ever see something and say, "I just have to have it"?

Niles: (HEAD SWIMMING) Where's my chair?

THE LIGHTS DIM. THE DANCE FLOOR IS ENGULFED IN COLORED LIGHT. A MIRRORED BALL DESCENDS FROM THE CEILING, SENDING SPOTS OF LIGHT AROUND THE ROOM. THE ORCHESTRA BEGINS TO PLAY A TANGO.

Daphne: Ah, a tango.

SHE STANDS, TAKES HIS HAND AND LEADS HIM TOWARD THE DANCE FLOOR.

Niles: But, you never taught me this.

Daphne: You'll love it. It's perfect for you. This is a passionate, hot blooded dance that rose up from the slums of Buenos Aires.

Niles: The parallels between me and an unemployed gaucho aside, maybe we should sit this one out.

HE HEADS OFF, BUT SHE GRABS HIS HAND AND PULLS HIM BACK VERY CLOSE TO HER.

Daphne: Nonsense! There's only rule in the tango. Our bodies must be in continuous contact with not a sliver of daylight between them.

Niles: I'll do my best.

THEY BEGIN TO DANCE.

Daphne: Loosen up. Don't be afraid. Daphne won't let anything happen to you.

Niles: I don't think . . .

Daphne: Don't think. Just feel. You're an Argentine slum-dweller. You have no house, no car, you don't know where your next meal is coming from, but none of that matters because tonight you have the tango.

Niles: Oh Mama, I've got it all!

NILES REALLY STARTS TO GET INTO IT.

Daphne: That's it. You're dazzling, you're brilliant. But I feel you're holding back.

Niles: I am.

Daphne: This is no time for inhibitions.

Niles: I know.

Daphne: Let it out, Niles. Let everything out.

Niles: Oh Daphne, I adore you.

AT JUST THAT MOMENT IN THE DANCE, THEY SWITCH DIRECTIONS AND
DAPHNE TURNS HER FACE AWAY. WE SEE NILES IS STRICKEN WITH
HORROR. HE JUST DID WHAT MARTIN WARNED HIM OF. THEN, TO HIS
AMAZEMENT:

Daphne: I adore you too.

Niles: What?

Daphne: (A LITTLE LOUDER) I adore you too.

Niles: Oh, how I've longed to hear those words.

Daphne: How I've longed to say them.

Niles: You're beautiful. You're a goddess.

Daphne: I don't ever want this moment to end.

Niles: Then let's not let it.

NILES, INSPIRED, TANGOS LIKE A MAN POSSESSED. THERE IS, IN FACT, NOT
A SLIVER OF DAYLIGHT BETWEEN THEM. OTHER COUPLES, INCLUDING
LACEY AND ANDREW, GIVE UP THE DANCE FLOOR TO WATCH THEM. THE
MUSIC REACHES A CRESCENDO. NILES DIPS DAPHNE, HIS FACE CLOSE TO
HERS. THE MUSIC ENDS. THE CROWD APPLAUDS.

Niles (CONT'D): This is the most glorious night of my life.

Daphne: Mine too.

NILES LOOKS INTO DAPHNE'S EYES, AND KISSES HER. SHE KISSES BACK.
THE LIGHTS COME UP. NILES PULLS DAPHNE UP AS THEY MOVE OFF THE
DANCE FLOOR, TOWARD THEIR TABLE. NILES IS WALKING ON AIR.

Niles: I'm a new man. Do you have any idea what I'm feeling?

Daphne: Of course I do. (SHE INDICATES THE LLOYDS) Your friends look positively
dumb struck. From now on there'll be no more of that "Oh, poor Niles" attitude.

Niles: Far from it.

Daphne: I knew you were a good dancer, but I had no idea you were such a good actor.
"I adore you, Daphne. You're a goddess, Daphne." We fooled everyone, didn't we?

Niles: Oh. Yes, we did, didn't we?

Moon Dance

Daphne: Rich people. You'd think they'd be a lot smarter. What a bunch of gits.

Niles: Go easy on them. Given the right circumstances anyone can be fooled.

Daphne: Well, what do you say, another dance?

Niles: No, thanks. It's getting late and I've done enough dancing for one night.

Daphne: All right. I'll just go powder my nose and we'll be off.

SHE EXITS. NILES WATCHES HER GO. AN ATTRACTIVE WOMAN IN HER LATE THIRTIES TAPS HIM ON THE SHOULDER. HE TURNS TO SEE CLAIRE BARNES.

Claire: Niles, Claire Barnes. I was an associate in your attorney's office.

Niles: Of course. Claire. It's good to see you again.

Claire: (HANDING HIM HER CARD) I heard about you and Maris and I just wanted to give you my card and let you know that you can call me any time.

Niles: Thank you, but I'm happy with my attorney.

Claire: I meant to go dancing.

Niles: Oh. Thank you.

CLAIRE SMILES AT HIM AND EXITS. NILES STARES AT THE CARD AS DAPHNE APPROACHES.

Daphne: Well, Dr. Crane, are you ready?

Niles: (LOOKING ACROSS THE ROOM AT CLAIRE) No . . . I don't think I am. (HE LEAVES HER CARD ON A NEARBY TABLE)

Daphne: I beg your pardon?

Niles: Oh, Daphne, yes, of course. Shall we?

DAPHNE GIVES HIM A CONFUSED LOOK, TAKES HIS ARM AND THEY START OUT.

Daphne: We had a time tonight, didn't we?

Niles: Yes, we certainly did.

Daphne: And to think you almost didn't come to the ball. It's such a shame when people let fear stop them from trying new things.

Niles: Excuse me.

NILES BREAKS AWAY FROM DAPHNE, RUNS BACK TO THE TABLE AND

GRABS THE CARD. HE RUNS BACK TO DAPHNE.

Niles (CONT'D): I'm ready now.

SHE TAKES HIS ARM AND <u>THEY EXIT</u>. AND WE:

FADE OUT.

<u>END OF ACT TWO</u>

SEASON FOUR

The Two Mrs. Cranes

Mixed Doubles

Ham Radio

THE TWO MRS. CRANES

#40570-073

Written by Joe Keenan
Created and Developed by David Angell, Peter Casey & David Lee
Directed by David Lee

ACT ONE

Scene A

FADE IN:

INT. FRASIER'S LIVING ROOM – DAY – DAY/1
(Frasier, Daphne, Martin, Niles)

FRASIER AND NILES SIT AT THE DINING ROOM TABLE. FRASIER READS A
NEWSPAPER WHILE NILES PROBES HIS MUFFIN WITH A PAIR OF TWEEZERS.

Frasier: (LOOKS UP FROM PAPER) Niles, what are you doing?

Niles: This fruit muffin contains a number of things I don't care for. Currants . . . A husk
of something . . . (FLICKING SOMETHING ONTO HIS PLATE) Away wrinkly thing.

Frasier: You know, if you and Maris reconcile, I'm going to miss these tranquil
mornings. Me reading my paper. You tweezing your muffin.

FRASIER GOES BACK TO HIS PAPER AS MARTIN AND DAPHNE ENTER
THROUGH THE FRONT DOOR. MARTIN HAS THE MAIL, DAPHNE CARRIES
GROCERIES. MARTIN SEEMS IN HIGH SPIRITS. THEY AD-LIB GOOD
MORNINGS.

Martin: Hey, I got a letter from my old army pal, Bud Farrell. The whole platoon's
getting together next weekend at his place in Rattlesnake Ridge. Remember I took you
boys camping there when you were small?

Frasier: Who could forget the birth of a lifelong reptile phobia? (TO DAPHNE)
Speaking of old chums, a certain Clive called while you were out.

Daphne: (CONCERNED) Clive? Did he sound British.

Frasier: No, he was one of those fiery Mexican Clives. He said he'd call back.

Daphne: I bet he will.

Martin: I can't wait to see the old gang.

Niles: Dad, you're not planning to drive to Rattlesnake Ridge. It's five hours away. You know how your hip stiffens up.

Martin: No problem. It says I can bring a guest. So, who's the lucky one?

Frasier: If my count is correct, Dad, two of us get to be lucky.

Martin: C'mon, they're great people . . . Stinky, Wolfman, Boom-Boom, Jim – mind you, Jim's not his real name. We call him that 'cause he drinks Jim Beam. Just like we call Hank "Bud" 'cause he drinks Budweiser . . . C'mon, you'd love these guys.

Niles: What sherry drinker wouldn't? Alas I have a conference that weekend.

Daphne: And I have my friend Megan's birthday party.

Martin: What about you, Fras?

SFX: THE PHONE RINGS

Frasier: Please let this be Lilith asking me to give her a kidney that weekend.

DAPHNE ANSWERS THE PHONE.

Daphne: Hello? (UNCOMFORTABLY) Oh, Clive . . . Yes, it has been a long time, hasn't it? . . . I'm sorry, I have dinner plans tonight. . . . Well, maybe just a drink then. Say six-thirty? . . . Me too. Bye. (HANGING UP) Oh hell.

Niles: Who is this Clive, anyway?

Frasier: No, wait, wait, I'm a bit psychic . . . ex-boyfriend?

Daphne: Worse. Ex-fiancé.

Niles: You were engaged?

Daphne: Yes, for years. We were mad for each other. He was very sweet, and had the most gorgeous eyes you ever saw.

Niles: But . . .?

Daphne: Oh yes, that too. I just couldn't see a future with him. The man was a total layabout. No ambition, no drive, couldn't hold a job. All he wanted to do was tinker about with his car. His hands were always black from the motor oil.

Niles: What a brutish habit. If God had intended me to work on my Mercedes, he wouldn't have given me Horst.

Daphne: I had to break it off, but I wanted to let him down easily, so I said if we were still free in five years we could try again. And here he is right on schedule. What do I say to him?

Frasier: Be honest. Tell him how you feel.

Daphne: What, and break the poor thing's heart all over again?

Frasier: In the long run it will spare you a lot of unnecessary anguish. A case in point – (TO MARTIN) Dad, I have no plans for next weekend but I don't wish to spend it in the middle of nowhere with Budweiser and Boilermaker and their liver-damaged friend, Seltzer.

Martin: Fine. They'll have another one someday.

Frasier: (TO DAPHNE) You see? No evasions. (TO NILES) No convenient conferences. Just simple honesty.

Martin: 'Course, I don't suppose Jim'll be there next time. (OFF LETTER) Says here he just had his third bypass. And poor old Bud –

Frasier: Well, off to work . . .

FRASIER CROSSES TO THE COAT RACK FOR HIS JACKET.

Martin: I guess I'll see Bud at Jim's funeral. Or vice versa. Unless I go first.

Frasier: Oh, for God's sake, all right! I'll drive you to your stupid reunion.

Martin: Thanks, son.

FRASIER EXITS.

Martin (CONT'D): Guess I should wait a few days before I mention the part about Stinky needin' a ride.

AND WE:

FADE OUT.

Scene B

A BLACK SCREEN. IN WHITE LETTERS APPEARS, "NEXT IN THE REPERTORY, 'COSI FAN TUSHY'."

INT. RADIO STUDIO – DAY – DAY/1
(Frasier, Roz, Gil)

FRASIER IS ON THE AIR. ROZ IS IN HER BOOTH.

Frasier: And in closing I'd like to send a message to Keith the narcoleptic I spoke to earlier. We can continue our conversation when you feel more alert, but meanwhile I urge you to reconsider applying for that air traffic controller position. This is Dr. Frasier Crane, KACL 780 AM.

FRASIER SIGNS OFF. <u>GIL ENTERS</u> THE BOOTH.

Gil: Brilliant show, Frasier. Chock full of pithy insights.

Frasier: What do you want?

Gil: A favor. Bonnie Weems, the Auto Lady, just asked me to a dinner party – one of her famous Bring-Your-Own-Antidote affairs. I told her I'd have to check my book. I'm planning to say you and I have ballet tickets that night, so do back me up.

Frasier: Sorry, I can't.

Gil: You've got to. Have you any idea how vile her food is? The local raccoons have posted warning signs on her trash bin.

<u>ROZ ENTERS</u> FRASIER'S BOOTH.

Frasier: No, I mean she already asked me. I told her I can't make it because I'm driving my dad to his army reunion in Rattlesnake Ridge.

Gil: Very clever. I'd use it myself, but I killed my father off to escape her Labor Day clam-bake.

<u>GIL EXITS</u>.

Frasier: Oh, Roz, I have opera tickets for tomorrow. I don't suppose you happened to remember –?

Roz: (SMITING HER FOREHEAD) Your opera glasses! I am so sorry, they completely slipped my mind.

Frasier: I wouldn't mind if you'd actually borrowed them to go to the opera, but no, you just wanted to ogle that bodybuilder across the street from you.

Roz: Hey, I've just looked once or twice. It's not like I copied his name off his doorbell so I could look up his number and call him when he's in the shower so he'd have to walk across his room naked to answer the phone by the picture window. That would be wrong.

Frasier: Roz, I want them back. I refuse to squint through *Pagliacci* just because you're trying to see *The Magic Flute*.

AS <u>FRASIER EXITS</u> WE:

FADE OUT.

Scene C

<u>INT. FRASIER'S LIVING ROOM – EVENING – DAY 1</u>
(Frasier, Niles, Daphne, Clive)

FRASIER IS IN THE LIVING ROOM.

Daphne (O.S.): Dr. Crane, I need your opinion on this outfit. I wanted something that sent no romantic signals whatsoever.

SHE ENTERS THE LIVING ROOM. SHE WEARS A LONG, HEAVY CARDIGAN OVER A DECIDEDLY DOWDY DRESS.

Frasier: I can't think how you could improve upon that short of wearing a cactus as a corsage. (THEN) You know, five years is a long time to carry a torch. The man may just be stopping by to say hello.

Daphne: I certainly hope so. The thought of rejecting the poor thing again is more than I can bear.

SFX: DOORBELL RINGS

Daphne (CONT'D): Oh dear, it's him. (TO FRASIER) Anything between my teeth?

Frasier: No.

Daphne: Do we have any spinach in the fridge?

Frasier: Oh, just go!

DAPHNE CROSSES AND OPENS THE DOOR TO NILES.

Daphne: Oh, Dr. Crane. I was afraid you were Clive.

Niles: ("FORGETFULLY") Clive? . . . Oh, yes Clive. Was that tonight? Well, don't I feel silly bringing over this thousand-piece jigsaw puzzle.

Frasier: Niles, I'm sure Daphne doesn't need us horning in on her reunion. We're going to dinner.

Niles: Can't we order in? I've already assembled the first kitten and two yarn balls.

Frasier: (FIRMLY) I'm getting my jacket.

FRASIER CROSSES UP TOWARD HIS BEDROOM.

SFX: THE DOORBELL RINGS

DAPHNE AND NILES BOTH TURN TOWARD THE DOOR.

Frasier (CONT'D): Oh, for God's sake Niles, give them some privacy.

NILES EXITS RELUCTANTLY TO THE KITCHEN. FRASIER EXITS TO HIS ROOM. DAPHNE OPENS THE DOOR AND THERE STANDS CLIVE. HE'S HANDSOME, SHY AND A BIT TONGUE-TIED.

Clive: Hello.

Daphne: Hello.

SHE GESTURES FOR HIM TO COME IN. HE DOES.

Clive: Look at you. You look wonderful.

Daphne: Oh, go on.

Clive: No, I mean it. Very pretty and . . . warm. (A MOMENT) So . . .

Daphne: So . . .

THEY HUG AWKWARDLY.

Clive: Oh, God.

Daphne: What?

Clive: I've gotten a spot of axle grease on your sweater.

Daphne: It's all right. It's just a ratty old thing. Please come in. Same old Clive I see.

Clive: (WIPING HIS HANDS WITH A HANKY) I suppose so.

Daphne: So, what brings you to Seattle?

Clive: My undying love for you. (THEN) Damn. I meant to lead up to that. Sorry.

Daphne: No, it's all right. Just a bit –

Clive: Abrupt. No "How are you?" No "Nice place you have here" – By the way, it's lovely. (POINTING AT THE VIEW) Is that the Space Needle?

Daphne: Yes.

Clive: Super. Anyway, I remembered what you told me five years ago. I thought my feelings would change. It is a long time, but –

Daphne: Clive . . .

Clive: No, let me finish. My feelings haven't changed. I think about you every day and every night. There comes a time in every man's life when he has to get up the courage to look a woman in the eye and say –

NILES ENTERS FROM THE KITCHEN WITH A SNACK BOWL.

Niles: Cheese Nips? (THEN "INNOCENTLY") Oh sorry, is this a bad moment?

Daphne: No, not at all. (TO NILES) This is my very dear old friend Clive Roddy. (TO CLIVE) Clive, this is Dr. Niles Crane . . . my husband.

Clive: Your husband?

Daphne: Yes. (SLIPPING AN AFFECTIONATE ARM AROUND NILES' WAIST) Six months next week.

Clive: Oh. Well – don't I feel a bit . . . Congratulations. (TO NILES) You're a very lucky man.

Niles: Believe me – (PUTTING AN ARM AROUND DAPHNE) it's like a dream come true.

AND WE:

FADE OUT.

END OF ACT ONE

ACT TWO

Scene D

BLACK SCREEN. IN WHITE LETTERS APPEARS: "A SWELL OF COUPLES."

FADE IN:

INT. FRASIER'S APARTMENT – CONTINUOUS – NIGHT/1
(Frasier, Martin, Daphne, Niles, Roz, Clive, Eddie)

THE ACTION IS CONTINUOUS.

Clive: I'm certainly happy for both of you. I see you don't wear wedding rings.

Daphne: We don't need rings, because we always have our arms around each other. Don't we, dear?

SHE GIVES NILES A PECK ON THE CHEEK. NILES GIVES HER ONE BACK, DECIDES HE LIKES IT AND GIVES HER ANOTHER.

Niles: I know it's sickeningly sweet, but it works for us.

Clive: Well, I suppose I should be going.

Niles: No! (OFF THEIR LOOKS) I mean, no, I'm so enjoying having you here.

Daphne: I did promise you a drink.

Clive: Well, I suppose I could stay for a beer.

Daphne: Oh, good. (TO NILES) Darling, could you give me a hand in the kitchen?

Niles: Certainly, my angel.

ANGLE ON KITCHEN

DAPHNE AND NILES ENTER. DAPHNE POURS BEER.

Daphne: I'm so sorry, Dr. Crane. It seemed the kindest way to let him down. I didn't mean to put you in such an awkward position.

Niles: When it comes to you no position's too awkward.

ANGLE ON LIVING ROOM

CLIVE HAS WANDERED UP TO THE WINDOW TO CHECK OUT THE VIEW. FRASIER ENTERS.

Frasier: Oh, hello. You must be Clive.

Clive: Yes. And you're –?

Frasier: Dr. Frasier Crane.

Clive: Oh, Niles' brother?

Frasier: Yes. You've met him?

Clive: Just now. Though I used to know his wife quite well.

Frasier: Really? You know Niles' wife?

Clive: Yes, she's one-of-a-kind, that one.

Frasier: Isn't she?

Clive: She certainly can light up a room.

Frasier: (LAUGHS) Usually by leaving it.

CLIVE REACTS. NILES AND DAPHNE RE-ENTER. THEY ARE ALARMED TO SEE FRASIER.

Niles: Frasier!

Daphne: Oh, Clive, I see you've met . . . my husband's brother.

Frasier: What?

Daphne: (TO CLIVE) He's not hard of hearing. He just doesn't listen. It must run in the family. My husband's the same way.

Niles: (DEMONSTRATING) What?

Clive: I'm not intruding on some family occasion, am I?

Daphne: No, not at all. Frasier lives here . . . I mean, temporarily. You see –

Niles: – He's had a little spat with his wife . . . Maris.

Clive: Oh. (TO FRASIER) Sorry to hear that.

Frasier: Yes, me too. (TO DAPHNE) Daphne, I'm parched. Could you show me again where you keep the wine?

Daphne: Of course. (TO NILES; SQUEEZING HIM AFFECTIONATELY) Can you spare me a minute?

Niles: Only if you pay the love toll.

HE LEANS TOWARD HER TOUCHING HIS CHEEK WHICH SHE DUTIFULLY KISSES.

Niles (CONT'D): Oops! Too much – here's your change.

HE KISSES HER BACK. FRASIER AND DAPHNE EXIT TO THE KITCHEN. NILES WAITS TILL THEY'RE GONE THEN TURNS IMMEDIATELY TO CLIVE.

Niles (CONT'D): Can you stay for dinner?

Clive: Are you sure? Daphne said you had plans.

Niles: They fell through. Daphne would be crushed if you said no.

Clive: Well, if you're sure . . .

ANGLE ON KITCHEN

Frasier: I told you just be honest but did you listen? No, you have to subject us to this ridiculous charade.

Daphne: Just play along. Please. I swear – one drink and he's out the door.

NILES ENTERS THE KITCHEN.

Niles: He's staying for dinner.

Frasier: What?

Daphne: How did that happen?

Niles: He just sort of invited himself. Pretty damned cheeky I thought.

Daphne: Oh, dear God.

Niles: Obviously, he still has hopes of winning you back. We'd better keep these displays of affection as realistic as possible.

165

NILES EXITS.

Daphne: What will I serve? (OPENING FREEZER) Do we still have that lasagna?

Frasier: You expect me to endure a whole evening of this nonsense?

Daphne: Just do this for me and anything you want, name it, it's yours.

Frasier: *Anything*?

Daphne: (REALIZING) Except Rattlesnake Ridge.

FRASIER SHRUGS THEN CALLS OUT TO THE LIVING ROOM.

Frasier: Oh, Clive . . .

Clive (O.S.): Yes?

Daphne: All right!

Frasier: (CALLING TO CLIVE) Is lasagna okay?

Clive (O.S.): Super.

Daphne: I'm warning you, one thing goes wrong the whole deal's off.

Frasier: Nothing can go wrong. We just have to keep our stories straight and avoid unnecessary complications.

AND WE HEAR MARTIN'S VOICE FROM THE LIVING ROOM.

Martin (O.S.): Hey, I see we got company.

FRASIER AND DAPHNE EXCHANGE PANICKED LOOKS.

ANGLE ON LIVING ROOM

DAPHNE AND FRASIER RACE IN. MARTIN IS REMOVING HIS COAT.

Niles: Dad!

Frasier: Dad!

Daphne: Dad!

MARTIN REACTS.

Daphne (CONT'D): Clive, I'd like you to meet my new husband's father.

Frasier: Or, as we sometimes say in this country, father-in-law.

Martin: What?

Daphne: You see? This listening problem all comes from their dad.

Clive: (EXTENDING HAND) I'm Clive Roddy.

MARTIN SHAKES CLIVE'S HAND.

Martin: (UNSURE) Hi. Marty Crane.

Niles: Oh, Daphne, how remiss we've been. We haven't even given Clive the tour.

Daphne: Oh, yes, quite right. Well, this is the living room . . .

Niles: I think Clive would be far more interested in the master bathroom, the shower being so large and Manchester being so rainy.

Daphne: Oh, it is lovely. Right through here.

DAPHNE LEADS CLIVE OFF. NILES CALLS AFTER HER.

Niles: Wait, you didn't pay the toll. (THEN, OFF FRASIER'S LOOK) Oh, never mind.

THEY'RE GONE. FRASIER TURNS TO MARTIN.

Frasier: Go away.

Martin: What for? What the hell's goin' on?

Frasier: Clive is Daphne's old boyfriend. She's trying to let him down easy by pretending she's married to Niles.

Niles: So, this is my place. Frasier's staying with us because he's separated from Maris.

Martin: (TO FRASIER) You couldn't stand her either, huh?

Niles: Very amusing.

Martin: Do I still live here?

Frasier: Yes, but it might be best if you just excused yourself. This is a very complex situation requiring quick thinking, improvisational skills and a knack for remembering details.

Martin: Gee, I never used any of those skills as an undercover cop.

Niles: Now, Dad, don't be offended.

Martin: We'd better be careful. This oatmeal brain of mine's liable to bungle everything.

FRASIER ROLLS HIS EYES AS DAPHNE AND CLIVE RE-ENTER.

Clive: (TO FRASIER) So, Daphne tells me you're both psychiatrists.

Frasier: Yes.

Clive: Fascinating. (TO MARTIN) Are you a psychiatrist as well, Marty?

Martin: Me? Nah, I'm retired.

Clive: What did you do?

Martin: I was an astronaut.

Clive: (FASCINATED) Really? You actually flew space missions?

Martin: A few. Me and Neil Armstrong, Buzz Aldrin. I was the one nicknamed him Buzz. People think it's 'cause he flew fast. Not true. He was scared of bees.

SFX: THE DOORBELL RINGS.

EVERYONE LOOKS TO THE DOOR WITH CONCERN. THEN FRASIER LEERILY CROSSES TO IT.

Frasier: Who is it?

Roz (O.S.): Open up. It's me.

Martin: What do you know? It's Maris!

FRASIER, NILES AND DAPHNE REGARD MARTIN WITH AS MUCH ENRAGED INCREDULITY AS THEY DARE DISPLAY IN FRONT OF CLIVE. MARTIN SMILES CONTENTEDLY. FRASIER OPENS THE DOOR. ROZ ENTERS AND THRUSTS A PAIR OF OPERA GLASSES AT FRASIER.

Roz: Here, I brought your stupid opera glasses. So are we friends, again?

FRASIER EMBRACES HER.

Frasier: Darling!

Clive: (TO DAPHNE) Well, I guess that little tiff's over.

ANGLE ON FRASIER AND ROZ

FRASIER WHISPERS INTO ROZ'S EAR.

Frasier: (WHISPERING) You're Maris.

Roz: (WHISPERING) What?

Frasier: (WHISPERING) We're married.

The Two Mrs. Cranes

Roz: (WHISPERING) What?

Frasier: (WHISPERING) Play along! (THEN, RECOVERING) Maris Crane, Clive Roddy.

Clive: It's a pleasure.

Roz: It certainly is.

Frasier: Cupcake . . . (TAKING ROZ'S ARM; TO ALL) Could you excuse me? We need a moment alone.

FRASIER AND ROZ CROSS UPSTAGE AND OUT ONTO THE BALCONY.

Niles: (TO CLIVE) Well, now you've met the whole Crane clan.

Clive: Yes, though, Daphne, I did notice in the phone book, you still go by Moon.

Niles: That must've been an old book. She hyphenates now. It's "Moon-Crane."

Martin: (REMINISCING) I remember the first time I drove a moon crane. Damn near rolled it in the Sea of Tranquility.

Niles: So Clive, what do you do?

Daphne: (INDICATING HIS HANDS) Still mucking about with cars I see.

Clive: Hmm? . . . Oh, my hands. No, I just helped a lady change a tire on my way here. I don't have as much time for cars as I used to. What with my business and all.

Daphne: Your business?

Clive: Yes. After you left I thought about the advice you used to give me and I decided it made sense.

Daphne: What advice?

Clive: You know, "Get a job, you lazy git." I had to grow up sometime. So I took a business course and opened a sporting goods shop. Next thing I knew I had three of them.

Daphne: Goodness. (TO NILES) Isn't this ironic? All those years I nagged him to make something of himself and now look at him. A captain of industry and still handsome as ever.

Niles: Yes, well send in the clowns.

FRASIER AND ROZ RE-ENTER THE LIVING ROOM.

Niles (CONT'D): Don't bother, they're here.

Frasier: Well, unfortunately my Maris has to say her goodbyes. She has a previous engagement.

Clive: Sorry to hear that.

Roz: Me too. I thought I was available, but apparently I'm not.

Martin: Ah, forget your plans, Maris. Stay for dinner.

Roz: Okay, Dad.

Clive: Lovely. We can celebrate you two being reconciled.

Roz: Well, it's still tentative.

DAPHNE EYES ROZ JEALOUSLY. JUST THEN EDDIE ENTERS AND TROTS RIGHT UP TO CLIVE.

Clive: Well, look who's here. What's his name?

EVERYONE LOOKS TO EVERYONE ELSE IN UNCERTAINTY OVER EDDIE'S OR ANYONE'S AGREED UPON IDENTITY BEFORE THEY ALL NOD AND SAY:

ALL (EXCEPT CLIVE): Eddie!

FADE OUT.

Scene E

FADE IN:

INT. FRASIER'S LIVING ROOM – LATER THAT EVENING NIGHT/1
(Frasier, Martin, Daphne, Niles, Roz, Clive)

NILES AND FRASIER CLEAR THE TABLE. NILES KEEPS A WATCHFUL EYE ON DAPHNE WHO, ALONG WITH ROZ, ONLY HAS EYES FOR CLIVE.

Martin: So there I am floating twenty feet up in the chamber when some idiot turns off the weightless button. Down I go, right on to this special pickax we used for moon rocks.

Clive: (SHAKING HIS HEAD SADLY) And you still walk with a cane?

Martin: Que sera sera. (RISING) Well, it's time I was hitting the ol' hay.

Frasier: Don't forget your warm glass of Tang.

Clive: (SHAKING HIS HAND) It was an honor to meet you.

Martin: I had fun too. 'Night all.

MARTIN EXITS TO HIS ROOM.

Clive: Delicious meal, Daphne. I don't remember the last time I ate so much.

Roz: That explains how you keep that fantastic physique.

Daphne: Yes. You are looking wonderfully firm. (PLAYFULLY PATTING HIS STOMACH) You used to have that little tummy.

Roz: Do you work out?

Clive: When I can. My shops keep me awfully busy.

Niles: Daphne and I have our own little exercise regimen. We work up quite a sweat, don't we, darling?

Daphne: (IGNORING HIM, TO CLIVE) I can't get over it. It's like you're a whole different person. (TO NILES, MEANINGFULLY) A whole different person.

FRASIER STANDS.

Frasier: Well, who's for coffee?

Roz: (HER EYES ON CLIVE) More importantly, who's for dessert?

Frasier: Gumdrop . . .

Roz: Just asking.

Daphne: I'll give you a hand.

ANGLE ON KITCHEN

DAPHNE AND FRASIER ENTER. THEY WHISPER FURIOUSLY AS THEY PUT PLATES IN THE SINK AND COFFEE AND COOKIES ONTO SERVING TRAYS.

Daphne: Would you please tell Roz to stop flirting? Has she forgotten she's a married woman?

Frasier: You're one to talk. If you batted your eyelashes any harder you'd blow out the candles.

Daphne: You get rid of her now or it's Rattlesnake Ridge for you.

Frasier: You wouldn't.

Daphne: Wouldn't I? By the way, Stinky needs a ride.

DAPHNE EXITS THE KITCHEN.

ANGLE ON LIVING ROOM

DAPHNE RE-ENTERS WITH A PLATE OF COOKIES FOR DESSERT. FRASIER FOLLOWS. ROZ IS READING CLIVE'S PALM.

Roz: And according to your love line . . .

Frasier: Maris darling, I don't know about you, but I'm completely exhausted.

Roz: See you at home. (EXTENDING HER GLASS TO DAPHNE) More wine, please.

Daphne: Are you sure that's wise, dear? Remember that blackout you had last month? (THEN, WITH A MERRY LAUGH) What am I saying? Of course you don't.

Niles: That's what I love about her, her sense of humor. (TO DAPHNE) Cookie, dear?

Daphne: No thanks. (WITH A GLANCE TO ROZ) Some of us do look after our weight.

Roz: Now, now, you have to keep your strength up. You are eating for two.

ALL REACT. DAPHNE STARES MURDEROUSLY AT ROZ.

Clive: (TO DAPHNE) You're having a baby? Well, when were you planning to spring that news?

Daphne: Well, we don't like to bring it up. It's a sore point around here what with my sister-in-law being barren and all.

Niles: Now now. It's not her fault. My brother is impotent.

Clive: (AT A LOSS) Well . . . congratulations. (THEN) Is there a loo I can use?

Niles: (POINTING) Right by the front door. We call that one Frasier's bathroom. That's why we've monogrammed the towels with his initials.

CLIVE CROSSES AND ENTERS THE POWDER ROOM. ALL WATCH HIM GO WITH TIGHT SMILES UNTIL THE DOOR CLOSES.

Frasier: Have you all taken leave of your senses.

Daphne: She started it. Hanging all over him. (TO ROZ) Oh, by the way, that was my foot you kept massaging.

Roz: What is your problem? Frasier told me we were doing this 'cause you wanted to brush him off.

Daphne: I changed my mind. Didn't you see my signals?

Roz: Gee, I missed them. It must've been during one of my blackouts.

Niles: No need to fight. I'll just flip a coin. (DOES SO) Good news, Roz.

Daphne: Sod off.

CLIVE, UNSEEN BY ALL FOUR, EXITS THE POWDER ROOM AND WATCHES THE FOLLOWING IN QUIET HORROR.

Daphne (CONT'D): (TO ROZ) You'd think with all your dozens and dozens of men you could leave at least one for me?

Roz: Dozens? (TO FRASIER) Did you tell her that?

Frasier: Well, forgive me for keeping track.

Niles: Why are you fighting over the man anyway? He's got all the charm of a cricket bat.

Roz: (TO DAPHNE) Hey, you want him so bad, fine, take him.

Daphne: Fat chance I've got now that you've told him I'm pregnant. How am I supposed to get rid of this bloody baby?

Frasier: (NOTICING CLIVE) Clive. Coffee?

Clive: No thank you. I really should be going.

Daphne: No, please. I know what you must think, but we're not what we seem.

Clive: You certainly aren't. Look, I know I'm a guest here so I've kept silent so far, but I'm sorry, I can't any longer. You are the most appalling family I have ever met. (TO FRASIER) You – breaking up with your wife over a pair of opera glasses. (TO NILES) And you – looking down your nose at me all the while you show off your posh flat. Well, for your information, I don't think there's anything remotely special about either of your bathrooms. (TO DAPHNE AND ROZ) And you two women, flirting shamelessly with me right in front of your husbands. (TO ROZ, THEN DAPHNE) You having just reconciled with Frasier, you carrying Niles' baby. I pity your child, Daphne . . . and I pity any good Manchester girl who comes here to this vile coffee-swilling Sodom and lets it change her the way it's changed you.

Daphne: But I haven't changed. Really. We're not the awful people you think we are.

Frasier: Yes. The truth is we've been lying to you all night.

Clive: Well, I don't care to be lied to anymore. Goodbye. I'll never understand how two men like you could have been spawned by that sweet, courageous old astronaut!

HE EXITS, AND WE:

FADE OUT.

Scene H

FADE IN:

INT. FRASIER'S LIVING ROOM – LATER THAT EVENING NIGHT/1
(Frasier, Niles, Daphne)

FRASIER, NILES AND DAPHNE ARE THERE. DAPHNE, NOW WEARING A RATTY BATHROBE, SITS GLUMLY EATING COOKIES FROM A LARGE PLATE ON HER LAP.

Niles: I've got another one. He would have wanted you to move.

Daphne: I would've moved.

Frasier: Daphne, I'm sure if you just bide your time a while he'll give you a second chance.

Daphne: This was my second chance.

Niles: You'll get another. I believe that if two people are meant to be together sooner or later they will be. Years may pass, years filled with frustration and missed connections. But the day will come when they just fall into each others' arms and jet off to a beautiful Caribbean Island, though France is nice too.

Daphne: I'm not sure I believe you, but thank you, Dr. Crane.

Niles: You're welcome . . . ("A JOKE") . . . Mrs. Crane.

Daphne: (LAUGHS THEN YAWNS) I guess it's bedtime. 'Night.

Frasier: Good night.

DAPHNE CROSSES TO HER ROOM. NILES RISES, STARTS TO TAKE HIS FIRST STEP TOWARD DAPHNE'S ROOM, THEN:

Frasier (CONT'D): Niles. You're annulled.

NILES SITS GLUMLY, TAKES A COOKIE AND EATS IT, AND WE:

FADE OUT.

END OF ACT TWO

MIXED DOUBLES

#40570-079

Written by Christopher Lloyd
Created and Developed by David Angell, Peter Casey & David Lee
Directed by Jeff Melman

ACT ONE

Scene A

FADE IN:

INT. FRASIER'S LIVING ROOM – DAY – DAY/1
(Niles, Frasier, Martin, Daphne, Roz, Eddie)

NILES AND FRASIER ARE UPSTAGE, AT THE TELESCOPE. FRASIER IS
LOOKING THROUGH IT, NILES IS WAITING SOMEWHAT IMPATIENTLY.

Niles: Don't be greedy. Your turn was up forty seconds ago. Tic, tic, tic, tic.

Frasier: Oh, all right. (THEY TRADE PLACES) It's the penthouse unit, second window
in from the right.

Niles: Scanning . . . scanning . . . (FINDING IT) Oh Mama! Utter perfection.

Martin: You two know what you're doing isn't right, don't you?

Frasier: We happen to be looking at an extremely rare Brancusi armchair, not a naked
woman.

Martin: That's what I'm talking about.

Frasier: By the way, Dad, I hope you're not settling in there. I have plans for the
television tonight. Roz is bringing over a quirky little Hungarian comedy she taped off
the satellite dish.

Martin: You know, I don't know why we can't get one of those dishes. Duke says they
got a channel that runs nothing but sports bloopers.

Frasier: Question asked and answered.

THE FRONT DOOR OPENS AND DAPHNE ENTERS.

Daphne: Evening.

Martin: Hey, Daph. You're home kinda early, aren't you?

Daphne: A bit. Something . . . sort of happened.

Martin: What was it?

Daphne: Well, Joe and I were having dinner, everything was nice as could be and I said, "Don't you like your potato?" And he said, "No, I'm not hungry for potato just now." And I said, "Well, if you don't like your potato you're welcome to try my potato –"

Frasier: Perhaps we could hasten to the post-potato portion of the dialogue.

Daphne: Well, that's when he said it. He said we'd been on-again, off-again for too long without making anything permanent. So maybe it was best if we just broke up.

Martin: Gosh, I'm sorry. But you're sure taking it well. If you'd told me Joe would end up dumping you tonight I'd have bet –

Daphne: Oh God. He dumped me!

AND WITH THAT, SHE BEGINS TO SOB UNCONTROLLABLY.

Frasier: Deftly done, Dad.

Martin: Well don't just stand there, you two – somebody comfort her.

Niles: Right.

THEY BOTH MOVE TOWARD HER, NILES LEADING THE WAY. HE'S OBVIOUSLY QUITE EAGER AT THE CHANCE TO HUG DAPHNE. BUT FRASIER BEATS HIM TO IT – TO NILES'S CONSTERNATION. THROUGHOUT THE FOLLOWING DAPHNE WILL REMAIN CRYING.

Frasier: That's it, Daphne. Let it all out.

Daphne: (THROUGH SOBS) This is so embarrassing.

Frasier: Never mind how it looks. Expressing our emotions is always beneficial even when it may come at the expense of our pride (NOTICES HIS LAPEL) – or a brand new Italian silk jacket.

SHE'S STILL BAWLING.

Frasier (CONT'D): I don't seem to be doing much good here. Maybe one of you should try.

Niles: Very well.

AGAIN, NILES STEPS FORWARD BUT MARTIN BEATS HIM TO IT.

Martin: Now Daphne, you're better off without that guy. He was a bum!

Daphne: He was the best thing in my life! (CRIES)

Martin: Oh. Well then maybe he just wasn't ready for a commitment.

Daphne: He's in love with someone else. (CRIES HARDER)

Martin: Oh. Well, then maybe you just weren't meant for each other. I mean, you're a champagne and caviar sort of girl – he's steak and potatoes.

Daphne: (SOBBING AT THE MEMORY) Potatoes! . . .

Martin: I'm making a mess of this too.

Niles: (STEPPING FORWARD) Here, Dad . . .

SFX: DOORBELL

Daphne: I'll get it.

SHE SLIPS AWAY FROM NILES AND OPENS THE DOOR TO ROZ WHO HAS ARRIVED WITH CASSETTE IN HAND.

Roz: Hi, Daphne.

Daphne: (CRIES) Roz.

Roz: Oh my God, you got dumped.

SHE HUGS DAPHNE.

Roz (CONT'D): (OVER DAPHNE'S SHOULDER, TO FRASIER) You made her open the door?

Frasier: It's what she does.

Martin: You're just in time, Roz. We're not doing such a good job of comforting her.

Roz: Don't worry about it. Come on.

THEY HEAD TO DAPHNE'S ROOM.

Daphne: (STARTING TO GATHER HERSELF) I'm sorry about all this. I guess I'm still at the point where I can't even hear his name without crying.

Niles: (SENSING AN OPPORTUNITY) Well, let's not give Joe that satisfaction.

DAPHNE BURSTS INTO TEARS AGAIN, NILES STEPS FORWARD TO COMFORT HER, BUT FRASIER HOLDS HIM BACK AS ROZ STEERS DAPHNE OFF TO HER ROOM.

Martin: Well, I don't know about you two, but I see emotion like that and it gets me all upset. Of course, if we had that sports blooper channel I'd be cheered up in no time.

Frasier: Well, if you're desperate, you could always dig up the home movie of Niles and me learning to play Frisbee.

Martin: Nah, that's just plain sad.

HE EXITS TO THE HALL FOLLOWED BY EDDIE. NILES HAS BEEN STARING OFF AFTER DAPHNE. FRASIER MOVES TO THE LIQUOR CABINET.

Frasier: Brandy, Niles?

Niles: (DISTRACTED) Yes, thank you. (AFTER A BEAT) Frasier, I think I just made an important decision.I'm going to tell Daphne how I feel about her.

Frasier: What?

Niles: I'm going to tell her tonight.

Frasier: You're serious about this.

Niles: I'm dead serious. Maris and I are nowhere near reconciling – she's being as intransigent as ever. I know this is the right decision because I'm perfectly calm about it. (HOLDS UP HAND, DEMONSTRATING. IT SHAKES) I'll take that brandy now.

Frasier: Niles, before you do anything this rash, you should consider it from all angles.

Niles: I've spent three years considering Daphne from all angles.

Frasier: Are you sure this is the right moment for this?

Niles: If you're trying to rattle me, it's not going to work. I've been rehearsing this for months. (GETTING INCREASINGLY NERVOUS) "Daphne, there's something you and I need to talk about. It's a matter of . . . For a long time now, I . . . well, you and I . . . we . . ." Exactly how is that brandy getting here, by Saint Bernard?

Frasier: I just think you should consider her state of mind. She's still reeling from her breakup with Joe.

Niles: Frasier, I'm not sitting on these feelings any longer.

Frasier: It won't kill you to wait a little longer. At least one more day.

Niles: A day? Oh, all right.

DAPHNE AND ROZ RE-ENTER.

Roz: If the jewelry's not that good and the sex isn't that good, what have you really lost here?

Daphne: I suppose you have a point.

Frasier: Well, I don't normally endorse the Gabor approach to therapy, but it seems to be working.

Roz: I'm going to take Daphne out and get her mind off her troubles.

Daphne: I want to thank you both for being so supportive. I'm feeling a bit better. Another few days and I'll have completely forgotten old what's-his-name.

Niles: (SENSING AN OPPORTUNITY) Joe.

IT HAS ITS DESIRED EFFECT – IT STARTS DAPHNE CRYING AND NILES MOVES IN TO OFFER A HUG, BUT ROZ STEPS IN THE WAY AND SHOOS NILES AWAY, AND WE:

FADE OUT.

Scene B

INT. LIVING ROOM – DAY – DAY/2
(Frasier, Niles, Martin, Daphne, Eddie)

MARTIN IS WITH EDDIE IN HIS CHAIR. HE'S READING THE SPORTS SECTION. FRASIER IS GOING THROUGH THE CD'S IN THE CABINET, LOOKING FOR ONE.

Martin: What were they thinking last night? If you're two for fifteen from behind the arc, why do you still give it to your two-guard instead of jamming it down to your big man in the paint?

Frasier: Eddie, I believe that question was directed at you.

Martin: You know, if you ever took an interest in sports, you'd probably like it. It's graceful, it's dramatic.

Frasier: (FINDING HIS CD) Thank you, Dad, but for now I'm quite satisfied with the likes of Pavarotti's *Pagliacci*. You have your big man in the paint and I have mine.

MARTIN EXITS TO THE KITCHEN.

SFX: DOORBELL RINGS

FRASIER CROSSES TO THE DOOR AND OPENS IT. NILES IS THERE, HOLDING FLOWERS TO HIS CHEST.

Frasier: Niles.

Niles: Frasier.

Frasier: Either your boutonniere is way over the top or you're here to pursue last night's plan.

Niles: Look, I know I don't have your support on this, but . . . how to put this?

Frasier: You don't care?

Niles: If you could work the phrase "rat's ass" into that you'd have it. The fact is, I'm tired of being lonely. And it makes no sense going on being lonely when the woman I long for is unattached.

Frasier: Well, as I said to you the time you tried to jump out of the treehouse with an umbrella, "I suppose you know what you're doing."

MARTIN RE-ENTERS FROM THE KITCHEN, AND RE-TAKES HIS SEAT.

Martin: Hey, Niles.

Niles: Hey, Dad.

SFX: PHONE RINGS

FRASIER GOES TO IT AND ANSWERS IT.

Frasier: Hello . . . Yes. Would you hold on please? (COVERS PHONE, THEN) Dad – is Daphne in her room?

Martin: Gee, I don't know. (THEN, SCREAMING) Daphne!! Hey, Daph! Daphne!!

Frasier: For God's sake, I can yell.

HE PUTS THE CALLER ON HOLD, AND EXITS TO THE HALL.

Martin: I've been waiting thirty years to do that.

Niles: So, you're probably wondering what I'm doing with these flowers.

Martin: Not really.

Niles: Well, I'll tell you. They're for Daphne. I've decided I'm going to tell her how I feel.

Martin: That's great, Niles.

Niles: "That's great?"

Martin: Yeah. You're single now, she's single. Why not?

Niles: Oh, my God. That is so funny.

Martin: (STARTING TO LAUGH) What is? Let me in on it.

Niles: I just never expected that reaction. I thought you'd say something more Dad-like. You know, like –

Martin: You're out of your mind?

Niles: Yes. (LAUGHS)

Martin: She'll never go for it in a million years?

Niles: (LAUGHING) Stop it!

Martin: Some day you'll look back on this as the stupidest, most idiotic –

Niles: (NOT LAUGHING) Dad, I said stop it.

<u>DAPHNE ENTERS</u> FROM THE HALL, <u>FOLLOWED BY FRASIER</u>. NILES COYLY HIDES THE FLOWERS BEHIND HIS BACK.

Daphne: Morning, Dr. Crane.

Niles: Hello, Daphne.

Daphne: Don't you look nice.

SHE PICKS UP THE PHONE, HITS THE BUTTON.

Daphne (CONT'D): (INTO PHONE) Hello . . . Yes, Rodney. I'm so glad you called . . . Yes, I enjoyed meeting you too. Uh-huh. Oh, well, yes, that would be lovely. I'll see you around four, then. Bye.

SHE HANGS UP.

Frasier: Rodney?

Daphne: You won't believe this. Last night, Roz insisted on taking me to this bar she calls the "Sure Thing."

Frasier: How flattering. They've named a bar after her.

Daphne: She told me whenever she takes a friend there they always end up meeting someone. Well, I wasn't there ten minutes and she spun my barstool around and I was face to face with this nice-looking man.

Martin: Rodney.

Daphne: Right. I suppose it's a bit soon for me to be seeing anyone else, but it's just coffee. Besides, if I wait he might not be available when I'm ready.

Niles: Timing is everything.

Daphne: I can't wait to tell Roz.

<u>SHE EXITS</u> TO THE HALL.

181

Niles: "Give it a day, Niles."

Frasier: Sorry. I don't know what to say.

Niles: Too bad you didn't have that problem last night.

Martin: Don't let this get you down.

Niles: I won't. I still have a fall back position. (TAKES OUT PHONE) I'm not particularly proud of what I'm doing right now. Given how strained our relationship is, I'm sure she'll make me grovel. But she's the only woman who can put an end to my loneliness.

Frasier: You're not going to call Maris.

Niles: Good God, no. (INTO PHONE) Hello Roz, about this sure thing bar of yours . . .

ON MARTIN AND FRASIER'S REACTIONS, WE:

DISSOLVE TO:

Scene C

INT. GRANVILLE'S - NIGHT - NIGHT/2
(Niles, Roz, Bulldog, Adelle)

AN UPSCALE PLACE WITH BOTH A BAR AND TABLES WITH CHAIRS. IT'S SPARSELY POPULATED. ROZ IS AT THE BAR. NILES ENTERS, A LITTLE FRAZZLED-LOOKING.

Niles: Well, I'm here. I forgot to gargle, I'm wearing mismatched socks, and I'm so nervous I could wet myself.

Roz: Well, we've got your opening line down.

Niles: You're going to have to be patient, Roz. This isn't exactly my milieu.

Roz: Let's make that lesson number one. If you're going to use words like "milieu" you might as well show up here with a sore on your lip and a couple of kids.

Niles: Point well taken.

HE TAKES OUT A HANDKERCHIEF AND BEGINS WIPING OFF HIS SEAT.

Roz: Guess what lesson number two is.

HE STOPS WIPING, SITS.

Roz (CONT'D): Will you relax? You're going to be fine. Just remember, every single woman here came for the same reason - to meet someone. They may be putting up a front that says "Go Away," but they're really praying someone will come talk to them.

Mixed Doubles

BULLDOG COMES UP BEHIND ROZ.

Bulldog: (IN AUSTRALIAN ACCENT) Hey there Sheila, you're looking good tonight.

Roz: Get bent. (SEES IT'S BULLDOG) Oh, it's you. Get bent.

Bulldog: I'm using my Australian tourist character tonight. (TO NILES) I've got a few of 'em I like to rotate, like crops. So what the hell are you doing here?

Niles: At the moment, contemplating the grim fact that you and I are peers.

Bulldog: You're just lucky you came on a night when you can observe the maestro. Watch and learn.

HE APPROACHES A WOMAN AT THE BAR.

Bulldog (CONT'D): (AS AUSTRALIAN) Hey there Sheila. You're looking pretty good up top. How are you down under?

THE WOMAN THROWS HER DRINK IN HIS FACE.

Bulldog (CONT'D): I'll check back with you later. G'day.

HE CROSSES TO THE BATHROOM TO DRY HIMSELF OFF.

Niles: I'm leaving.

Roz: Hey – I didn't come all the way down here to see you wimp out.

Niles: No, you came all the way down here because I promised you the keys to my cabin for the weekend. (GIVES HER KEYS) There you are. There's a bear skin rug in protective cellophane in the closet behind the wet bar.

HE STARTS TO LEAVE, SHE GRABS HIM BY THE ARM.

Roz: Look, I have a perfect matchmaking record in this bar and you are *not* breaking my streak. Now sit.

HE DOES.

Roz (CONT'D): There's just a few rules you need to know. First, when you introduce yourself be as casual as possible. Second, you cannot say enough nice things about her hair. I know it's shallow, but it works. Third, hang on her every word. Be fascinated. Now go.

Niles: What do you mean "go?"

Roz: It's time.

Niles: Are you insane? I'm not ready, I'm not nearly ready.

Roz: Look, I've thrown a lot of babies into the water and they all came up swimming. Go.

Niles: But there's no possible way I can –

SHE SPINS HIS BARSTOOL AROUND BRINGING HIM FACE TO FACE WITH AN ATTRACTIVE BLOND WOMAN WHO SITS ALONE. THIS IS <u>ADELLE</u>.

Niles (CONT'D): Hello.

Adelle: Hello.

Niles: I hope I'm not bothering you.

Adelle: No, not at all. I'm Adelle.

Niles: Niles. So, Adelle – is that with one "l" or two?

Adelle: Two.

Niles: (FASCINATED) Really.

AS THEY CONTINUE, WE:

FADE OUT.

END OF ACT ONE

ACT TWO

Scene D

FADE IN:

<u>INT. FRASIER'S LIVING ROOM – NIGHT – NIGHT/3</u>
(Frasier, Martin, Niles, Adelle, Daphne, Rodney, Eddie)

FRASIER IS AT THE TABLE; EDDIE IS A FEW FEET AWAY. THEY ARE STARING AT EACH OTHER – INTENTLY. IT'S A STARE DOWN. <u>MARTIN ENTERS</u> FROM THE KITCHEN.

Martin: You're wasting your time.

Frasier: No, I'm not.

Martin: You're not going to win.

Frasier: It's time he learned what it feels like to be stared at. (TO EDDIE) So bring it on. You can't touch me. You've got nothing. I'm – (THEN, BREAKS, CLUTCHING HIS EYES) Gaah! It was as though his eyes turned into sorcerer's pinwheels and started spinning.

Martin: Just shake hands and say good fight.

SFX: DOORBELL RINGS

MARTIN CROSSES TO IT, OPENS IT. NILES IS THERE, WITH ADELLE.

Niles: Hey, Dad.

Martin: Hi, Niles. Come on in.

Niles: I'd like you to meet Adelle Childs. Adelle, my father, Martin, and my brother, Frasier.

ALL AD-LIB HELLOS.

Niles (CONT'D): (TO FRASIER) Are you all right? Your eyes look funny.

Frasier: I'm fine. So Adelle – it's nice to finally meet you.

Adelle: It's nice to meet you too.

Frasier: (HANDING NILES TICKETS) Here are your opera tickets.

Niles: Thank you.

Frasier: Do you have time for coffee before you go?

Adelle: That would be nice.

Frasier: Splendid. I can debut my Limoges coffee set. There are six unique cups, each representing a different wife of Henry the Eighth. Only last week my antique dealer finally located an Anne of Cleves to complete the set.

Martin: (TO ADELLE) He loves to rub it in – I'm still looking for a Wilma to complete my juice glass set.

Niles: (TO FRASIER) I'll give you a hand.

FRASIER AND NILES START TO THE KITCHEN. EDDIE JUMPS ONTO ADELLE'S LAP.

Martin: Don't mind him. He'll lie down anyplace that's nice and warm. Not that I meant to imply that . . . well that – (HIS ONLY WAY OUT) Eddie, get off of there!

IN THE KITCHEN, FRASIER AND NILES BEGIN MAKING COFFEE.

Niles: So: What do you think?

Frasier: She seems nice.

Niles: She's fabulous! I know it's only been three dates, but I feel as though I've been rescued. I no longer have to worry about becoming one of those pitiful losers embittered by a failed marriage, leading a lonely, pathetic life of . . . (OFF FRASIER'S WITHERING LOOK) fulfillment and good times.

Frasier: Shouldn't you make a beeping noise when you back up like that?

THEY EXIT TO THE LIVING ROOM. MARTIN AND ADELLE HAVE BEEN SITTING IN UNCOMFORTABLE SILENCE.

Frasier (CONT'D): Coffee will be ready in a moment.

Adelle: So what were you two whispering about?

SFX: DOORBELL

NILES CROSSES TO ANSWER IT.

Niles: Oh, nothing. Just about how whenever you think you've got your life figured out something unexpected happens.

HE OPENS THE DOOR TO DAPHNE AND RODNEY BANKS.

Daphne: Sorry, forgot my keys. Hello, all. Everyone, this is Rodney Banks.

Niles: How do you do?

HE AND RODNEY SHAKE HANDS.

Rodney: The pleasure is mine.

HE REMOVES A HANDKERCHIEF AND WIPES HIS HAND. NILES DOES THE SAME.

Rodney (CONT'D): No offense, but it is the flu season.

Niles: Yes, you can't be too careful.

Daphne: This is Frasier Crane, and his father Martin, and . . .

Niles: (MOVING ADELLE TOWARD DAPHNE) Adelle Childs.

Daphne: Hello. We've just had the most wonderful day at the marina.

Martin: Oh, you've got a boat?

Rodney: Actually, no. I have an inner ear curvature that makes me prone to motion sickness. But there's a bistro there that serves a bouillabaise that's an exact duplicate of the one at Tour D'Argent in Paris.

Frasier: A duplicate you say.

Martin: Can you join us for coffee?

Daphne: Yes, that would be nice.

Frasier: I'll get it. Daphne, you like yours black. Rodney?

Rodney: Generally I take it with one percent milk and just a nuance of cinnamon.

Frasier: I had a feeling you might.

Martin: I'll give you a hand.

FRASIER CROSSES INTO THE KITCHEN. MARTIN FOLLOWS. THEY BEGIN POURING COFFEE.

Martin (CONT'D): What the hell was that?

Frasier: I know. We should put a red mark on the real Niles so we can tell them apart.

Martin: Niles must be going nuts.

NILES ENTERS.

Niles: Can I lend a hand?

MARTIN AND FRASIER JUST STARE AT HIM.

Martin: No thanks. Niles, what do you think of Rodney?

Niles: Well, so far I'm not very impressed. Kind of a pretentious fop, isn't he?

Martin: He doesn't remind you of anyone?

Niles: Remind me of anyone?

RODNEY ENTERS.

Rodney: So Niles – Adelle tells me you're headed to the opera tonight.

Niles: Yes, *Khovanshchina*.

Rodney: A masterwork.

Niles: I don't think there's a more haunting moment in all of opera than when Shaklovity poisons the prince.

Rodney: Agreed. Although I believe he stabs him.

Niles: No, he poisons him.

Rodney: Well, no sense arguing. Oh, about my coffee, I neglected to mention that I like my milk steamed. But just a dollop of foam, such as might give the effect of a cumulus cloud reflected in a still pond.

Niles: Consider it done.

RODNEY EXITS. THERE'S A BEAT, THEN:

Niles (CONT'D): I want to kill myself.

Martin: Oh come on, Niles. It's funny.

Niles: No, it's not remotely funny. Frasier talked me out of approaching Daphne on the same night she fell for that man.

Frasier: You can't really be mad at me.

Niles: Mad at you? What for? For denying me any chance at a happiness I have only ached for for the last three years of my life? No, Frasier, I'm grateful. Come closer, I'll show you how grateful.

HE GRABS A KNIFE FROM THE COUNTER.

Frasier: Are you mad?

Martin: (STEPPING BETWEEN THEM) Niles!

Frasier: He's got that same look in his eyes that Eddie had!

DAPHNE ENTERS, NILES QUICKLY HIDES THE KNIFE.

Daphne: Isn't Rodney just great?

Martin: Oh, yeah.

Frasier: Yes, great.

Daphne: I think it was the moment Joe broke up with me I heard a voice say, "Daphne, it's time you went for a completely new type of man."

ALL WE HEAR IS THE COLD SLAP OF A KNIFE BLADE AGAINST THE COUNTER BEHIND NILES' BACK. DAPHNE EXITS.

Frasier: I should really be getting Rodney his coffee.

HE STARTS OUT, BUT RODNEY RE-ENTERS, CARRYING A REFERENCE BOOK.

Rodney: Niles, I've taken the liberty of looking up that opera point we were disputing. It says right here it was a stabbing. You don't forget a stabbing.

Niles: No, you don't.

Frasier: (EXITING) Well, we all have our coffee now. No sense staying in here when we have wide open spaces in the living room.

FRASIER ENTERS THE LIVING ROOM, FOLLOWED BY RODNEY AND MARTIN.

Rodney: (SMELLS HIS COFFEE) Mmm – nothing on earth smells quite so heavenly as a freshly brewed cup of coffee. Well, perhaps one thing does.

HE MAKES A MOVE TOWARD DAPHNE.

Daphne: Stop that. He loves to smell my hair.

FROM THE KITCHEN WE HEAR A CRASH, OBVIOUSLY FRASIER'S COFFEE SET IS NO LONGER COMPLETE.

Frasier: (DEFLATED) Anne Boleyn?

Niles (O.S.): Catherine of Aragon.

FADE OUT.

Scene E

INT. CAFE NERVOSA – DAY – DAY/4
(Niles, Frasier, Adelle, Rodney)

NILES IS AT A TABLE ALONE. FRASIER ENTERS, A BIT SHEEPISHLY, AND APPROACHES HIM. NILES SEES HIM, THEN LOOKS THE OTHER WAY. FRASIER STRIDES OVER AND TAKES A SEAT.

Frasier: Oh for heaven's sake, Niles, not returning my calls, and trying to ignore me is the behavior of a pouting adolescent. Are you quite finished? (THEN REALIZING) You put gum on my chair, didn't you?

Niles: Yes, and now I'm finished.

FRASIER WORKS TO REMOVE THE GUM.

Frasier: I'm sorry if I steered you wrong, but let's remember, you do have someone wonderful in your life now, don't you?

Niles: I suppose I do.

Frasier: Adelle does make you very happy, doesn't she?

Niles: Yes. Yes, she does.

Frasier: Well then, if you're ever going to follow another piece of advice I give you, follow this one: Adelle is your path to happiness.

AT THAT MOMENT, ADELLE AND RODNEY ENTER THE CAFE ARM-IN-ARM.

FRASIER SEES THEM, NILES DOESN'T.

Frasier (CONT'D): But let's say I'm wrong.

FRASIER GINGERLY REMOVES THE KNIFE FROM NILES' PLACE-SETTING.

Niles: But you're not wrong. Adelle is a wonderful, affectionate woman.

FRASIER SEES ADELLE GIVE RODNEY A KISS.

Frasier: She *is* affectionate.

Niles: And she's clearly drawn to a man of my type. Just thinking about her is lifting my spirits. Thank you, Frasier.

Frasier: Niles . . . look.

HE INDICATES THE TABLE WHERE ADELLE AND RODNEY HAVE TAKEN SEATS AND ARE NOW HOLDING HANDS. NILES LOOKS.

Niles: I don't believe it! The betrayal! *No one* treats Daphne like that!

HE STANDS, FRASIER GRABS HIM BY THE ARM.

Frasier: Niles! Whatever you do, don't engage him in a physical fight. The whole thing would just look too weird.

FRASIER LETS GO OF HIM. NILES STRIDES OVER TO ADELLE AND RODNEY'S TABLE.

Niles: Hello, Adelle.

Adelle: (STARTLED) Oh no.

Rodney: I know this may look a tad incriminating, but the truth is –

Niles: Oh, spare me, you ludicrous popinjay. I know exactly what's going on. I was watching you from my table.

Adelle: I was going to call you. You see, Rodney and I, well we . . . well, you saw from your table. I'm sorry.

Niles: I'm sorry too, Adelle. But I'm mostly sorry for Daphne. (TO RODNEY) How do you intend to handle that small matter?

Rodney: I was planning to tell her tonight. We're meeting for drinks at Granville's.

Niles: Why don't you do her a favor and let me tell her? It will be better coming from a friend.

Rodney: Yes, I suppose it would. Please tell her I'm sorry. Sometimes when a man finds the woman he's meant to be with (TAKES ADELLE'S HAND) he's powerless to resist. I hope she understands that.

Niles: I hope she understands it too.

NILES HEADS OUT THE DOOR. FRASIER WALKS OVER TO THE TABLE.

Frasier: (TO RODNEY) I just have one question for you. Do you have an older brother?

Rodney: As a matter of fact I do. He's the pride of the family. Handsome, successful, brilliant. I've always been rather jealous of him.

Frasier: Spooky.

AS FRASIER HEADS OUT, WE:

FADE OUT.

Scene H

INT. GRANVILLE'S - NIGHT - NIGHT/4
(Daphne, Niles)

DAPHNE IS THERE WITH A GLASS OF WINE. NILES ENTERS.

Niles: Evening, Daphne.

Daphne: Hello, Dr. Crane.

Niles: You don't seem surprised to see me.

Daphne: I was running late so I called Rodney on his cel phone. He told me everything.

Niles: Oh. I'm sorry.

Daphne: Sorry for you, too. (RE: THE WINE) Join me in a little sorrow-drowning?

Niles: Yes, I believe I will. (TO BARTENDER, RE: HER WINE) One more of these, please. (THEN) You know, I can't say I really blame Adelle. Rodney is that type of man that women seem to go for.

Daphne: (SADLY) Yes, he is.

Niles: I didn't mean to upset you.

Daphne: You didn't. I guess I'm just more in the mood to hear about his negative qualities right now.

Niles: Well, he is a bit of a know-it-all, and kind of fussy.

Daphne: . . . has to have everything just so, he's a nut about cleanliness, then there's his clothes, his precious shoes . . .

Niles: I don't like this road we're on. (OFF HER LOOK) I mean, wouldn't we be better off discussing what's in our future?

Daphne: I suppose. I'll tell you one thing, after the run I've had lately I pity the next man I date – I'll probably rip him to shreds.

Niles: What about the man after that?

Daphne: It's not that I hate all men, but they are an unfeeling lot. Look at Rodney. The minute he heard I'd just broken up with someone he moved right in for the kill. Is that how all men are?

Niles: Not all men, no.

Daphne: Of course they aren't. You're not. You're kind, sensitive. If you ask me, you were too good for that Adelle.

Niles: Thank you, Daphne. But the truth is my heart was never really in that relationship.

Daphne: I thought it might not be.

Niles: There's someone else who's been on my mind too much.

Daphne: I had a feeling, Dr. Crane.

Niles: You did?

Daphne: Yes. As long as you still have feelings for your wife, you know you can't be involved with anyone else. It makes sense to me. I know I'd never get involved with a man who was separated.

Niles: Even if he'd worshiped you since the day he laid eyes on you?

Daphne: And don't think that's not just how they'd put it, too. (LAUGHS) No. I think I need to do a bit of separating myself. From Joe, I mean. I'll wait a good long time before I do any more dating.

Niles: I'm glad to hear you say that.

Daphne: It's funny when you think about it: the two of us both coming to this same singles bar this week. This is the very stool I was on when I met Rodney.

Niles: I was right here when I met Adelle.

NILES POINTS TO THE EMPTY STOOL NEXT TO DAPHNE. DAPHNE LAUGHS TO HERSELF.

Niles (CONT'D): What?

Daphne: Oh, I was just thinking: if it had been a different time in both of our lives, we might have actually met. How do you suppose that would have gone?

Niles: What, our conversation?

Daphne: Yes. Just for fun – we could both use a smile.

Niles: Well, I suppose I would have said "Excuse me, is this seat taken," you'd have said "No." Then you'd have said "My name's Daphne," and I'd have said "I'm Niles." Then I'd have said, "What are you doing for the rest of your life?"

Daphne: (LAUGHS) You always know just the right thing to say. (THEN, AS A FRIEND WOULD SAY IT) I love you, Dr. Crane.

Niles: I love you too, Daphne.

AND WE:

FADE OUT.

END OF ACT TWO

HAM RADIO

#40570-089

Written by David Lloyd
Created and Developed by David Angell, Peter Casey & David Lee
Directed by David Lee

ACT ONE

Scene A

FADE IN:

INT. CAFE NERVOSA - DAY - DAY/1
(Frasier, Niles, Martin)

NILES AND MARTIN ARE SEATED AT A TABLE DRINKING COFFEE. THERE IS A SLIGHTLY STRAINED FEELING.

Martin: This is great, spending time like this.

Niles: We don't do it enough.

Martin: Yep, just the two of us.

THERE'S AN AWKWARD BEAT, THEN FRASIER ENTERS, CARRYING A FOLDER. MARTIN AND NILES BOTH EXCITEDLY WAVE HIM OVER.

Martin (CONT'D): Hey, Fras! Frasier!

Niles: Come join us!

Frasier: (TO THE COUNTER PERSON) Double cappuccino to go.

FRASIER CROSSES TO JOIN THEM.

Frasier (CONT'D): Thank you. But I can only stay a moment. I've taken on a very exciting project. This is KACL's fiftieth anniversary. I did some research and found that they used to specialize in live dramas. You must remember those, Dad.

Martin: Oh sure.

Frasier: (TO NILES) People of Dad's generation would sit around the radio each night, absolutely mesmerized.

Martin: We were a simple people. It was that little orange glow that got us.

Frasier: I happen to think radio drama was marvelous. People actually had to use their imagination. Then TV came along and ruined it.

Martin: Yeah, and it scared us too. We kept wondering how all those little people got trapped in that box.

Frasier: All right, Dad. Anyhow, I've persuaded the station manager to give me thirty minutes of air time to recreate the very first mystery KACL ever aired. "Nightmare Inn."

Martin: Let me guess: Bunch of people get caught in a storm and everybody wonders who's going to be murdered first.

Frasier: Exactly. And I'm going to direct it.

Niles: Then we can stop wondering.

Martin: What, you don't think your brother knows how to direct?

Niles: No, the trouble is he doesn't know how to stop directing. During our prep school production of "Richard III," he drove the entire cast crazy with his constant critiquing. I seem to recall a delay on opening night while our Richard chased Frasier around the dressing room, beating him with his hump.

Frasier: It was just a little backstage horseplay to relieve tension.

Niles: You have an Orson Welles complex. By the end of the week, you'll not only be directing, you'll have rewritten the script and be playing the lead.

Frasier: Nonsense. I have no intention of performing. And the only "rewriting" I've done is some cutting – to get it down to thirty minutes.

MARTIN HAS TAKEN THE SCRIPT OUT OF THE FOLDER AND NOW READS THE TITLE.

Martin: "Frasier Crane's Nightmare Inn."

Frasier: It's just a working title.

ON THEIR REACTIONS, WE:

FADE OUT.

Scene B

FADE IN:

INT. RADIO STUDIO – THE NEXT DAY – DAY/2
(Roz, Frasier, Gil, Bulldog, Ian)

Frasier: Well, that's it for today, but don't forget to tune in Saturday night for KACL's presentation of "Nightmare Inn." So set your dials for goosebumps. Till then, this is

Frasier Crane reminding you that – (PLAYFULLY) – you never know what's lurking in the shadows.

HE GIVES AN EVIL CHORTLE LIKE "THE SHADOW" AND CLICKS OFF. HE TAKES OFF HIS HEADPHONES AND ROZ COMES IN THE BOOTH.

Roz: Well that should certainly comfort that woman who called about her paranoia. Listen – have we found a leading man, yet?

Frasier: No.

Roz: Well, you could do it.

Frasier: Don't be silly, Roz. It is a juicy role, and a strong voice is required, but I've got my hands full as it is.

HIS DOOR SWINGS OPEN AND GIL CHESTERTON ENTERS.

Gil: Oh Frasier, I've had a quick peek at your script and I think I'd be perfect as "Bull" Kragen, the brutish gamekeeper.

Frasier: Um, actually, Gil, I think that might be . . . a little too on the nose. But you know what part you could do? (CONSULTING SCRIPT) "Nigel Fairservice, drummed out of the Royal Air Force under mysterious circumstances."

Roz: With him playing it they may not seem so mysterious.

Gil: I'll take it. After all, Nigel does have that divine speech in the second act about his boyhood in Surrey, "romping with his school chums in the fens and spinneys, when the twilight bathed the hedgerows like a lambent flame."

THEY BOTH GIVE HIM A JAW-DROPPED STARE.

Gil (CONT'D): Actually I had rather a long peek at the script.

GIL EXITS.

Roz: (CHECKING SCRIPT) Gosh, we've still got a lot of these supporting roles to cast, don't we?

Frasier: I'm working on that. Jennifer in accounting is married to a professional actor who specializes in dialect parts. I'm hoping he'll do six or seven of the smaller roles.

BULLDOG ENTERS.

Bulldog: Hey Doc: Need one more for your play?

Frasier: Absolutely, Bulldog. But you've got to promise you'll promote us during your show.

Bulldog: Actually I wasn't talking about me. I'm talking about a friend of mine, Maxine.

Gifted girl. Athletic, too. I fell in love with her the minute I saw her doing laps.

Frasier: She's a swimmer?

Bulldog: No, a dancer. Come on Doc, you'd really be helping me out.

Frasier: Well we still need a maid and she's only got one line: "Look out – he's got a gun!"

Bulldog: Maxine could knock that line right out of the park.

Frasier: Okay. She can have it – but only if you play a part too. We need someone for the sinister silk merchant.

Bulldog: (THINKS, THEN) All right, deal. Maxine's going to be so excited. I gotta remember to pick up one of those cute little maid outfits on my way home from work.

Frasier: She doesn't have to appear in costume.

Bulldog: Maybe here she doesn't.

BULLDOG EXITS.

Roz: Well, we're getting there.

Frasier: Except for the lead. I haven't seen anyone even remotely qualified to play a wily old Scotland Yard inspector. You may be right, Roz. With time running short, I may have to bite the bullet and take on the burden myself.

THERE IS A KNOCK ON THE DOOR. FRASIER OPENS IT TO REVEAL IAN FROM ACCOUNTING, AN ENGLISHMAN WITH GREY HAIR AND MUSTACHE, TWEEDY, SMOKING PIPE – HE COULD PASS AS A SCOTLAND YARD INSPECTOR.

Ian: Excuse me, Dr. Crane. Is it too late to read for the role of the inspector?

Frasier: I'm afraid that part has already been cast.

AND, AS FRASIER QUICKLY CLOSES THE DOOR ON IAN, WE:

FADE OUT.

Scene C

FADE IN:

INT. FRASIER'S LIVING ROOM – THAT EVENING – NIGHT/2
(Frasier, Roz, Mel, Daphne, Gil, Bulldog)

FRASIER IS GOING OVER THE SCRIPT WITH ROZ AND MEL (HUSBAND OF JENNIFER IN ACCOUNTING) AS DAPHNE ADMITS GIL AND BULLDOG. AS

THEY CROSS DOWN TO FRASIER, DAPHNE STARTS SETTING OUT SOFT DRINKS AND CHEESE-AND-CRACKERS.

Frasier: Ah, Bulldog, Gil. Right on time. We have to be on our toes tonight, we have a professional actor with us. This is Mel White, our man of a thousand voices.

THEY AD-LIB GREETINGS, TAKE SCRIPTS, SIT DOWN.

Frasier (CONT'D): Mel will be doing Hans, the German butler, both McCallister sisters and Peppo the dwarf – (READING) "a little man with a big secret."

Bulldog: The same guy's playing all those parts?

Frasier: Yes, plus "Bull" Kragen and O'Toole the handyman. (TO MEL) Think you can handle it?

Mel: Just so they don't all talk at once.

Frasier: (BUBBLING) What a joy to work with a professional. Bulldog – where's Maxine?

Bulldog: She's home with food poisoning.

Frasier: Oh, I'm sorry.

Bulldog: Ah, nothing serious. I think she just wrestled in some bad jello.

Frasier: Never mind. She only has one line: "Look out – he's got a gun!" Daphne can do that for tonight.

GIL, WHO HAS BEEN THUMBING THROUGH HIS SCRIPT, LOOKS UP.

Gil: Oh Frasier . . . (POINTING) one of Nigel's lines seems to be missing.

Frasier: I had to take out twenty minutes.

Gil: Yes, yes, but that line so neatly defined Nigel's character.

Frasier: (INCREDULOUS) Saying "gesundheit" when the butler sneezed?

Gil: It shows he's a caring person.

Frasier: It's cut, Gil. Learn to let go.

Gil: (SIGHS) Oh very well. Just so I still have that delicious speech about my boyhood in Surrey . . .

Frasier: Yes, that's still in.

Gil: Romping with my school chums in the fens and –

Moon Dance

A passionate
embrace on the
dance floor ...

But is it all an act?

The Two Mrs. Cranes

Daphne and Roz battle for the attention of Daphne's ex-boyfriend, Clive.

Face off between the two 'Mrs. Cranes'.

Mixed Doubles

The Crane brothers spy on the neighbor's ... furniture.

Niles encounters his
doppelgänger.

Ham Radio

The show must go on ... Frasier, Niles and Roz make a crisis out of a radio drama.

Bulldog freezes up on air.

Season's greetings from the *Frasier* cast.

The Wise Man.

Room Service

A surprise visit from Frasier's past.

Frasier discovers his brother and breakfast for two in his ex-wife's hotel bathroom.

The Ski Lodge

Two men, two women and a lot of confusion.

A lust triangle.

A Valentine's date for Frasier, or just a business meeting?

Frasier is confused about the dress code in Cassandra's hotel room.

Frasier: (IMPATIENT) Yes, yes, that one. Now – I fear we may still be long so I'm going to ask Daphne to time us tonight. And Noel hasn't rounded up all the sound effects yet so I'm also going to have her read those. That's a lot of responsibility for you, but I'm sure you can handle it. Start the watch. Sound effect.

DAPHNE STARTS STOPWATCH.

Daphne: (DECLAIMING) "Sound of door opening."

ROZ, WHO HAS BEEN EATING, DOES HER LINE WITH HER MOUTH FULL.

Roz: "Inspector – thank God you've come."

Frasier: Stop the watch. Roz, I have a line that says "when she opened her lips I caught a hint of some exotic accent." You'll notice it does not say "when she opened her lips cheese fell out."

Roz: (HUFFY) I was hungry, okay? Sorry.

Frasier: Start the watch. (THEN) "This is a grisly business, Miss Thorndyke."

Daphne: (DECLAIMING) Sound of door closing.

Roz: "I can't believe any of my guests could be a multiple-murderer."

Frasier: "That's easy for you to say, but my job is to suspect everyone. Please introduce your guests."

Roz: "This is the silk merchant, Mr. Wang."

BULLDOG STARTS TO GIGGLE.

Frasier: Stop the watch! What's your problem?

Bulldog: Wang? You gotta give me another name. I'll crack up every time I hear that.

Frasier: (STRUGGLING FOR PATIENCE) All right. All right. What about "Wing?" That's a good Chinese name. Everybody: Change Wang to Wing in your scripts.

Daphne: (DECLAIMING) Sound of people changing Wangs to Wings.

Mel: Look, could we move this along?

Frasier: Certainly. (TO OTHERS) That's a professional speaking. (TO ROZ) From your line. (TO DAPHNE) Start.

Roz: "This is the silk merchant, Mr. Wing."

Frasier: "Did you witness anything suspicious this evening, Wing?"

Bulldog: "Me no lookee. Me go beddy-by, chop-chop."

Roz: Whoa. Chinese Embassy on line one. You can't say that.

Frasier: Don't worry. I'll adjust his dialogue later. (TO DAPHNE) Start.

Gil: "I'm Nigel Fairservice, inspector. I was strolling in the garden when this dreadful tragedy occurred."

Frasier: "Did anyone see you?"

Gil: "Several people. Hans, the German butler –"

Mel: (GERMAN ACCENT) "Ja, I saw der gentleman."

Frasier: (TO DAPHNE) Stop. (TO MEL) That's wonderful, Mel, but to my ear he's coming across just a bit more Austrian than German.

Mel: (ANNOYED) I've done that accent on both Broadway and London stages.

Frasier: (AIRILY) Yes, well, perhaps they have different standards than I do. All right, let's do it again. But this time, people, I want you to make it real. From the dwarf's entrance . . .

INTERIOR DISSOLVE TO:

INT. FRASIER'S LIVING ROOM – TWO HOURS LATER – NIGHT/2

FOOD IS EATEN, EMPTY GLASSES ARE SCATTERED AROUND, TIES HAVE BEEN LOOSENED OR REMOVED, PEOPLE ARE SEATED OR STANDING IN DIFFERENT PLACES THAN WHEN WE LEFT.

Frasier (CONT'D): (READING SCRIPT) ". . . And so, the case was closed and with a grateful shudder I swore I'd never return to Nightmare Inn." (TO DAPHNE) Stop. Time?

Daphne: (CHECKING) Thirty-two minutes, forty seconds.

Frasier: Damn. I'll have to trim some more before we try again.

Roz: Again? We've done it four times.

Frasier: We'll keep doing it until I'm satisfied. Which reminds me, Mel: I'm not entirely happy with the second McCallister sister.

Mel: (DANGEROUSLY) Oh . . .?

Frasier: Yes, she still doesn't sound sufficiently post-menopausal.

Mel: (RISING) I see. You also told me my gamekeeper sounded too cultured, my Irishman sounded more Protestant than Catholic, and my dwarf sounded too tall. So let me try this and you tell me how it sounds: (GERMAN) "I qvit!"

MEL CROSSES TOWARD DOOR BEHIND FRASIER.

Frasier: Wait, you can't leave.

MEL EXITS SLAMMING THE DOOR.

Daphne: (DECLAIMING) . . . And with a grateful shudder he swore he'd never return to Nightmare Inn, either.

Bulldog: What do we do now, boss?

Frasier: Not to worry. I have a plan.

FRASIER GOES TO THE TELEPHONE AND BEGINS DIALING.

Roz: Oh yeah, right. We're doing this thing tomorrow night. Where are you going to find an idiot willing to do six dialect parts unrehearsed?

Frasier: (INTO PHONE) Niles – I love this new message on your machine. What an expressive voice you have . . .

AND WE:

FADE OUT.

END OF ACT ONE

ACT TWO

Scene D

FADE IN:

INT. BROADCAST STUDIO – THE NEXT NIGHT – NIGHT/3
(Frasier, Noel, Gil, Niles, Bulldog, Maxine, Roz)

IT'S A LARGER STUDIO THAN FRASIER'S, WITH A PHONE ON ONE WALL, OLD-FASHIONED STAND MIKES ON THE FLOOR AND A TABLE ON WHICH NOEL IS SETTING UP HIS SOUND EFFECTS WHILE FRASIER GOES OVER THE SCRIPT WITH GIL.

Gil: There's your brother. How is he enjoying the prospect of playing all those parts?

Frasier: Actually, he doesn't know about that yet. If he did he never would've agreed.

NILES ENTERS, A BIT AGITATED, AND CROSSES TO THEM.

Niles: Frasier, I thought you said you were going to messenger the script to me this morning.

Frasier: I'm so sorry, Niles. I ended up tinkering with it until the very last minute. But not to worry, with your natural gift you'll be fine. Now come see this. (QUICKLY DISTRACTING) Noel was just giving us a demonstration of the sound effects.

Noel: Okay. This is my door sound (OPENS LITTLE DOOR), my thunder screen (SHAKES IT), balloons for gunshots (POPS ONE) –

Gil: Why not a blank pistol?

Noel: Guns scare me.

Frasier: The mic was picking up his whimpering.

Noel: (INDICATES TAPE PLAYER) This has various kinds of organ music.

SFX: NOEL PLAYS TAPE, WHICH GIVES A CHILLING ORGAN STING

Noel (CONT'D): I've also got bells, wind-machine, gravel bag, and a coffee thermos.

Niles: What does that do?

Noel: Keeps my coffee warm. Duh.

NOEL INFLATES SEVERAL MORE BALLOONS FROM THE HELIUM TANK AS BULLDOG ENTERS WITH MAXINE, HIS STATUESQUE PROTEGEE.

Bulldog: This is Maxine, everybody. Baby, you go up in the booth and work on your part.

Maxine: Okay.

MAXINE OBLIGINGLY GOES INTO THE BOOTH WITH A SCRIPT.

Frasier: (SOTTO) "Work" on it? Bulldog, she only has one line.

Bulldog: Yeah, but she's got – what do you call it, begins with a "dis?"

Niles: Distemper?

Bulldog: Dyslexia. That's it, she's dyslexic.

Frasier: I wish you'd told me.

Bulldog: She'll be great, it's me I'm worried about. I've got some serious butterflies here.

Frasier: You're on the radio all the time.

Bulldog: That's me being me. This is acting. It's scary.

Frasier: That's all part of the thrill of live performance: butterflies in the stomach, sweaty palms, dry throat, pounding heart. I imagine you have all of those.

Bulldog: I do now.

ROZ ENTERS WITH A LIP FULL OF NOVOCAINE AND SPEAKING ACCORDINGLY.

Roz: Forry I'm wait, Fravier – I just fpent two hourf in va dentist's chair. An emergenfy. Ooh!

Gil: What is the matter?

Roz: Novocaine. He faid it would weah off by now. I keep biting by vip.

Frasier: Dear God. (CHECKS WATCH) And we start in five minutes.

Niles: I don't even know who I'm playing.

Frasier: I'll just cue you once we're on the air.

Niles: But shouldn't I at least prepare a little?

Frasier: Oh Niles, your spontaneity is your greatest asset as an actor. What was it the Yale Daily News said about your Tartuffe?

Niles: Oh, I don't know. Something about my having the magnetism of Marlon Brando, the charm of Danny Kaye, and the range of Laurence Olivier.

Frasier: Yes. (SOTTO, TO ROZ) He'll need all of them.

AND WE:

CUT TO:

Scene E

INT. FRASIER'S LIVING ROOM – CONTINUOUS – NIGHT/3
(Martin, Daphne, Frasier [V.O.])

DAPHNE IS SEATED BY THE RADIO.

Daphne: Hurry up, it's starting.

SHE TURNS UP THE VOLUME AS MARTIN ENTERS FROM THE KITCHEN WITH A BIG BOWL OF POPCORN. WE HEAR FRASIER'S VOICE DOING THE INTRO.

Frasier (V.O.): Good evening. This is Frasier Crane welcoming you to KACL's recreation of the original Mystery Theater. We invite you to follow us – if you dare – through the looming portals of . . .

SFX: THERE IS A WONDERFUL BURST OF SPOOKY ORGAN MUSIC

Frasier (V.O.) (CONT'D): . . . Nightmare Inn.

Daphne: I already know the plot but I'll try not to blurt out the name of the murderer.

Martin: Good. As a cop I hated it when people did that.

CUT TO:

Scene H

INT. BROADCAST STUDIO - CONTINUOUS - NIGHT/3
(Frasier, Roz, Niles, Noel, Gil, Bulldog, Maxine)

ALL ARE STANDING AT MICS, SCRIPTS IN HAND. FRASIER IS READING.

Frasier: . . . In all my years at The Yard I doubt I'd ever seen a fouler night –

CUES NOEL, WHO GIVES HIM THUNDER.

Frasier (CONT'D): – than that on which I was called out to investigate a double murder at the old inn on the moors.

HE CUES NOEL AGAIN, WHO GIVES HIM A DOOR KNOCK.

Frasier (CONT'D): The door was answered by Miss Carlotta Thorndyke.

FRASIER CUES NOEL TO GIVE A DOOR OPENING EFFECT.

Frasier (CONT'D): Her face was unfamiliar, and when she opened her lips I caught a hint of some exotic accent.

ROZ READS HER LINE HOLDING HER LIP IN HER FINGERS TO KEEP FROM BITING IT, GIVING HER AN EVEN WEIRDER SOUND.

Roz: Inthpector, fank God youf come.

HE CUES NOEL WHO MAKES DOOR SHUTTING SOUND.

Frasier: This is a grisly business, Miss Thorndyke.

Roz: I campf bewiewe any of by guesps coulb be a mububle-mububer.

SHE BITES HER LIP, WINCES, DROOLS, CLAPS A KLEENEX TO HER MOUTH.

Frasier: That's easy for you to say – (ROLLS HIS EYES) – but my job is to suspect everybody. Please introduce –

HE REALIZED ROZ IS MINISTERING TO HER LIP AND VAMPS.

Frasier (CONT'D): – No never mind. I know your guests by reputation. This must be Mr. Wing, the silk merchant. Did you witness anything suspicious, Wing?

HE CUES BULLDOG, WHO FREEZES, STARING AT HIS SCRIPT. FRASIER CUES HIM AGAIN. HIS MOUTH MOVES BUT NO SOUND EMERGES.

Frasier (CONT'D): Ah yes . . . the inscrutable Mr. Wing . . .

HE CUES BULLDOG MORE FURIOUSLY. BULLDOG CONTINUES TO STARE AT HIS SCRIPT AS THOUGH HYPNOTIZED, MOVING HIS MOUTH SILENTLY.

Frasier (CONT'D): (VAMPING WILDLY) . . . Of course, the inscrutable and *mute* Mr. Wing, who – who –

HE LOOKS WILDLY AROUND, SEES THE SOUND EFFECTS TABLE, HAS AN IDEA.

Frasier (CONT'D): – Who wears a bell on his hat. Did you witness anything suspicious, Wing?

FRASIER SHAKES THE BELL WHILE SHAKING HIS HEAD "NO" VERY AGITATEDLY.

Frasier (CONT'D): No, eh? I'll remember you said that. (CUES GIL)

Gil: I'm Nigel Fairservice, inspector. I was strolling in the garden when this dreadful tragedy occurred.

Frasier: Did anyone see you?

Gil: Several people. Hans, the German butler –

FRASIER CUES NILES. NILES REACTS WITH SOME SURPRISE.

Niles: Ja, I saw der gentleman.

Gil: O'Toole, the gardener –

FRASIER AGAIN CUES NILES, WHO REACTS, SURPRISED, PANTOMIMING "ME?" FRASIER NODS AND CUES HIM AGAIN. NILES ASSAYS A BROGUE.

Niles: T'was himself and no mistake.

Gil: – As well as Prudence McCallister.

Frasier: Is that true?

FRASIER CUES NILES, WHO HUFFS IN SILENT ANGER BUT MAKES A GAME ATTEMPT AT A MATRONLY VOICE.

Niles: Yes, I was taking a breath of air.

Frasier: (NARRATING) I tried to shake Nigel's alibi but each witness was adamant. O'Toole – (CUES)

Niles: Faith and it's true.

Frasier: – Hans – (CUES)

Niles: Jawohl.

Frasier: – Miss McCallister – (CUES)

Niles: Mercy, yes.

Frasier: There remained one suspect whose whereabouts had not yet been established . . . Peppo the dwarf, a retired circus performer.

FRASIER CUES NILES, WHO THROWS UP HIS HANDS, GIVING UP. THE HELL WITH IT.

Frasier (CONT'D): Exactly where were you when the murders occurred, Peppo?

FRASIER CUES. NILES SHRUGS. FRASIER CUES AGAIN. NILES PANTOMIMES "HOW?" FRASIER LOOKS AROUND, SPOTS THE HELIUM TANK, POINTS TO IT. GRITTING HIS TEETH, NILES GOES AND TAKES A HIT OFF THE TANK.

Frasier (CONT'D): Peppo? I'm waiting . . . exactly where were you?

Niles: (HELIUM VOICE) I was at the movies.

REELING AND COUGHING, NILES GOES AND SLUMPS IN A CHAIR AND TAKES A LONG DRINK OF WATER FROM A GLASS ON THE TABLE.

Frasier: At the movies, you say? Well, one quick phone call can verify that. What's this? Dear God! The phone lines have been cut.

HE CUES NOEL FOR ORGAN MUSIC.

SFX: ORGAN MUSIC

Frasier (CONT'D): Now we're really stranded. Totally and completely isolated from any contact with the outside world.

SFX: THE ACTUAL PHONE IN THE STUDIO RINGS

NOEL, ACTING ON INSTINCT, PICKS IT UP.

Noel: Studio five. (REALIZING) Sorry.

Frasier: Apparently, the phone's been repaired. Hello?

HE PULLS THE CORD FROM THE BOTTOM OF THE PHONE.

Frasier (CONT'D): It's gone dead again. Who knows what other surprises this night may bring?

AND WE:

CUT TO:

Scene J

INT. FRASIER'S LIVING ROOM – CONTINUOUS – NIGHT/3
(Frasier [V.O.], Martin, Daphne)

Frasier (V.O.): Nightmare Inn will continue after these words from our sponsor.

MARTIN TURNS DOWN THE VOLUME.

Martin: I didn't remember the plots of these things being so goofy.

Daphne: Mr. Wing wasn't mute last night. Dr. Crane must have written that.

Martin: Too bad he isn't playing it.

CUT TO:

Scene K

INT. BROADCAST STUDIO – CONTINUOUS – NIGHT/3
(Frasier, Roz, Noel, Gil, Niles, Bulldog, Maxine)

FRASIER IS SCRIBBLING IN THE SCRIPTS AS NILES BERATES HIM.

Niles: Six different roles and six different accents? I have half a mind to walk out of here.

Frasier: I had no choice, but you're doing brilliantly. Although your Hans could be a bit gruffer.

Niles: Don't direct me.

Frasier: Right, right. Sorry. My bigger problem is we're running way over time. (TO GIL) Gil, at the bottom of page fourteen, after you're shot, just say "I'm dying." Cut the rest.

Gil: (STRICKEN) That's my boyhood in Surrey speech.

Frasier: Yes, I know.

Gil: You can't cut that. You can't.

Frasier: Stop whining. We have a play to do.

Gil: I don't care anymore.

Frasier: Quiet. Ten seconds, everybody. Maxine, watch for your cue. And let's pick the pace up, people.

FRASIER CLAPS HIS HANDS AND EVERYONE TAKES THEIR PLACES. THE ON-AIR LIGHT GOES ON.

Frasier (CONT'D): (NARRATING) "Nightmare Inn" – Act Two – I was baffled. They all had alibis. Suddenly Miss Thorndyke pointed, her eyes wide with alarm . . . (CUES ROZ)

Roz: There's someone outside that window!

FRASIER CUES NOEL WHO HITS TAPE. INSTEAD OF ORGAN MUSIC, HOWEVER, LOUD, JINGLY CALLIOPE MUSIC COMES OUT.

SFX: CALLIOPE MUSIC

Noel: (SOTTO) I forgot to rewind.

HE SHUTS OFF THE TAPE.

SFX: CALLIOPE MUSIC STOPS

Frasier: (STRUGGLING) Why yes . . . Miss Thorndyke . . . it . . . it appears to be an ice-cream truck . . . but – but never mind that . . . (FLIPS AHEAD A PAGE) Suddenly the storm put the lights out and we were left in darkness. Then, a scream.

FRASIER CUES MAXINE, WHO STEPS FORWARD AND READS HER ONE LINE, GIVING IT HER BEST SHOT.

Maxine: (SCREAMS, THEN) Look out – he's got a nug.

Frasier: (BESIDE HIMSELF) A *gun*. A gun is what he's got.

FRASIER CUES NOEL WHO POPS TWO BALLOONS. BANG! BANG!

Frasier (CONT'D): Just then the lights came back up. A smoking gun lay on the table, the maid lay dead, unable to name her killer. And Nigel Fairservice lay mortally wounded.

Gil: I'm dying –

Frasier: Poor man was gone.

Gil: (STUBBORNLY) – Never again to revisit the scene of my boyhood in Surrey –

FRASIER MAKES FRANTIC "CUT" GESTURES WITH FINGER AND THROAT. GIL POINTEDLY IGNORES HIM.

Gil (CONT'D): – Romping with my school chums in the fens and spinneys – FRASIER GRABS A BALLOON . . .

Frasier: Then the lights went out again. (POPS BALLOON) Nigel had been shot again.

Gil: Only grazed me. – When the twilight bathed the hedgerows –

Frasier: (POPPING ANOTHER BALLOON) The final bullet blew his head clean off his shoulders. (THEN) People, let's try to keep calm. Although it's hard when the killer is among us.

GIL WORKS THE "DOOR" SOUND EFFECT, KNOCKING AND "ENTERING."

Gil: (NOW TOTALLY AD-LIB) Hi-ho. I'm Nigel's brother Cedric. I haven't seen him since we were boys in Surrey, romping –

FRASIER POPS ANOTHER BALLOON.

Frasier: And so died the last surviving member of the Fairservice family.

CUT TO:

Scene L

INT. FRASIER'S LIVING ROOM – CONTINUOUS – NIGHT/3
(Martin, Daphne, Gil [V.O.])

Martin: Boy, I didn't see that one coming.

WE HEAR THE ONGOING DRAMA ON THE RADIO AS THEY LISTEN. FIRST THERE IS ANOTHER KNOCK AND ANOTHER DOOR OPENING.

SFX: KNOCK AND DOOR OPENING

Gil (V.O.): Hello, I'm the ice-cream man. Years ago I went to school with Nigel Fairservice. We used to romp in the fens and spinneys –

SFX: THE SOUND OF ANOTHER BANG

Daphne: This is turning into a bloodbath.

Martin: See – that's why I prefer TV. You want to see that stuff.

CUT TO:

Scene N

INT. BROADCAST STUDIO – CONTINUOUS – NIGHT/3
(Frasier, Roz, Niles, Noel, Gil, Bulldog, Maxine)

Frasier: By this time I was more baffled than ever so I played a hunch. Hans, may I see your fingernails?

Niles: Why?

Frasier: They seem a bit ragged for a butler's.

Niles: All right, all right, I'm not what I appear. None of us is. I'm not a butler, I'm not even (LOSING ACCENT) German.

SFX: NOEL PLAYS AN ORGAN STING

DURING THE FOLLOWING, FRASIER CAN'T HELP HIMSELF AND BEGINS GESTICULATING LIKE AN ORCHESTRA CONDUCTOR DIRECTING NILES' PERFORMANCE.

Niles (CONT'D): Sit down, inspector. You're about to hear a fascinating tale. Each of us holds a piece of the puzzle to relate to you. When we've finished you'll know the full, dark secret of Nightmare Inn.

FRASIER GESTICULATES THAT NILES SHOULD EMOTE FROM THE HEART. NILES GIVES FRASIER A LOOK THAT SAYS, "YOU'D BETTER STOP THAT."

Roz: Are you sure we should, Hans?

Niles: Be quiet, Mother.

SFX: NOEL PLAYS ANOTHER ORGAN STING

Niles (CONT'D): Mother and I moved here when I was a small boy after the tragic death of my father.

FRASIER INDICATES FOR MORE EMOTION.

Niles (CONT'D): I kept the pain of that loss buried deep within me like a serpent coiled within a damp cave.

FRASIER INDICATES AGAIN FOR MORE EMOTION. NILES GIVES HIM A LOOK THAT SAYS, "THAT'S IT," AND TOSSES THE SCRIPT ASIDE.

Niles (CONT'D): Okay, that's it. Never mind all that. I think I'll just take that gun off the table. (POPS BALLOON) Sorry about that, O'Toole. I guess we'll never hear your fascinating piece of the puzzle. (TWO MORE BALLOON POPS) Or yours, Kragen and Peppo. Could you McCallister sisters stand back-to-back? I'm short on bullets. (ANOTHER POP) Thank you. (TO ROZ) What was your name again, dear?

Roz: Miss Thorndyke.

Niles: Thank you. (BALLOON) Also Wing, (BALLOON PLUS BELLS) and of course one final bullet for myself, so the mystery will die with me. (FINAL BALLOON POP) Hah.

NILES FOLDS HIS ARMS AND BEAMS AT FRASIER.

Frasier: (FLOUNDERING) Well, then . . . that . . . pretty much wrapped things up. The case was closed and with a grateful shudder I swore I'd never return to Nightmare Inn.

SFX: ORGAN STING

Frasier (CONT'D): Well, we still have . . . (LOOKS AT HIS WATCH) nine minutes remaining. Perhaps we could have a little post-play discussion.

AND WE:

CUT TO:

Scene P

INT. FRASIER'S LIVING ROOM – CONTINUOUS – NIGHT/3
Martin, Daphne, Frasier [V.O.], Gil [V.O.])

Martin: What?

MARTIN AND DAPHNE EXCHANGE A LOOK.

Frasier (V.O.): I suppose, to me, it stands as a morality play about the futility of using violence to solve our problems.

Gil (V.O.): I agree. It reminds me of a lesson my mother taught me when I was still a boy in Surrey, romping with my –

GIL'S VOICE CUTS OFF. HE IS BEING STRANGLED. WE THEN HEAR THE SOUND OF GIL BEING RESTRAINED. FRASIER IS OBVIOUSLY SOLVING HIS PROBLEM WITH VIOLENCE. THE MAYHEM BUILDS: THERE ARE SOUNDS OF A TUSSLE, THEN GENERAL ANARCHY. ON MARTIN AND DAPHNE'S REACTION, WE:

FADE OUT.

THE END

Scene R

(END CREDITS)

INT. BROADCAST STUDIO – LATER THAT NIGHT – NIGHT/3

(Roz, Noel)

NOEL IS CLEANING UP, PUTTING THE SOUND EFFECT ITEMS INTO A BOX. HE NOTICES SOME PAGES FROM A SCRIPT, PICKS THEM UP, CROSSES TO THE MIC, AND DRAMATICALLY BEGINS TO PERFORM. IN THE HALLWAY, ROZ WANDERS BY, SEES HIM, SNEAKS IN, CROSSES TO THE PROP TABLE AND POPS A BALLOON WITH HER PENCIL. NOEL THROWS HIS PAGES IN THE AIR, HITS THE DECK, AND WE:

FADE OUT.

END OF SHOW

SEASON FIVE

Perspectives On Christmas

Room Service

The Ski Lodge

PERSPECTIVES ON CHRISTMAS

#40570-106

Written by Christopher Lloyd
Created and Developed by David Angell, Peter Casey & David Lee
Directed by David Lee

ACT ONE

Scene A

FADE IN:

A BLACK SCREEN. IN WHITE LETTERS APPEARS, "MASTER CLASS."

Martin (V.O.): Yow! Easy!

INT. MASSAGE ROOM – NIGHT – NIGHT/2
(Martin, Masseur)

A SMALL, LOW-LIT ROOM WITH A MASSAGE TABLE IN THE CENTER. A
MASSEUR WORKS ON MARTIN, WHO IS ON HIS BACK.

Masseur: Sorry – your neck is tight.

Martin: Yeah, well, I've had a tense couple of days.

Masseur: Well, the holidays will do that to you.

Martin: Yeah, well, this was the worst Christmas ever . . .

CUT TO:

Scene B

INT. FRASIER'S LIVING ROOM – DAY – DAY/1 (MARTIN'S VERSION)
(Martin, Frasier, Daphne, Niles, Eddie)

Martin (V.O.): It started yesterday . . .

AS IN THE PAST, THE ROOM IS ABUNDANTLY DECORATED IN CHRISTMAS
REGALIA. FRASIER AND MARTIN ARE DECORATING THE TREE. NILES
IS NEARBY WITH A CUP OF EGGNOG. THERE'S MISTLETOE OVER THE
DOOR.

Martin: You know the only part about Christmas I don't like? How quickly it's all
over.

Frasier: Yes, come December 26th it's all a memory, with nothing but your light decorating touch to remind us.

DAPHNE ENTERS THE FRONT DOOR, WITH EDDIE ON A LEASH. SHE PAUSES TO REMOVE HIS LEASH, DIRECTLY BELOW THE MISTLETOE.

Daphne: Afternoon, all.

THEY ALL AD-LIB HELLOS.

Niles: That's awfully dangerous, Daphne, standing there under that mistletoe.

Frasier: That's enough eggnog, Niles.

Daphne: The oddest thing just happened. I was walking Eddie past that church over on Chestnut, and he turned to go in, like he assumed that's where we were going.

Frasier: That's strange. He did exactly the same thing when I was walking him yesterday.

Daphne: You're kidding. Mr. Crane – any idea why he'd do that?

Martin: Not a one.

Daphne: Well, don't you think it's strange?

Martin: Look, that dog does a lot of weird things. Yesterday when we were taking a bath together he spent fifteen straight minutes pushing the soap around with his nose, like an otter. Weird.

MARTIN MOVES TO THE KITCHEN.

Frasier: Yes, if he gets any weirder we may have to send "Eddie" to a home.

FRASIER CROSSES INTO THE KITCHEN. MARTIN IS THERE, POURING HIMSELF A GLASS OF EGGNOG.

Frasier (CONT'D): Well, I'm off. I've still got all my shopping to do.

Martin: All of it?

Frasier: Yes, I'm determined not to settle this year. I want to give gifts that will be remembered and cherished long after the holidays.

Martin: Well, there's nothing more cherished than the gift of laughter.

Frasier: Dad, if you want that "Highway Patrol Bloopers" tape you'll have to buy it yourself. (OFF MARTIN'S EGGNOG) You're not going to drink that naked, are you? The first mistake in eggnog preparation is failing to garnish it properly with a dash of nutmeg.

FRASIER GRABS A SPICE CONTAINER AND SPRINKLES SOME IN MARTIN'S

CUP. MARTIN TAKES A SIP AND INHALES THE SPICE, SENDING HIM INTO A COUGHING AND WHEEZING FIT.

Frasier (CONT'D): (CHECKING SPICE CONTAINER) Of course the second mistake is placing the nutmeg next to the paprika on the spice shelf.

Daphne (O.C.): Mr. Crane, are you all right?

Frasier: We're fine, Daphne. (THEN) Sorry, Dad.

FRASIER STARTS OUT.

Martin: Oh, Fras – can I talk to you a minute?

Frasier: Sure. What is it?

Martin: Well, the thing Daphne was talking about . . . there is a reason Eddie knows that church. I've been taking him there.

Frasier: Well, I guess the family that bathes together prays together.

Martin: No, there's this priest, Father Curtis, who knows Eddie from the park. One day he asked if Eddie could be in their Christmas pageant. Well, I said okay, then he roped me into playing a shepherd. Then Dutch Gansvört came down with bronchitis and I got promoted to wise man.

Frasier: Dad – apart from stirring my sympathy for someone named Dutch Gansvört, I'm not sure why you're telling me this.

Martin: It turns out the wise man has to sing a song. I told him I could do it, but the song is a killer. I'm going to humiliate myself.

Frasier: Well, you probably just need a little rehearsal. Why don't we work on it tonight?

Martin: You really think that will help?

Frasier: Absolutely. You're a good singer, you're just rusty. We'll start at eight.

Martin: I'm more than rusty. The first time I sang it, the kid playing the Angel Gabriel laughed so hard he wet his cloud.

Frasier: Maybe we'll start at seven. (CALLS OFF) Niles, hold the elevator.

DISSOLVE TO:

Scene C

INT. FRASIER'S LIVING ROOM – THAT NIGHT – NIGHT/1
(Martin, Frasier, Niles, Eddie)

FRASIER AND NILES ARE AT THE PIANO AND EDDIE IS ON THE COUCH.

MARTIN ENTERS WITH SHEET MUSIC.

Martin: All right, this is the song – "O Holy Night". You know it?

Frasier: Of course, Dad. It's a classic. It all builds to that one wonderful note at the end (SINGING) "O NIGHT DIVINE!"

Martin: Yes, yes, that's exactly the note I can't hit. I practice in my room and Eddie ends up burying his head under a pillow.

Niles: Well, not to worry, Dad. We'll get you there. Now, the whole key to singing is learning to control your throat.

Frasier: That's one school of thought.

Niles: (PRODUCES A BOW TIE) A good exercise you can do is put this bow tie on and practice making it go up and down by moving your Adam's apple.

Frasier: It will also come in handy should you sing "O Holy Night" with a barbershop quartet.

Niles: Do you mind?

AND THEY GO INTO AN OVERLAP FIGHT, THEN:

Martin: Can I just try singing? I want to be done with this when Daphne gets home. I don't want her knowing anything about this or she'll insist on coming to the pageant and I'm nervous enough as it is.

Niles: Fine. Why don't we just see what we're working with? (INDICATES MUSIC) We'll start right here. And I really want to see you attack that note.

NILES BEGINS TO PLAY AND MARTIN BEGINS TO SING.

Martin: "O NIGHT WHEN CHRIST WAS BORN . . . O NIGHT DIVI-I-I-I –"

ON THE SYLLABLE "-VINE," MARTIN MISSES BADLY AND HIS VOICE TRAILS OFF.

Niles: Sometimes the note sees the attack coming and retreats.

THEY THEN HEAR A BANGING COMING FROM ABOVE.

Martin: (LOOKING UP) Hey, shut up! This bozo upstairs bangs his broom handle against the floor whenever I sing.

Frasier: Ignore him, Dad. You know, there is another voice exercise that helped me immensely when I sang the role of Colonel Fairfax in "The Yeoman of the Guard". The principle is to distract yourself with a physical exercise, thus freeing your voice. You hit a note, then slide up the octave as you descend slowly to a crouch position. Observe.

FRASIER DEMONSTRATES THE EXERCISE.

Frasier (CONT'D): It works.

Niles: That's interesting. I wonder if the reverse is true.

NILES SQUATS DOWN AND RISES UP AS HE SINGS A DESCENDING OCTAVE. FRASIER AND NILES CONTINUE SQUATTING AND STANDING, GOING UP AND DOWN THE OCTAVES.

Frasier: Come on, Dad.

Martin: No, I'm afraid with three people doing it it might look stupid.

Frasier: We're just trying to help.

Niles: I'm starting to think your problem is all psychological. You've convinced yourself you can't hit that note.

Martin: I've convinced the guy upstairs, too.

Frasier: Niles may be right. You may just need some positive reinforcement. Let's try it again, but this time concentrate on eliminating any negative thoughts. All right?

Martin: Okay.

NILES BEGINS TO PLAY, AND MARTIN TO SING.

Martin (CONT'D): "FALL ON YOUR KNEES."

Frasier: You've got it, Dad.

Martin: "OH, HEAR . . ."

Frasier: I hear sweet music.

Martin: ". . . THE ANGELS' VOICES . . ."

Niles: I hear one angel . . .

Martin: "O NIGHT . . ."

Frasier: It's a good night!

Martin: "DIVINE . . ."

Frasier: Something's divine!

Martin: "O NIGHT . . ."

Niles: Yeah, Dad!

Martin: "WHEN CHRIST WAS BORN . . ."

Frasier: A star is born!

Martin: "O NIGHT . . ."

Frasier: Bring it on home.

Martin: "DIVI-I-I-I -"

HE TRIES FOR THE NOTE, MISSES AGAIN, NILES AND FRASIER CRINGE, AND SOON MARTIN'S BELLOWED NOTE TRAILS OFF. EDDIE BURIES HIS HEAD UNDER A CUSHION.

Frasier: Well, that was better.

FROM ABOVE WE AGAIN HEAR THE BROOM BANGING.

Niles/Frasier/Martin: Oh, shut up!!

CUT TO:

Scene D

INT. MASSAGE ROOM - NIGHT - NIGHT/2
(Masseur, Martin)

MARTIN IS BEING MASSAGED.

Masseur: So, how'd you end up doing? Whoa - your neck tensed up again, didn't it?

Martin: That answer your question?

FADE OUT.

Scene E

FADE IN:

INT. MASSAGE ROOM - NIGHT - NIGHT/2
(Masseur, Daphne)

WE'RE CLOSE ON THE MASSEUR.

Masseur: These shoulders are awfully tight.

WE WIDEN TO REVEAL IT'S DAPHNE HE'S MASSAGING.

Daphne: It's been a stressful few days.

Masseur: I'd be happy to listen.

Daphne: Oh, no . . . Well, it started yesterday. I had something on my mind . . .

CUT TO:

Scene H

<u>INT. FRASIER'S LIVING ROOM - DAY - DAY/1 (DAPHNE'S VERSION)</u>
(Daphne, Niles, Frasier, Martin, Eddie)

IT'S THE SAME SCENE AS BEFORE. MARTIN IS DECORATING THE TREE.
FRASIER AND NILES ARE NEARBY. NILES HAS AN EGGNOG. THERE'S
MISTLETOE OVER THE DOOR. <u>DAPHNE ENTERS WITH EDDIE</u> ON A LEASH.

Daphne (V.O.): Lucky for me, Dr. Crane's brother was over. He's always such a good
friend to me.

Daphne: Afternoon, all.

THEY ALL AD-LIB HELLOS, THEN:

Niles: You know, Daphne, that's awfully dangerous standing under that mistletoe - a
piece could fall into your eye.

Frasier: Let me freshen that.

FRASIER TAKES NILES' EGGNOG.

Daphne: Oh, thank you, Dr. Crane. (THEN) The oddest thing just happened. I was
walking Eddie past that church on Chestnut and he turned to go inside - as though
that's where he thought we were going.

Frasier: That's strange. He did the same thing yesterday when I was walking him.

Daphne: Any idea why he'd do that, Mr. Crane?

Martin: Nope. Dogs are weird.

<u>MARTIN EXITS TO THE KITCHEN, FOLLOWED BY FRASIER.</u>

Daphne: You know, that worries me a bit.

Niles: What does?

Daphne: Well, I think your father's been going to that church. I had an uncle who did
the same thing. Had no interest in church his whole life, then he started going every day.
Turns out he'd gotten some bad news from his doctor. He didn't even last the year.

Niles: Well, first of all, I can see you're upset, so come here.

HE OPENS HIS ARMS TO HER AND SHE HUGS HIM.

Daphne: Thank you, Dr. Crane. You're always so supportive.

Niles: Second of all, I think you're worrying over nothing. I've never known my father to have so much as a hangnail without letting everyone know about it.

Daphne: That's true. Maybe I just got myself worked up remembering my Uncle John.

Niles: Look at you – just saying his name gets you upset. Come here.

HE REACHES OUT TO HUG HER.

Daphne: I'm fine.

Niles: No, you need a hug.

Daphne: Well, all right.

NILES HUGS HER AGAIN. FROM OFF-STAGE WE HEAR THE SAME SCARY-SOUNDING, NUTMEG-INDUCED COUGH FROM MARTIN IN THE KITCHEN.

Daphne (CONT'D): Mr. Crane, are you all right?

Frasier (O.C.): We're fine, Daphne.

Niles: You see, nothing to worry about. Well, I've got to run. Now, what did I do with my keys?

DAPHNE STARTS LOOKING AROUND, THEN:

Daphne: Oh, here they are.

THEY ARE ON THE FLOOR ABOUT A FOOT AWAY, BUT IN ORDER FOR DAPHNE TO GET THEM SHE HAS TO BEND OVER DIRECTLY IN FRONT OF NILES. SHE DOES SO, AND NILES DOES NOT LOOK AT HER BUTT. SHE HANDS THEM TO HIM.

Niles: Thank you, Daphne.

Daphne: Honestly, Dr. Crane, I've never known anyone who lost his keys the way you do . . .

NILES STARTS OUT AS FRASIER AND MARTIN ENTER FROM THE KITCHEN.

Frasier: Hold the elevator, Niles. Dad, don't worry. Niles and I will be there for you.

Daphne: What's that about?

Martin: Never mind.

FRASIER AND NILES EXIT.

Daphne: Well, I know it's time for your exercises, but what if we played a game of cribbage instead? We could even have a beer.

Martin: Thanks anyway, Daph, but I'm not in the mood. I'm just going to go lie down.

Daphne: Mr. Crane, did you ever call Dr. Stewart for the results of your physical?

Martin: Oh, yeah, couple of days ago. I'm fine. Come on, Eddie.

EDDIE RUNS TO JOIN MARTIN AS HE HEADS FOR THE HALL. MARTIN STOPS IN FRONT OF THE CHRISTMAS TREE, STARING AT IT.

Daphne: Is everything all right?

Martin: Oh, yeah. It's just all over so fast.

MARTIN HEADS OFF, AND OVER DAPHNE'S VERY CONCERNED LOOK, WE HEAR:

Daphne (V.O.): Well, that was enough to convince me I was right. And the next twenty-four hours were a living hell.

CUT TO:

Scene J

INT. FRASIER'S LIVING ROOM – NEXT DAY – DAY/2 (DAPHNE'S VERSION)
(Daphne, Martin, Niles, Eddie)

MARTIN IS THERE, ON THE PHONE.

Daphne (V.O.): . . . The worst came the next day.

DAPHNE ENTERS THE FRONT DOOR, UNSEEN BY MARTIN. SHE WEAR A LONG RED DRESS AND CARRIES SEVERAL BAGS.

Martin: (INTO PHONE) I'm just terrified about this, Father. It all came about so suddenly. I'm not prepared . . . Tell me again what I'm supposed to say when I see Jesus the first time . . .

DAPHNE'S HORROR-STRICKEN.

Martin (CONT'D): (INTO PHONE) All right . . . Yeah, I'll see you in a little while. Goodbye.

HE HANGS UP. DAPHNE TRIES TO PUT A GOOD FACE ON THINGS.

Daphne: Hello.

Martin: Oh, hi.

Daphne: You know, Mr. Crane, I'm so excited about the gift I just got for you – why don't you open it now?

Martin: Well, we usually wait 'til Christmas, but to tell you the truth, I could use a little cheering up.

MARTIN TAKES THE BOX AND BEGINS OPENING IT.

Daphne: You know, if there's something on your mind, I'm always here to talk about it . . .

Martin: You're nice to offer, but no thanks. This is one of those things a man's gotta do alone.

HE REMOVES A SWEATER. IT'S A RED, GREEN AND GOLD PULLOVER – A LITTLE GARISH, YES, BUT VERY MARTIN.

Martin (CONT'D): Wow, look at this!

Daphne: You like it?

Martin: Are you kidding? I love it. I'm never taking this sweater off – they'll have to bury me in it.

DAPHNE STARTS TO TEAR UP.

Martin (CONT'D): Daph, are you all right? It looks like you're crying.

Daphne: Oh, Mr. Crane, I know why you've been going down to that church.

Martin: You do?

Daphne: Yes. I'm just so worried for you.

Martin: Well, it'll all be over soon enough. What're you getting so upset for?

Daphne: Because I care about you and I can't believe you were going to let this whole thing happen without ever telling a soul.

Martin: Well, it's embarrassing.

Daphne: Embarrassing?

Martin: You think I want a bunch of people looking at me up there, stiff as a board, a lot of stupid make-up on my face? . . .

Daphne: So how much time have you got?

Martin: (CHECKS WATCH) About twenty minutes.

Daphne: Twenty minutes?

Martin: And I can't wait 'til it's over. This is the last Christmas pageant I'm ever signing up for.

Daphne: You're in a Christmas pageant? I thought you were dying.

Martin: Why'd you think that?

Daphne: Well, you just got your test results, you're down at the church all the time . . .

MARTIN STARTS LAUGHING.

Daphne (CONT'D): Why are you laughing?

Martin: Because it's funny.

Daphne: Well, I don't think it's so bloody funny.

Martin: Are you kidding? It's hysterical. Ooh – I'm dying.

Daphne: You will be.

DAPHNE PICKS UP THE BOX THE SWEATER CAME IN AND HURLS IT AT MARTIN.

Martin: Hey, watch it.

Daphne: Don't you tell me what to do!

AND THEY GO INTO AN OVERLAPPING FIGHT: "I WAS WORRIED SICK," "WELL IT'S NOT MY FAULT," "IT BLOODY WELL IT," ETC. MEANWHILE, THE FRONT DOOR OPENS AND A STRICKEN-LOOKING NILES ENTERS, HIS JACKET RIPPED AND COVERED IN GREASE STAINS AND PINE NEEDLES, AND HIS HAIR MUSSED. HE MAKES HIS WAY ACROSS THE ROOM THEN BENDS OVER TO TIE HIS SHOE. FINALLY MARTIN NOTICES HIM.

Martin: Niles – you okay?

CUT TO:

Scene K

INT. MASSAGE ROOM – NIGHT – NIGHT/2
(Masseur, Niles)

NILES IS ON THE TABLE.

Masseur: You can talk about it if you like.

WE SEE NILES' SQUISHED FACE THROUGH THE FACE HOLE.

Niles: I'm not ready just yet.

FADE OUT.

END OF ACT ONE

ACT TWO

Scene L

FADE IN:

INT. MASSAGE ROOM – NIGHT – NIGHT/2
(Niles, Daphne)

WE ARE CLOSE ON NILES.

Niles: I can't tell you how good that feels. I don't think I've ever had a massage like this.

WE WIDEN TO REVEAL IT'S DAPHNE WHO'S MASSAGING HIM.

Daphne: Well, I'm glad. (THEN) As long as you're so relaxed, maybe I ought to just give you my Christmas present right now.

SHE STARTS TO LIE DOWN ON TOP OF NILES.

Niles: Umm. Oooh.

Niles (V.O.): Yeow!

CUT TO:

Scene N

INT. MASSAGE ROOM – CONTINUOUS – NIGHT/2
(Niles, Masseur)

NILES' SHOULDERS ARE BEING MASSAGED BY THE MASSEUR.

Niles: Ow. You woke me up!

Masseur: Sorry. I guess this ankle is a bit tender.

Niles: Yours would be too if you'd had the day I'd had . . .

CUT TO:

Scene R

INT. FRASIER'S ELEVATOR/HALLWAY – LATE AFTERNOON – DAY/2
(Niles, Albert, Jane, Doris, Vern [V.O.], Woman, Man)

Niles (V.O.): I went out to do some shopping, then I arrived at Frasier's building . . .

Perspectives On Christmas

NILES STANDS BEFORE AN ELEVATOR. ITS DOORS OPEN AND WE REVEAL A MIDDLE-AGED WOMAN, <u>DORIS</u>, AND A COUPLE IN THEIR SEVENTIES, <u>ALBERT AND JANE</u>. ALBERT IS A DOUR-FACED MAN, WHO FINDS THE WORST IN EVERYTHING. THERE IS ALSO A VERY LARGE CHRISTMAS TREE. NILES STEPS IN AND MOVES NEAR DORIS, AWAY FROM THE TREE.

Niles: Excuse me, I don't want to crowd you, but this is a brand new hand-tailored Italian suit. You know how hard it is to get sap out of virgin wool.

Albert: Another reason we didn't need this tree.

Jane: Oh, Albert.

Albert: Well, we're leaving for Florida in three days. Besides, this thing's a fire hazard.

Jane: Mr. Doom and Gloom.

Niles: You know, they make a chemical now that you can use to fireproof a tree.

Albert: Causes cancer.

Niles: Happy holidays, then.

THE ELEVATOR STOPS.

Jane: What just happened?

Doris: I think the elevator stopped.

NILES PUSHES SOME BUTTONS.

Niles: Not to worry – I'm sure we can get it going again.

Albert: We've probably got about twenty minutes of oxygen.

Niles: Sir – you're only going to alarm everyone.

Doris: I work in an E.R.

Niles: Ah, then maybe you can instruct these people on how to stay cool in a crisis.

Doris: I was on duty that night the elevator cable snapped in the Bing building. They brought these people in on cookie sheets.

NILES PUSHES THE INTERCOM BUTTON.

Niles: Hello? Is someone there?

Vern (V.O.): Yeah, who is it?

Niles: There's a group of us stuck in one of your elevators. We've pushed all the buttons, but the doors won't open and we can't seem to move off the eighth floor.

Vern (V.O.): All right, where are you calling from, Sir?

Niles: The Elliott Bay Towers.

Vern (V.O.): Well, both my crews are out – they're on the other side of town. Could be a good hour and a half before I can get anybody there.

Doris: Well, I can't wait that long – my children are upstairs alone in the apartment.

Albert: Haven't got a gas stove up there, have you?

Niles: Shut up, Albert.

Vern (V.O.): Well, there is another way. If somebody felt like climbing through the trapdoor on top of your car, there's a manual release switch up there that would open up your doors.

Doris: Well, that's what we have to do then. Someone's got to go up there.

Albert: That's a pretty small opening.

Niles: Well, obviously I have more confidence in your wife than you do. There you go, ma'am. Alley-oop.

NILES FORMS A BASKET WITH HIS HANDS, AND OFFERS JANE A LEG-UP.

Doris: (TO NILES) It's got to be you.

Niles: Did I mention this is virgin wool?

Doris: My children are alone.

Niles: Exactly how do you expect me to get up there?

Doris: You could climb up the tree.

Niles: What?

Doris: Surely you climbed plenty of trees when you were a boy?

Jane: That's Dr. Crane's brother.

Doris/Albert: (KNOWINGLY) Oh.

Niles: Fine.

NILES REMOVES HIS COAT AND HANDS IT TO DORIS. HE STARTS CLIMBING UP THE TREE.

Niles (CONT'D): I suppose in times of crisis, someone has to step forward and be a hero. Today, that man is Niles Crane. Ow! Dammit. Tomorrow it will be Mr. Li, my dry cleaner.

Albert: All right. Grab his feet and we'll push him through.

THEY DO SO.

Niles: Not so fast, not so fast!

NILES VANISHES THROUGH THE OPENING AND WE HEAR A THUD.

Niles (V.O.): Yow! Not to worry. I landed in a nice, soft puddle of grease. I'm looking for the release switch, just bear with me . . . This might be it.

THE DOORS OPEN.

Doris: Quick!

THEY ALL RUN OUT, DORIS STILL CARRYING NILES' COAT.

Niles (V.O.): Did that do anything? Hello? People? Lady with my coat?

NILES STICKS HIS HEAD BACK INSIDE THE ELEVATOR, UPSIDE-DOWN.

Niles (CONT'D): Where did you all go?

THE DOORS CLOSE AGAIN, AND WE HEAR THE ELEVATOR START TO MOVE UPWARD.

Niles (CONT'D): Oh my God! We're going up. Someone stop this thing!

RESET TO:

INT. HALLWAY – SECONDS LATER

A MAN AND A WOMAN ARE ROUNDING THE CORNER, AS THE ELEVATOR DOORS OPEN AND NILES CRAWLS OUT. HIS SUIT IS TORN AND COVERED WITH GREASE, AND HE HAS PINE NEEDLES ALL OVER HIM.

Woman: Why is that man crawling?

Man: That's Dr. Crane's brother.

Woman: (KNOWINGLY) Oh.

Niles (V.O.): I was slightly shaken by what I had done . . .

CUT TO:

Scene S

INT. FRASIER'S LIVING ROOM – MOMENTS LATER – DAY/2 (NILES' VERSION)
(Niles, Daphne, Martin, Eddie)

Niles (V.O.): But I'd completely composed myself as I arrived at Frasier's.

NILES CALMLY ENTERS TO FIND DAPHNE AND MARTIN IN MID-FIGHT, DAPHNE HURLING A BOX AT MARTIN. DAPHNE WEARS A SHORTER, SEXIER VERSION OF THE RED DRESS WE SAW HER IN EARLIER. MARTIN'S SWEATER IS RED, BLUE, GOLD, YELLOW, ORANGE, GREEN, WHITE, MAGENTA, TURQUOISE AND FUCHSIA.

Niles (V.O.) (CONT'D): But before I could tell my story, my father was out the door to his Christmas pageant and it was some time later, after Frasier returned home, that I finally brought them up to speed.

CUT TO:

Scene T

INT. FRASIER'S LIVING ROOM – LATER – DAY/2 (NILES' VERSION)
(Niles, Frasier, Roz, Daphne, Eddie)

NILES IS ON THE COUCH, WITH DAPHNE AT HIS SIDE. FRASIER IS THERE.

Niles: Of course, I don't know what you use to get elevator grease out of virgin wool.

Frasier: Well, brown suede seems to be leeching it out nicely.

NILES BEGINS TENDING TO THE COUCH WITH HIS HANDKERCHIEF.

SFX: DOORBELL RINGS.

FRASIER CROSSES TO IT.

Frasier (CONT'D): Anyway, no Christmas is complete without a bit of tumult. But now we can all relax and enjoy this beautiful holiday evening together.

FRASIER OPENS THE DOOR TO ROZ, WHO STANDS THERE SCOWLING AT HIM, HOLDING A PRESENT.

Roz: Merry Christmas.

SHE THROWS THE PRESENT INTO THE ROOM AND STALKS BACK OUT.

CUT TO:

Scene V

INT. MASSAGE ROOM – NIGHT – NIGHT/2
(Roz, Masseur)

ROZ IS ON THE TABLE.

Roz: You sure you want to hear about this?

Masseur: Why not?

Roz: Okay. Well, I've been a little depressed because of all the weight I've been putting on.

Masseur: Oh, everyone gains weight around the holidays. You'll drop it all in January.

Roz: Actually, I'm pregnant. I'm not dropping this weight until the middle of May. Anyway, I was getting a cup of coffee . . .

CUT TO:

Scene W

INT. CAFE NERVOSA – DAY – DAY/2 (ROZ'S VERSION)
(Roz, Niles, Martin, Frasier, Daphne, Eddie)

FRASIER IS AT A TABLE WITH NILES AND MARTIN. THERE'S A PIECE OF CHEESECAKE ON THE TABLE. ROZ ENTERS.

Roz: Hey, guys.

THEY AD-LIB HELLOS.

Roz (CONT'D): (TO NILES) That's a nice suit.

Niles: Yes, and it's brand new. So since you're probably going to be ordering some food, I'd rather not risk getting it stained.

Roz: What do you mean I'll probably be ordering some food? Is that a crack about my weight? I'm pregnant. Pregnant people gain weight.

Niles: Well, I see our little hormone cocktail was mixed extra-strong today.

NILES EXITS.

Martin: Well, I should get going too. I've still got a couple of hours before my pageant and I need the time to rehearse.

Frasier: Look on the bright side, Dad. Tomorrow morning it'll all be a memory.

DAPHNE ENTERS AND CROSSES TOWARD THEM. SHE OVERHEARS THE

FOLLOWING:

Martin: Yeah, but even when it's all over, I still have to make peace with the man upstairs.

DAPHNE WHIMPERS INTO HER HAND AND HEADS TO THE LADIES' ROOM AS <u>MARTIN HEADS</u> TO THE DOOR AND <u>OUT</u>.

Roz: Frasier, are you sure we have to do this thing this afternoon?

Frasier: Come on Roz, it's an hour out of your life to a good cause. There's no better feeling than that of giving to others.

Roz: Then you're about to feel great. Give me that.

SHE SLIDES OVER HIS CHEESECAKE AND BEGINS EATING IT.

<u>SFX: FRASIER'S CEL PHONE RINGS</u>

HE ANSWERS IT.

Frasier: (INTO PHONE) Hello . . . Well, yes, Mrs. Doyle, she is. Hold on. (COVERS PHONE; TO ROZ) It's your mom. They forwarded her from the office.

ROZ TAKES THE PHONE.

Roz: (INTO PHONE) Hello . . . No, it's no bother, Mom. (ROLLS HER EYES) I'll pick you up at the airport . . . yup, ten a.m. . . . . I'm looking forward to it, too. Bye.

Frasier: Oh, wait. Let me wish her a merry Christmas.

Roz: (INTO PHONE) Hang on, Mom.

<u>ROZ</u> HANDS HIM THE PHONE AND <u>MOVES TO THE COUNTER</u>.

Frasier: (INTO PHONE) Mrs. Doyle, it's Frasier again. I just wanted to say happy holidays. And also, just a word to the wise – Roz has put on quite a few pregnancy pounds of late and she's rather sensitive about it, so you might want to be careful about what you say. (SEES ROZ COMING) Anyway, looking forward to seeing you. Bye-bye.

FRASIER HANGS UP AS <u>ROZ REJOINS HIM</u>.

Roz: You know, Frasier, I think I'm going to meet you over there. I still have some gifts to get.

Frasier: I still have all of mine to get. I don't know what it is this year – nothing I see seems to be quite right.

Roz: It's really sweet that you're trying to make your gifts so special. You know, I'm sorry if I've seemed irritable lately. I'm just nervous about my mom coming. I just can't figure out how I'm going to tell her I'm pregnant.

Frasier: You mean you haven't told her?

Roz: No. And I just know she's going to go insane. I've wanted to talk to her, it's just . . . well, you know how it is when you've got something to tell someone but you're not quite sure how to put it?

Frasier: Yes, I do.

SFX: FRASIER'S CEL PHONE RINGS AGAIN.

Roz: Well, I'll let you get that. See you in a bit.

SHE STARTS OUT AS FRASIER ANSWERS THE PHONE.

Frasier: (INTO PHONE) Hello . . . Yes, I had a feeling you might call back . . .

CUT TO:

Scene X

INT. SHOPPING MALL - AFTERNOON - DAY/2
(Frasier, Roz, Sally, Billy, Vic)

A SMALL AREA DECORATED AS "SANTA'S VILLAGE". THERE'S A LARGE CHAIR FOR SANTA, A BAG OF TOYS, ETC. FRASIER, DRESSED AS SANTA, IS THERE, AS ROZ, DRESSED AS MRS. CLAUS, ARRIVES.

Frasier: Hey - I was beginning to worry about you.

Roz: Well, you should have. I'm on the verge of a complete breakdown. Shopping was a disaster - then, when I went to slip into this darling little costume, the pants split.

Frasier: I'm sorry. Did you try to put too much padding in? (OFF HER LOOK) You didn't put any padding in, did you?

Roz: Of course, on top of all that, I keep thinking about my mom - how am I going to tell her?

Frasier: Well, that may be easier than you think.

Roz: Ha! You don't know my mom.

Frasier: If you like, I could tell her for you.

Roz: Are you kidding? She'll be mad enough knowing that I didn't tell her for a full three months. The only worse thing would be hearing it from someone else.

Frasier: Maybe we should discuss this later.

Roz: Discuss what?

Frasier: Oh, nothing.

Roz: Oh my God! When you talked to her in the cafe you told her, didn't you? Frasier!

Frasier: Hello, children. Ho, ho, ho! Who's first?

Roz: I'm gonna kill you.

A LITTLE GIRL, SALLY, STEPS UP. FRASIER QUICKLY SEATS SALLY IN HIS LAP.

Sally: You're gonna kill Santa?

Frasier: No, little girl. Mrs. Claus said she wanted to kiss me.

Roz: Yeah, I'll kiss you. Come here, I'll kiss you good.

Frasier: No, not yet Mrs. Santa - we have to give out some toys. (TO SALLY) Were you a good girl this year?

Roz: Don't tell him if you weren't. He'll blab it to everyone. (HANDING HER A GIFT) Here, run along.

SALLY GOES.

Roz (CONT'D): Frasier . . .

Frasier: Well, you talk to your mom about everything, how was I supposed to know?

A LITTLE BOY, BILLY, COMES UP.

Billy: Hi, Santa. I'm Billy. I want a pony for Christmas.

Roz: You got it. Now beat it.

Billy: Mommy - mommy - I'm gonna get a pony!

BILLY RUNS TO HIS MOTHER, WHO GLARES AT ROZ.

Frasier: Roz, can't we talk about this later?

Roz: No, we can't.

A BIG KID, VIC, STEPS UP.

Vic: Hi, Santa.

Roz: Oh my God, what are you, twenty? Get out of here.

Frasier: Will you try to stay calm?

Roz: No, I will not, because I'm not calm. I am completely freaked. I'm pregnant, and you told my crazy mother, and my Christmas is ruined, and I'm too fat to even be Mrs. Santa! I hate this holiday!

SHE KICKS THE BIG SACK OF PRESENTS, KNOCKING IT OVER, AND STRIDES OFF. A GROUP OF PARENTS AND CHILDREN LOOK ON IN HORROR.

Frasier: Mrs. Claus was up very late helping me make all these toys . . .

CUT TO:

Scene Y

INT. FRASIER'S LIVING ROOM/HALLWAY – NIGHT – NIGHT/2 (ROZ'S VERSION)
Roz, Frasier, Martin, Daphne, Niles, Eddie)

Roz (V.O.): Of course, I still had to stop by Frasier's. I had to give him his champagne glasses . . .

WE SEE FRASIER OPEN THE DOOR TO ROZ, WHO THROWS HIS PRESENT INTO THE ROOM. SHE TURNS TO GO, FRASIER GOES AFTER HER.

RESET TO:

INT. HALLWAY – CONTINUOUS

Frasier: Roz, please stop. I'm sorry about what happened, but it was a mistake. And I can't let you go. How would it look if I turned a pregnant woman away on Christmas Eve when there's so much room here at the inn?

Roz: Just give me my present and I'll get out of here.

Frasier: Fair enough.

HE STEERS HER INTO THE APARTMENT.

RESET TO:

INT. FRASIER'S LIVING ROOM – CONTINUOUS

Frasier (CONT'D): Niles, Daphne – Roz is here.

THEY MURMUR LACKLUSTER HELLOS.

Frasier (CONT'D): Oh, come on, people. Let's liven things up in here – it's Christmas Eve. For heaven's sake, what are the Cranes known for, if not their legendary holiday spirit?

THE FRONT DOOR OPENS AND MARTIN ENTERS, DRESSED AS A WISE MAN. EDDIE IS WITH HIM.

Martin: I hate singing, and I hate Christmas, and I'm going to bed.

MARTIN STARTS TO THE HALL.

Frasier: Dad, I take it you didn't quite hit that high note?

Martin: No. And as usual, Eddie buried his head. Only this time he buried it in the Christ child's cradle. Then I guess he mistook the Christ child for one of his chew toys 'cause he picked it up in his mouth and started shaking it. Mary and Joseph went ballistic, Eddie took off with it still in his mouth, and half the population of Bethlehem went chasing off after him. I never should have agreed to be in that pageant.

Daphne: You would have saved me a lot of grief.

Martin: Hey, don't start that again.

Frasier: Now, now, let's not say anything we're going to regret.

Roz: You're one to talk.

Frasier: Oh, now, Roz.

DAPHNE AND MARTIN BEGIN FIGHTING, ROZ AND FRASIER CONTINUE FIGHTING. NILES LIES LOW ON THE COUCH WITH HIS WASHCLOTH. FINALLY:

Frasier (CONT'D): Oh, now that is enough! This is the night we celebrate peace and togetherness, and I will not let that be ruined. I intend to get us all in the right frame of mind by giving you all my gift. I was determined this year to do something a little more meaningful, and after a great deal of effort, I have. My gift doesn't come from some fancy store, all wrapped in glittery paper – my gift comes from my heart. Tonight, I intend to sit each one of you down and tell you, in my own words, just how much you mean to me.

THEY ALL STARE AT HIM IN HORROR – THIS IS THE WORST IDEA THEY'VE EVER HEARD.

Frasier (CONT'D): Or, I could get someone over to give us all massages.

AS THE GROUP MUMBLES "THAT'S A BETTER IDEA," "MORE LIKE IT," ETC., WE:

FADE OUT.

END OF ACT TWO

ROOM SERVICE

#40570-113

Written by Ken Levine & David Isaacs
Created and Developed by David Angell, Peter Casey & David Lee
Directed by David Lee

ACT ONE

Scene A

FADE IN:

INT. RADIO STUDIO/HALLWAY - DAY - DAY/1
(Frasier, Betsy [V.O.], Lilith, Roz)

FRASIER IS ON THE AIR. ROZ IS IN HER BOOTH, SCRAWLING A NOTE ON A PIECE OF PAPER.

Frasier: Good morning, Betsy. I'm listening.

ROZ HOLDS UP HER SIGN THAT SAYS "BATHROOM" AND TAPS ON THE GLASS. FRASIER SEES HER AND GESTURES FOR HER TO WAIT FOR A MINUTE.

Betsy (V.O.): Hi, Dr. Crane. My problem is, my husband wants to take me on a cruise for our anniversary.

Frasier: Sounds enchanting.

ROZ CONTINUES WAVING.

Betsy (V.O.): Yes, except I keep having this dream where I'm in our cabin and all of a sudden I see a few drops of water leaking in. At first it's just a trickle, then it's a stream, then it's gushing, pouring, water everywhere, and nothing in the world can stop the flow.

NO LONGER ABLE TO STAND IT, ROZ EXITS HER BOOTH.

Frasier: That's a very powerful image, wouldn't you say, Roz?

FRASIER TURNS AND SEES ROZ IS GONE FROM HER CHAIR.

Frasier (CONT'D): Roz agrees.

RESET TO:

INT. RADIO STUDIO HALLWAY - CONTINUOUS

AS ROZ EXITS HER BOOTH, SHE ENCOUNTERS <u>LILITH</u>.

Lilith: Excuse me, I'm looking for Frasier Crane. They said he'd be in here.

Roz: Lilith, it's me, Roz Doyle.

Lilith: Oh, yes – Frasier's fun-loving producer. (NOTICING HER STOMACH) Who, apparently, has been having a bit too much fun . . . loving.

Roz: I'd love to send one back your way but I've got to pee.

<u>ROZ DASHES OFF</u>. <u>LILITH ENTERS ROZ'S BOOTH</u>.

RESET TO:

<u>INT. FRASIER'S BOOTH – CONTINUOUS</u>

DURING THE FOLLOWING LILITH WILL DRIFT OVER TO THE CONSOLE. FRASIER RELAXES IN HIS CHAIR WITH HIS BACK TO ROZ'S BOOTH.

Frasier: Betsy, perhaps this exercise will help. Visualize being on that boat. You're in your cabin – no cracks, no leaks, it's dry as a bone. You go to your door, open it, and –

FRASIER NONCHALANTLY TURNS HIS CHAIR TOWARD THE GLASS AND SEES LILITH.

Frasier (CONT'D): Aaah!!

Betsy (V.O.): What is it? The water's coming in through the door?

Frasier: No, Betsy. Someone just walked in and frightened me. It's my ex-wife so if you're a regular listener you know what I'm talking about.

Betsy (V.O.): That's it. We're going to Vegas.

Frasier: Thanks for your call. Stay tuned for the news.

EXASPERATED, FRASIER TURNS OFF THE MIC AND <u>STRIDES INTO ROZ'S BOOTH</u>.

Frasier (CONT'D): Hello, Lilith.

Lilith: Surprise.

Frasier: I think we're a little past that now, aren't we? What brings you to Seattle?

Lilith: I'm attending the National Conference on Self Psychology.

Frasier: Really? Are you sure you want to hold up that mirror, Lilith? (OFF HER LOOK) Well, whatever. You're in town and I'm glad you're here. How's Freddie?

Lilith: Fine. We have an amazing child.

Frasier: Yes, we do. And Brian?

Lilith: Fine. I have an amazing husband.

Frasier: Yes. Did you two get the gift basket I sent for the holidays?

LILITH PUTS HER HANDS TO HER FACE AND BEGINS TO BREAK DOWN. ROZ ENTERS.

Roz: Frasier, what did you do?

Frasier: Nothing, I sent her a gift basket. Fruits and festive nuts.

Lilith: It's not the basket, you nit. It's Brian. He left me.

Frasier: He left you?

Roz: Maybe I should go.

Lilith: No, everyone else knows it, you might as well know it too. How can I put this succinctly? . . . Brian was looking for someone more . . . feminine. And he found him.

Frasier/Roz: "Him"?

Lilith: Stan Jablonsky, that little hussy.

FRASIER CROSSES TO LILITH.

Frasier: Oh Lilith. I'm genuinely sorry.

Lilith: I didn't know where to turn but I knew that you would somehow be here for me.

Frasier: So you didn't just come for the conference?

Lilith: No.

Frasier: Well, you shouldn't be alone tonight. Niles and I are attending a reception at the Union Club. Why don't you join us?

Lilith: Thank you, Frasier, I'd love to. (TAKING FRASIER'S HANDS) I don't know if I deserve your compassion but I already feel better just holding your strong, comforting hands.

IT'S AN AWKWARD MOMENT FOR FRASIER. HE'S NOT QUITE SURE HOW TO REACT.

Frasier: Yes, well, it's good to hold you, Lilith, but if you'll excuse me, I have an appointment. Station manager. Very important. Can't break it. See you tonight. 'Bye.

LILITH SQUEEZES HIS HANDS. FRASIER SMILES AND QUICKLY EXITS.

Roz: Boy, that's rough, leaving you for a man. You really had no idea?

Lilith: None at all. Stan was a contractor we hired to expand our master bedroom. Ironic, isn't it? No sooner do I get the closet of my dreams, than my husband comes out of it.

DISSOLVE TO:

Scene B

INT. CAFE NERVOSA - LATER THAT DAY - DAY/1
(Frasier, Niles)

NILES IS AT A TABLE, EATING PASTRIES. FRASIER ENTERS.

Frasier: Hello, Niles. (RE: PASTRY) That bun looks good.

Niles: Now, now. Remember your diet.

Frasier: Of course. Thank you. (HE SITS) Speaking of buns I could do without, Lilith is back.

Niles: Oh, that explains why blood was pouring from my faucets all morning.

Frasier: Go easy on her, Niles. Her husband has left her. And get this . . . for a man.

Niles: Damn. I owe Dad five dollars.

Frasier: The poor thing. She's obviously devastated. Her whole world's been turned upside-down. Of course, look who I'm telling - no one knows better than you how a messy divorce can leave a person . . .

FRASIER NOTICES THAT NILES HAS NODDED OFF TO SLEEP.

Frasier (CONT'D): . . . Strangely relaxed.

FRASIER SHAKES NILES.

Frasier (CONT'D): Niles? Niles?

Niles: Huh? What? Yes?

Frasier: Am I boring you?

Niles: Damn - did I do it again? I'm sorry, Frasier. Seems I'm suffering from a bout of narcolepsy.

Frasier: Good Lord. When did this start?

Niles: After the divorce. I checked with my doctor. I'm fine, it's just a reaction to stress – my way of escaping the frustration of the whole ugly mess. But please, go on with what you were saying.

Frasier: Well, Lilith is deeply distressed and she's come to me to help her make some sense of all this. I must say I find it all a bit disconcerting.

Niles: How so?

Frasier: We have a destructive pattern. Whenever Lilith comes to me in need, I find her vulnerability highly desirable. Against my better judgement, we wind up in bed and I always have terrible regrets.

Niles: And you felt this way about her today?

Frasier: Ohh, baby!

Niles: Well, do your best to avoid her.

Frasier: I can't. She's joining us at the reception tonight.

Niles: What? <u>She's</u> going to be there?

<u>NILES' CEL PHONE RINGS</u>.

Frasier: Niles. It's nothing but a bunch of stuffed shirts talking about their portfolios and prostates.

Niles: Exactly. And you've ruined it. (THEN) Excuse me. (INTO PHONE) Hello . . . (TO FRASIER) Damn, it's one of Maris' cadre of lawyers. (INTO PHONE) Yes, we've been over that . . . No, I can't . . . How dare you. She already has the house. I'm not even allowed to visit the koi pond . . . uh-huh . . . uh-huh . . .

NILES FALLS ASLEEP AGAIN.

Frasier: Niles . . . Niles . . .

Niles: (WAKING UP, ON PHONE) I'm not even allowed to visit the koi pond.

FRASIER SNATCHES THE PHONE AWAY.

Frasier: (INTO PHONE) He'll call you back. (FOLDS UP PHONE) Well look at us. A narcoleptic and a weak-willed sexual obsessive. Don't we look like a couple of brothers in an O'Neill play? (THEN) Niles, help me. I need the power to resist her.

Niles: You know you can. And if I sense any wavering I'll be by your side, ever vigilant.

Frasier: Thank you.

NILES PICKS UP A PASTRY.

Niles: Think of Lilith as this pastry. It may satisfy a momentary craving, but in the end you'll regret it. Much like my situation with Maris – it wasn't easy, but I did find the courage to stand up to her and say . . . I'm trying to remember my exact words. I think it was . . . uh . . .

NILES NODS OFF TO SLEEP. FRASIER TAKES THE PASTRY FROM HIS HAND AND BITES INTO IT. IT IS AS DELICIOUS AS HE HOPED. HE ADDRESSES A PASSING WAITRESS.

Frasier: (RE: PASTRY) Two more of these.

DISSOLVE TO:

Scene C

<u>INT. FRASIER'S LIVING ROOM – THAT NIGHT – NIGHT/1</u>
(Martin, Daphne, Niles, Frasier, Lilith, Eddie)

<u>MARTIN</u> IS TRYING TO GET <u>EDDIE</u> TO DO A TRICK, HOLDING OUT A TREAT, AS <u>DAPHNE ENTERS</u>.

Martin: Hey Daph, look. I've taught Eddie a trick.

Daphne: Oh, I love animal tricks. I was reading in a movie magazine that there's a stunt dog they taught to ride a motorcycle into a burning building, pick up a baby in his teeth, and then jump out a window to safety. What did you teach Eddie?

Martin: To roll over.

Daphne: You must be very proud.

<u>SFX: THE DOORBELL RINGS</u>. DAPHNE MOVES TO ANSWER IT.

Martin: Oh forget it, Eddie.

DAPHNE OPENS THE DOOR TO <u>NILES</u> AS <u>FRASIER ENTERS</u> THE LIVING ROOM.

Niles: Good evening, Daphne . . . Dad.

Frasier: Oh hello, Niles. Sherry? It'll give you a chance to relax while we wait for Lilith.

Martin: (PANICKED) You never said she was coming up here.

Daphne: You just said you were going to dinner.

Martin: You never said she was coming up here.

Frasier: It's just to rendezvous. She'll be here for two minutes.

Martin: But you never told me. You were home an hour. You never told me. Not a word. (TO DAPHNE) Did he say anything to you?

Daphne: No, nothing. (TO FRASIER) You could have told us, you know. We could have made plans to be elsewhere.

Frasier: (HE'S HAD ENOUGH) She's coming. Both of you suck it up! She's been through a devastating week. Her husband left her. I'd like you both to show a little compassion. Unless, of course, you have to go hide in your rooms because two minutes of polite conversation with a woman who needs you is too much to ask.

SFX: THE DOORBELL RINGS. MARTIN AND DAPHNE START HURRIEDLY EXITING.

Martin: Out of my way!

Daphne: Me too!

IN HIS HASTE, MARTIN DROPS HIS CANE. DAPHNE STARTS TO GO BACK TO RETRIEVE IT.

Martin: Leave it!

MARTIN AND DAPHNE EXIT.

Niles: Now remember, Frasier. I'm here for you if you feel yourself starting to weaken.

Frasier: Fear not. I'm completely in control.

FRASIER OPENS THE DOOR. IT'S LILITH AS WE'VE NEVER QUITE SEEN HER BEFORE. SHE'S A KNOCKOUT. HER LOOK IS SOFT AND SEDUCTIVE. HER HAIR IS OUT OF ITS CUSTOMARY BUN. HER FIGURE IS REVEALED. NOTE: SHE WEARS A FASHIONABLE WRAP AROUND HER SHOULDERS.

Frasier (CONT'D): (IMMEDIATELY) Ohh, baby.

Lilith: Thank you, Frasier. I needed that. I treated myself to a little makeover this afternoon. Probably just an attempt to compensate for the battering my ego's taken recently. Pretty transparent, huh?

Frasier: No, but if you stand in front of the light –

Niles: Frasier!

Lilith: Niles, sorry to hear your marriage ended in a shambles.

Niles: Ditto.

Frasier: Well, now that the pleasantries are out of the way – let me take your wrap.

LILITH TAKES OFF HER WRAP, REVEALING HER BARE SHOULDERS. THE LOOK IS NOT LOST ON FRASIER.

Frasier (CONT'D): Yowsa. Lilith, what is that intoxicating fragrance you're wearing?

Niles: Frasier, can I see you in the kitchen?

Frasier: No!

Lilith: It's something new, called "Encore."

Frasier: Bravo. I can almost feel the curtain rising.

Niles: Frasier! (TO LILITH) Excuse us. We'll be right back . . . Eddie will keep you company.

NILES HUSTLES FRASIER INTO THE KITCHEN.

Lilith: (TO EDDIE) Hello, Eddie. Remember me?

EDDIE SEES LILITH AND RUNS OUT OF THE ROOM.

RESET TO:

INT. KITCHEN - CONTINUOUS

Frasier: Thank you, Niles. This is going to be tougher than I thought.

Niles: Just calm down. Let me get you a bottle of water.

NILES OPENS THE REFRIGERATOR AND LEANS IN. WE CAN'T SEE HIS FACE.

Frasier: Damn her lily-white hide. She knows what she's doing, dressing like that. The woman plays me like a lute. Look at me – I have all the resistance of a horny stag. Niles, what am I going to do? Niles? . . . Niles? . . .

NILES HAS FALLEN ASLEEP IN THE REFRIGERATOR. FRASIER SHAKES HIM AWAKE.

Niles: I did it again?

Frasier: You fell asleep with your cheek right against the ice tray.

Niles: That's strange. I dreamt I was tangoing with Maris.

Frasier: I need your help resisting Lilith.

Niles: All right, I think I've got the answer. When you feel yourself yielding to her, summon an image so repellent you're incapable of any sexual desire. Do you remember that summer at Uncle Henry's farm, when we found that dead horse lying in the hot sun, crawling with maggots?

Frasier: Of course I do.

Niles: Well hold on to that picture. You can ride that horse to safety.

Frasier: Thank you, Niles, that might do the trick. When it comes to an ugly image, you can't beat a dead horse. Lilith can bat her eyes and push her breasts up to Canada and I won't budge.

FRASIER AND NILES EXIT TO THE LIVING ROOM.

CUT TO:

Scene D

INT. LILITH'S HOTEL ROOM - NEXT MORNING - DAY/2
(Lilith, Niles)

TWO PEOPLE ARE IN BED SLEEPING. WE CAN'T MAKE OUT WHO THEY ARE. THE WOMAN TURNS OVER. IT'S LILITH. HER ARM FALLS OVER HER COMPANION.

Lilith: (EYES STILL CLOSED; MURMURING)

Morning.

HER BEDMATE TURNS OVER. IT'S NILES.

Niles: (EYES STILL CLOSED; SLEEPILY)

Morning.

AS THE REALIZATION HITS, THEIR EYES POP OPEN - AND IF THAT'S NOT AN ACT BREAK WE DON'T KNOW WHAT IS.

FADE OUT.

END OF ACT ONE

ACT TWO

Scene E

FADE IN:

INT. LILITH'S HOTEL ROOM/BATHROOM - CONTINUOUS - DAY/2
(Lilith, Niles, Waiter, Frasier)

NILES AND LILITH IN BED.

Lilith: My God. What did we do? What did we do?

Niles: Well, first we –

Lilith: I know what we did. What do we do now?

Niles: Let's just try to stay calm. These things happen. They happen every day. (LOSING IT) Every day in France and people die for it! Frasier's going to kill us. (THEN) Why did you have to look so damned bewitching all evening?

Lilith: Oh, so it was my fault, Mr. Sweet-and-Attentive? Why'd you have to drive me home and walk me to my door?

Niles: The way the moonlight bathed your alabaster shoulders –

Lilith: Your sensitive and manly touch –

Niles: Yours too.

Lilith: Take me.

THEY DIVE FOR EACH OTHER BUT THEN PULL UP SHORT.

Niles/Lilith: No!!

Lilith (CONT'D): We've got to resist this. It's wrong.

Niles: Of course it is. Last night was simply two wounded people acting out of loneliness and confusion.

Lilith: Not to mention four bottles of wine. But for whatever reasons we're here, we must never let this happen again.

Niles: Yes, of course. (BEAT) But just to clarify . . . because of the ramifications of our indiscretion or, because, you know . . .?

Lilith: You were fine. My God, you Crane men.

THERE'S A KNOCK AT THE DOOR.

Niles: (PANICKING) Who's that?

Lilith: Don't panic. No one knows we're here.

Niles: I told Frasier I was driving you home.

Lilith: (NOW PANICKING) Why did you do a stupid thing like that?

Niles: It wasn't stupid at the time. How did I know the minute we got inside this room you'd be on me like a hawk on a titmouse?

THERE'S ANOTHER KNOCK AT THE DOOR.

Lilith: (SOTTO) Just be quiet.

LILITH GETS UP, THROWS ON HER ROBE AND CROSSES TO THE DOOR.

Lilith (CONT'D): (TENTATIVELY) Who is it?

Waiter (O.C.): Room service, Ma'am.

Lilith: (TO NILES, RELIEVED) Oh that's right. We ordered breakfast last night.

LILITH OPENS THE DOOR AND LETS IN THE ROOM SERVICE <u>WAITER</u>. HE <u>ENTERS</u>, ROLLING A BREAKFAST CART INTO THE ROOM. HE'S A CHIPPER FELLOW.

Waiter: Good morning, Ma'am, Sir.

THE WAITER STARTS TO SET UP BREAKFAST AT THE TABLE.

Waiter (CONT'D): I have Eggs Benedict and Eggs Florentine.

Lilith: Did you bring ketchup?

Waiter: Oh, No, I'm sorry. Let me go get that for you right now.

Niles: Ketchup on Eggs Florentine?

Waiter: (JOKING) Oh, your first breakfast together?

Lilith: Just get it!

THE <u>WAITER EXITS</u>. NILES GETS OUT OF BED AND SLIPS ON A BATHROBE.

Niles: Now I remember ordering this. It's the breakfast I always order after a night of passion.

Lilith: Eggs Benedict . . . very rich.

Niles: Well I only have it once a year. (THEN) Let's dig in.

THEY SIT AT THE TABLE. THERE'S A <u>KNOCK AT THE DOOR</u>.

Lilith: Well, that was quick.

LILITH CROSSES TO THE DOOR AND IS JUST ABOUT TO OPEN IT WHEN THEY HEAR:

Frasier (O.C.): Lilith, are you awake?

A STARTLED LILITH AND NILES SPEAK IN HUSHED TONES.

Lilith: It's Frasier!

Niles: What do we do?

NILES NEARLY KNOCKS THE TRAY OVER GETTING UP.

Frasier (O.C.): Lilith?

Lilith: Just a second.

Niles: Why did you answer?!

Lilith: I don't know. I'm not very good at this. Hide in the bathroom.

THEY BOTH DART FOR THE BATHROOM.

Niles: No, not you!

Lilith: Here, take the cart with you.

NILES STARTS TO PUSH THE CART INTO THE BATHROOM. THEN:

Niles: Food in the bathroom?

Lilith: Go!

LILITH SHOVES <u>NILES</u> AND THE CART <u>INTO THE BATHROOM</u>, KNOCKING NILES DOWN.

Frasier (O.C.): Lilith? Lilith?

Lilith: Coming.

LILITH RUNS TO THE DOOR, FEIGNS COMPLETE INSOUCIANCE AND OPENS THE DOOR.

Lilith (CONT'D): Hello, Frasier. What are you doing here?

Frasier: Surrendering, Lilith.

<u>FRASIER ENTERS</u>. HE HEADS TOWARD LILITH AND TRIES TO KISS HER.

Lilith: But Frasier –

Frasier: Oh, don't punish me because I played hard to get last night. It took everything I had to resist you.

Lilith: But Frasier, this is wrong.

Frasier: Who cares? Can you honestly say when you were lying in bed last night you weren't thinking about me?

Lilith: (CONSIDERS A MOMENT) Yes.

Frasier: Oh, drop the mask, Lilith. We both know why you came to Seattle. We both know why you dressed so enticingly last night.

FRASIER HEARS <u>THE TOILET FLUSH</u>.

Frasier (CONT'D): Is someone in your bathroom?

Lilith: No, it's a . . . defective toilet. Did that all night long. I'd better check it.

<u>LILITH DASHES INTO THE BATHROOM</u>.

RESET TO:

<u>INT. LILITH'S BATHROOM - CONTINUOUS</u>

<u>LILITH ENTERS</u>. NILES IS SITTING ON THE TOILET, ASLEEP. THEY TALK IN WHISPERS.

Lilith (CONT'D): Niles!

Niles: (STARTLED AWAKE) Yes?

Lilith: You fell asleep and flushed the toilet.

Niles: Damn. Is he still here?

Lilith: Yes.

Niles: What does he want?

Lilith: He wants to make love to me.

Niles: Does the man have no scruples? He specifically asked me last night to keep him away from you and then the minute my back is turned he sneaks over here and yes, I'm aware of the irony.

Lilith: I'll just ask him to leave.

RESET TO:

<u>INT. LILITH'S HOTEL ROOM - CONTINUOUS</u>

<u>LILITH RETURNS TO THE HOTEL ROOM</u>. FRASIER HAS REMOVED HIS CLOTHES AND IS NOW IN A BATHROBE.

Lilith (CONT'D): Oh dear God.

Frasier: Oh, drop this charade, Lilith - you're not even convincing.

Lilith: I think I'm going to be sick.

Frasier: Well, that had a ring of truth to it . . .

THERE'S <u>A KNOCK AT THE DOOR</u>.

Waiter (O.C.): Room service.

Lilith: Go away.

Waiter (O.C.): I have your ketchup, Ma'am.

Lilith: Not necessary.

Waiter (O.C.): Okay, but I need the bill.

Lilith: Later.

Frasier: Let's just take care of this.

FRASIER OPENS THE DOOR. THE <u>WAITER ENTERS</u> WITH A BOTTLE OF KETCHUP. DURING THE FOLLOWING THE WAITER NOTICES THERE'S A DIFFERENT MAN IN A BATHROBE.

Waiter: Sorry to disturb you. Here's your ketchup . . . Sorry it took so long.

LILITH, WHO'S STANDING BEHIND FRASIER, SIGNALS THE WAITER NOT TO SAY ANYTHING.

Waiter (CONT'D): I'll still need the bill. Where's the cart?

Lilith: In the bathroom.

Frasier: Why is the breakfast cart in the bathroom?

Lilith: Uh . . . I was going to take a hot bath while I ate.

Frasier: Still, Lilith . . . food in the bathroom?

Lilith: Be back in a second.

<u>LILITH GOES INTO THE BATHROOM</u>.

Frasier: This is a little embarrassing. My ex-wife. We're sort of reconnecting.

Waiter: Yes Sir. That's wonderful.

Frasier: And who knows? It might work out this time.

Waiter: Ohh-kay.

<u>LILITH COMES BACK</u> WITH THE BILL.

Lilith: There you go. There's a generous, *generous* tip there for you.

Waiter: Thank you, Ma'am.

Frasier: Listen, while you're here, would you please bring me up some Eggs Benedict? Silly for her to eat alone.

Waiter: Ohh-kay.

THE WAITER NODS AND EXITS.

Frasier: Now where were we?

Lilith: Look, I don't think it's a good time for this.

FRASIER TAKES LILITH'S HANDS.

Frasier: Why not, my darling? We're here. We're finally alone. You need your Frasier.

FROM THE BATHROOM WE HEAR A LOUD CRASH AS THE BREAKFAST CART GOES OVER.

Frasier (CONT'D): (CROSSING TO THE BATHROOM) What the hell was that?

Lilith: Frasier, stop. Don't go in –

FRASIER OPENS THE BATHROOM DOOR. NILES IS LYING SPRAWLED ON THE TOPPLED BREAKFAST CART.

Frasier: Niles!

Niles: (SITTING UP) Yes?

Frasier: Oh my God!

Lilith: I'm so sorry. We didn't mean for this to happen.

Frasier: Oh my God!

Niles: She's telling the truth. It was a mistake. A stupid, misguided –

Frasier: Stop it, Niles. I don't want to hear how or why or – I just want to get out of here.

FRASIER EXITS THE HOTEL ROOM.

Lilith: Frasier, Frasier!

BUT HE'S OUT THE DOOR.

Niles: This is my worst nightmare.

Lilith: You have egg on your face.

Niles: That's an understatement. I'm mortified. I –

Lilith: No. Actual egg. It's in your hair, too.

THERE'S <u>A KNOCK AT THE DOOR</u>. LILITH OPENS IT AND <u>FRASIER COMES BACK INTO THE HOTEL ROOM</u>.

Niles: I knew you couldn't stay mad at us.

Frasier: I'm in a bathrobe, you jackass.

FRASIER BEGINS COLLECTING HIS CLOTHES AS SOMETHING DAWNS ON LILITH.

Lilith: I can understand your shock and – believe me, if I could erase everything that happened last night I would. But if you look at this rationally for a moment, we didn't technically do anything wrong.

Frasier: What?! You didn't do anything wrong?

Niles: I'm a little unclear on that myself but I'm willing to go along with it.

Lilith: You and I are no longer married. Neither is Niles. I won't say this is my shining hour but we're not responsible to you or anyone else for our actions.

Niles: (JUMPING ON THE BANDWAGON) Right! And I'm frankly a little insulted by your outburst.

Frasier: I can't believe this! You're actually defending what you did?

Lilith: Just listen. The past few days have been the worst of my life. I've never felt less self-assured, more in need of validation, both as a person and as a woman. And Niles was feeling the same thing.

Niles: Exactly. (REALIZING) Wait a minute.

Lilith: (TO FRASIER) Our physical reaction to each other was nothing more than a desperate attempt to reaffirm our own worth.

Frasier: Very impressive, Lilith. But I happen to be a psychiatrist too. Let me tell you what really transpired. This is a passive-aggressive manifestation of the deep resentments that you both have toward me. You were punishing me for my notoriety. My successful adjustment after our marriage. It is this shared bond that brought you two to your palace of sweet revenge.

Lilith: Allow me to rebut: What a crock.

Frasier: It is not!

Lilith: This is yet another example of your complete self-absorption and the reason we could not stay together in the first place.

Frasier: I think I have a right to - why am I defending myself?

Niles: If you ask me, you're both off the mark. Last night was all about two people ruled by very strong superegos, tortured by them, who had a chance, however misguided, to break through and rediscover their ids together. Call me an old softy, but that's how I see it.

Frasier: (A BEAT; THEN) Okay then . . . the three of us have certainly analyzed the crap out of this.

Lilith: Where does that leave us?

Niles: Yes. Where do we all go from here?

Frasier: (AFTER A BEAT) I don't know.

THERE'S AN AWKWARD SILENCE. <u>A CEL PHONE RINGS</u> IN THE CLOSET.

Niles: Oh, that's mine.

NILES GOES TO THE CLOSET TO SEARCH FOR HIS CEL PHONE.

Lilith: You realize if you had simply given in to me last night instead of this morning, the three of us wouldn't be in this hell?

Frasier: No, it would be the two of us in a whole different hell. Well, we're young - our best hells are still ahead of us.

Niles: (INTO PHONE) Niles Crane . . . Absolutely not. We agreed on a figure . . . Well that's too damned bad. I've been manipulated enough by you jackals. I'll see you in court. (HANGS UP) The very idea that Maris would still think - (REALIZES) Hey, wait a minute . . . I'm not sleeping. By all rights the strain of that conversation should have caused me to go out like a light. And instead I feel alert. Almost invigorated.

Lilith: It's not surprising. Your experience with Maris over the past few months has been emasculating. Last night may have gone a long way toward restoring your self-confidence.

Niles: Yes. And by the same token, you can give up the neurotic assumption that Brian left you because you're not attractive. You've had ample evidence to the contrary.

Lilith: Yes, I have. To hell with Brian. If he wants a doting little wife he can keep Stan.

Frasier: Well, this just worked out great for everyone, didn't it? You two solved your problems. The waiter got a handsome tip. Come on, everyone, on my cue . . . a rousing chorus of "Oh Happy Day."

Lilith: Please try to understand.

Niles: Yes, what happened was nothing more than -

Frasier: Oh, stop it, both of you. Enough. It happened, and I'm going to have to deal with it . . . (THEN) I suppose in a twisted way there is one positive in this for me. You see, Lilith, I have never stopped desiring you, even though we are completely wrong for each other. But now, from this day forward, whenever I look at your face, I'll see the back of my brother's head, and that's better than a dead horse any day.

Lilith: Well I'm glad to hear that . . . I suppose. You know, Frasier –

Frasier: Enough, Lilith.

Lilith: All right. Maybe I'll just go have some breakfast.

LILITH GOES INTO THE BATHROOM. THERE'S AN AWKWARD SILENCE. FRASIER AND NILES DON'T KNOW WHAT TO SAY TO EACH OTHER. FINALLY:

Niles: Are we okay?

Frasier: No, we're not. (BEAT) But we will be.

Niles: Well that's enough for now. (THEN) We're an odd little family, aren't we?

Frasier: Yeah, like the one in "Deliverance."

THERE'S A KNOCK AT THE DOOR.

Waiter (O.C.): Room service.

FRASIER OPENS THE DOOR. THE WAITER ENTERS WITH ANOTHER BREAKFAST CART.

Waiter (CONT'D): Here's the Eggs Benedict, and –

THE WAITER LOOKS AROUND AND NOTICES THERE'S NO LILITH, JUST TWO MEN IN BATHROBES.

Waiter (CONT'D): Ohh-kay.

AND AS HE TURNS AND EXITS, WE:

FADE OUT.

END OF ACT TWO

THE SKI LODGE

#40570-114

Written by Joe Keenan
Created and Developed by David Angell, Peter Casey & David Lee
Directed by David Lee

ACT ONE

Scene A

FADE IN:

INT. RADIO STUDIO - DAY - DAY/1
(Frasier, Roz, Connie)

FRASIER IS IN HIS BOOTH AFTER THE SHOW. ROZ ENTERS FROM HER BOOTH.

Frasier: Good show today, Roz. I particularly thought –

ROZ NOTICES A WOMAN, CONNIE, TALKING TO AN EMPLOYEE IN THE HALL.

Roz: Oh God, it's Connie from promotions. She drives me up the wall. Every time I see her she hits me up for another charity.

Frasier: Well, Roz, maybe it's time you set some limits. How hard can it be to say no just once? (THEN) Well, look who I'm talking to.

ROZ SHOOTS FRASIER A LOOK AS CONNIE ENTERS.

Connie: Hi, Frasier. Roz, I was looking for you.

Roz: Listen Connie, before you say anything, I've got to get this off my chest. I've bought Girl Scout cookies from you, helped pay for your kid's band uniforms, and bought tickets for every raffle your church ever had . . . I'm tapped out. So whatever you came for, I'm not interested.

Connie: Well then, I'll just go. By the way, my church had its raffle drawing yesterday. You won the grand prize. (PLACING ENVELOPE ON TABLE) Sorry to bother you.

CONNIE EXITS.

Roz: (CALLING AFTER) Oh Connie, Connie don't – Oh, forget it. What did I win?

ROZ RUNS TO THE ENVELOPE AND OPENS IT.

Roz (CONT'D): Oh my God, this is incredible. It's a one-weekend rental of a deluxe private ski lodge on Mt. Baker, complete with lessons from a former Olympic champ.

Frasier: That is a grand prize, indeed. I must admit, I'm a bit envious. Well, I hope you have a wonderful weekend.

Roz: Thank you, Frasier.

Frasier: Though I don't suppose you'll have much use for those ski lessons.

Roz: There'll be other stuff to do.

Frasier: Oh, tons. Just because you can't ski – or for that matter hike, sled or snowboard – doesn't mean you can't relax by the fire with a nice warm snifter of . . . Oh, sorry.

Roz: Well, the scenery will be nice.

Frasier: Breathtaking . . . though I hope you can enjoy it after that four-hour drive, and you so carsick these days –

Roz: Frasier, I know what you're hinting at here. But this is the first thing I've ever won in my life. It means something to me. I'm not about to give it away, or sell it, or trade it for a . . .

Frasier: Big-screen TV?

ROZ HANDS FRASIER THE ENVELOPE.

Roz: The key's in the mailbox.

FADE OUT.

Scene B

FADE IN:

INT. FRASIER'S LIVING ROOM – EVENING – NIGHT/1
(Daphne, Martin, Niles, Frasier, Eddie)

MARTIN SITS WATCHING A GAME ON TV. EDDIE SITS NEARBY. THE SOUND IS UP VERY LOUD.

SFX: THE DOORBELL RINGS. DAPHNE ENTERS FROM THE KITCHEN AND CROSSES TO THE DOOR.

Daphne: What do you need that so loud for? I swear you've gone deaf as a post.

Martin: It's just a cold stopping up my ears. I'm fine.

DAPHNE OPENS THE DOOR TO NILES, WHO'S ON HIS CEL PHONE.

The Ski Lodge

Niles: (INTO PHONE) Good God, man, whose lawyer are you, anyway? No, I will not calm down. (TO DAPHNE, CALMLY) Hello, Daphne. (ON PHONE) They call that a settlement? Call them and turn it down. (LOUDER, OVER TV) I said turn it down, you ninny!

Martin: (TURNING DOWN THE TV) Okay! Geez, you could ask a person nicely.

Niles: (HANGING UP) I have got to find a new divorce lawyer. Claude is clearly no match for Maris' team.

Daphne: Real sharks, are they?

Niles: When I was courting Maris I sent her a Valentine that read "You're the girl my heart adores. Everything I have is yours." Now they insist it's a pre-nup.

Daphne: That's terrible. (TO MARTIN) Can you imagine using that as a weapon – a Valentine?

Martin: Sure, I'd love a Ballantine.

Daphne: That does it. You're getting a hearing aid whether you like it or not.

Martin: I don't need a hearing aid. My ears will be back to normal in no time.

Daphne: You said that two days ago. Soon you won't be able to hear a word I say.

Martin: Gee, we wouldn't want that. There'd be no reason to keep living.

DAPHNE SCOWLS AND TURNS AWAY.

Martin (CONT'D): (TAKING A SHOT) I heard that.

Daphne: I didn't say anything!

FRASIER ENTERS.

Frasier: Well, what's everyone standing around for when you should all be packing?

Daphne: Packing for what?

Frasier: For the fabulous ski trip I'm taking us on this weekend.

Niles: You're kidding. You won the raffle?

Frasier: In a manner of speaking. We have a gorgeous ski lodge with an Olympic champ in residence to give us lessons.

Daphne: It sounds like heaven. Skiing all day, then warming up with a nice hot rum drink, curled up under blankets in front of a roaring fire.

Niles: Yes, I feel the steam rising from my toddy already.

Daphne: Oh, damn . . . I can't go.

Niles: (STRICKEN) Why not?

Daphne: My friend Annie. It's her birthday Saturday and I promised I'd spend it with her.

Niles: Well, bring her along.

Daphne: (TO FRASIER) Could I? I know she'd love it. She's very gung-ho for sports. She was captain of my girls' rugby team at school.

Frasier: (LEERY) Well, I'm not sure how many bedrooms there are.

Niles: If we're short she can have mine.

Daphne: Where will you sleep?

Niles: Oh, I'll find someplace.

Daphne: (TO FRASIER) You're sure you don't mind?

Frasier: Not at all. What could be more fun than a gung-ho girls' rugby captain?

DAPHNE EXITS TO HER ROOM.

Frasier (CONT'D): (TO NILES) I'll kill you for this.

Niles: I'm sorry, it's the only way Daphne will come. And if you think I'm letting a moonlit ski lodge go to waste, think again.

Frasier: Niles, you just filed for divorce last week. Can't you wait a while?

Niles: Wait? I've waited five long years for this. (TO MARTIN) Dad, wouldn't you say it's time?

Martin: (CHECKS HIS WATCH) I've got ten past twelve. That can't be right. Oh, wait, I put it on upside-down again.

Frasier: (A BEAT, THEN) If you want to make a fool of yourself with Daphne, that's your affair. But you're not ruining this ski trip by asking along a girl who sounds to me like a serious avalanche risk. I'm telling Daphne forget it – no guests.

DAPHNE RE-ENTERS.

Daphne: I called Annie and she's all excited. Turns out she just bought new skis with the money she made from her last swimsuit calendar.

DAPHNE EXITS TO THE KITCHEN.

Frasier: (TO NILES) Well, I hope you're happy. We're stuck with her now.

The Ski Lodge

FADE OUT.

Scene C

FADE IN:

INT. SKI LODGE LIVING ROOM – DAY – DAY/2
(Niles, Martin, Frasier, Daphne, Annie, Guy)

THE LODGE HAS A LIVING AND DINING ROOM AREA WITH A FIREPLACE.
OFF THIS IS A SMALL KITCHEN. ANOTHER DOWNSTAGE DOOR LEADS TO A
BEDROOM. DOORS LEADING TO TWO MORE BEDROOMS FACE EACH
OTHER UPSTAGE. STAIRS BEYOND THIS LEAD TO A SECOND FLOOR
LANDING WITH DOORS TO THREE MORE BEDROOMS.

MARTIN AND NILES ENTER CARRYING LUGGAGE.

Niles: Wow, look at this place.

Martin: Nothing like a change of scenery. (THEN) Where do you suppose the TV is?

Niles: At this altitude I'm surprised my ears haven't stopped up. How's it affecting your
ears, Dad?

NO RESPONSE.

Niles (CONT'D): Dad?

Martin: What?

Niles: How are your ears?

Martin: (COVERING BADLY) Great. Never been better. No hearing aid for me.

BEHIND NILES' BACK MARTIN MADLY FLEXES HIS JAW TO MAKE HIS EARS
UNPOP. HE HAS NO LUCK. FRASIER ENTERS CARRYING BAGS.

Frasier: (CALLING BACK OVER HIS SHOULDER) No need to struggle with that,
Annie. I'll be back to help you in a moment. (REACTS TO LODGE) This is some place,
isn't it?

Niles: I'm just glad we made it all right, the way you kept taking those curves so sharply.
Poor Annie kept being thrown up against you.

Frasier: (NAUGHTILY) What can I say? I'm a bad driver.

Niles: I'll grant you she's comely, but don't you find her a tad – what would a polite
euphemism be? – stupid?

Frasier: She's just unschooled, like Liza Doolittle. Give her the right Henry Higgins and
she'll be ready for a ball in no time.

Niles: Leave it to you to put the "Pig" back in "Pygmalion".

DAPHNE AND ANNIE ENTER WITH THEIR BAGS. THEY ALL AD-LIB HELLOS.

Daphne: Goodness. This place is just lovely.

Niles: And lovelier still now that you're in it.

Frasier: (TO ANNIE) Stunning vista. Makes one think of the Matterhorn, doesn't it?

Annie: I wouldn't know, I'm not very musical.

MARTIN OPENS ONE OF HIS BAGS AND REMOVES TWO LARGE BOTTLES OF RUM.

Martin: There's a relief. With all that swerving you did on the drive up, I was afraid these might break. I'm going to make us all a batch of my special hot buttered rum.

Frasier: You're actually going to put butter in the rum?

Martin: It's cold in these mountains – you need a little fat in your booze.

MARTIN CROSSES INTO THE KITCHEN.

Frasier: Good thinking, Dad. When we're done with the buttered rum I'll whip us up a nice hearty batch of Pork Nog.

Annie: (EARNESTLY) None for me, thanks, I'm a vegetarian.

Niles: Daphne, let me help with your luggage. Which room do you want?

Daphne: (POINTS) That one on the left upstairs should have a nice view.

Niles: What a coincidence. That's right next to my room.

Annie: I'll take the one next to that.

Frasier: Allow me.

NILES AND FRASIER TAKE THE BAGS AND EXIT INTO THE BEDROOMS. ANNIE WATCHES NILES GO.

Annie: That Niles is quite a cutie. Now he's the one getting divorced?

Daphne: Poor thing's been just miserable.

Annie: Well, I may just have to cheer him up.

Daphne: You just leave Dr. Crane alone. No offense, but I've seen the way you go through men. The last thing he needs is for someone else to break his heart.

The Ski Lodge

Annie: But it's my birthday. Besides, you're not his nanny.

UNSEEN BY THEM, <u>GUY ENTERS</u> CARRYING GROCERIES. HE'S IN HIS MID-THIRTIES, FRENCH AND VERY GOOD-LOOKING.

Daphne: Can't we just have a nice relaxing ski trip? Does the whole weekend have to be about sex?

Guy: Hello.

DAPHNE AND ANNIE TURN AND SEE GUY. DAPHNE IS VERY IMPRESSED.

Daphne: Hello.

Guy: I am Guy.

Daphne: Daphne.

Annie: Annie.

Guy: I hope you're ready to ski tomorrow. I'm going to work you very hard.

<u>GUY EXITS TO THE KITCHEN</u> WITH THE GROCERIES.

Daphne: Dibs on the Frenchman.

Annie: You can have him. He's not half as cute as Dr. Crane.

<u>FRASIER HAS EMERGED FROM HIS ROOM</u> JUST IN TIME TO OVERHEAR THIS.

Frasier: Enough! My ears are burning.

<u>NILES EMERGES FROM HIS ROOM</u> JUST AS <u>GUY RE-ENTERS FROM THE KITCHEN,</u> FOLLOWED BY MARTIN.

Daphne: Everyone, did you meet Guy, our ski instructor?

Guy: I will also be your chef. Tonight, Entrecôte à la Guy.

Niles: A ski champion and a gourmet – *vous êtes formidable.*

Guy: *Parlez français?*

Niles: *Oui. J'ai habité six mois à Paris quand j'étais en étudiant.*

Guy: You speak very well.

Annie: *Oui.*

Frasier: Oh, you speak French as well?

Annie: No, all I know how to say is "oui."

Frasier: Well, I'm sure that'll be enough to get you through the weekend.

MARTIN GLANCES OUT THE WINDOW.

Martin: Well, ain't that a postcard. Look – two deer in the snow, just kinda nuzzling each other.

THEY ALL LOOK OUT AND SEE IT AND SAY "AWWW," "HOW CUTE," ETC.

Daphne: How romantic.

Frasier: Enough to put ideas in one's head.

FRASIER STEALS AN APPRAISING GLANCE AT ANNIE.

Annie: Isn't it?

ANNIE GLANCES AT NILES.

Niles: Yes.

NILES GLANCES AT DAPHNE.

Daphne: I should say so.

DAPHNE GLANCES AT GUY.

Guy: *Absolument.*

GUY STEALS A GLANCE AT NILES. THEY ALL STARE OUT THE WINDOW.

Martin: Well, I better start that rum cooking.

FADE OUT.

END OF ACT ONE

ACT TWO

Scene D

FADE IN:

INT. SKI LODGE LIVING ROOM/KITCHEN – EVENING – NIGHT/2
(Daphne, Guy, Niles, Annie, Frasier, Martin)

DINNER IS OVER. DAPHNE AND ANNIE SIT IN THE LIVING ROOM AREA FINISHING THEIR RUM DRINKS WHILE WATCHING GUY SKILLFULLY STOKING THE FIRE.

Daphne: Look at you – you're handy, a chef, a ski champ . . . is there anything you don't do?

Guy: There are a few things. (TURNING) Niles – you look *très élégant.*

NILES HAS EMERGED FROM HIS ROOM, WEARING SILK PAJAMAS AND A DRESSING ROBE, AND COMES DOWNSTAIRS.

Niles: I simply had to change. After that meal I felt I was going to burst out of my trousers.

Annie: (SAUCILY) Ooh my!

Daphne: Annie.

FRASIER COMES OUT OF HIS ROOM HAVING ALSO CHANGED INTO A HANDSOME DRESSING GOWN AND PAJAMAS.

Daphne (CONT'D): Dr. Crane, what a smashing robe. (TO ANNIE) Doesn't he look handsome?

Annie: Oh, yes, quite. Well, look at this – I've finished my buttered rum.

Frasier: Never let it be said that Frasier Crane would permit a lady to go thirsty. (TO DAPHNE) Daphne, go see if Dad's finished with that second batch.

RESET TO:

INT. KITCHEN – CONTINUOUS

MARTIN STANDS AT THE STOVE WHERE A LARGE POT OF RUM SITS, STEAM RISING FROM IT. HE'S STILL TRYING TO UNPOP HIS EARS. DAPHNE ENTERS. HE HURRIEDLY TURNS AND STIRS THE RUM.

Martin: Almost there. I just need to replace the rum that's boiled off.

MARTIN ADDS MORE RUM TO THE POT.

Daphne: Just what Annie needs. (PEERING BACK THROUGH THE DOOR) She's all over poor Dr. Crane as it is, and after I begged her to leave him be. (TURNS TO MARTIN) Why couldn't she be hot for Frasier?

Martin: Who?

Daphne: (LOUDLY, ANNOYED) Annie. Oh, I should just forget about those two and concentrate on Guy. I could sure go for that tall drink of water.

Martin: That what?

Daphne: Tall drink of water.

MARTIN OBLIGINGLY GETS DAPHNE A TALL DRINK OF WATER. DAPHNE, NOT NOTICING THIS, EXITS. FRASIER ENTERS. MARTIN TURNS AROUND WITH THE DRINK OF WATER AND FRASIER TAKES IT.

Frasier: Thanks, Dad, but it's the rum I really need. I'm hoping it'll help clinch things with Annie.

Martin: Annie?

Frasier: Yeah.

Martin: Well, I know a little something about her – she's hot for you.

Frasier: Says who?

Martin: Daphne. She said, "Annie's hot for Frasier."

Frasier: I knew my charm would win her over. I really should register this dressing gown with the love police.

RESET TO:

INT. SKI LODGE LIVING ROOM – CONTINUOUS

ANNIE HAS SEATED HERSELF NEXT TO NILES, A SYMPATHETIC HAND ON HIS KNEE. NILES IS UNCOMFORTABLE. DAPHNE HOVERS DISAPPROVINGLY.

Annie: I know the pain you're going through. I mean, I've never been divorced myself, but my last boyfriend was . . . eventually.

Niles: Well, you know, c'est la vie.

Annie: What you need is something to take your mind off it. I'll tell you what always works for me –

Daphne: (GRABBING ANNIE) Time to go upstairs.

Annie: What for?

DAPHNE DRAGS ANNIE UP THE STAIRS.

Daphne: I need to give you your birthday present. It's in my room.

Annie: (CALLING TO NILES) See you in a bit.

THEY DISAPPEAR INTO DAPHNE'S ROOM. GUY SITS CLOSER TO NILES.

Guy: Your friend Daphne – she did not like the way Annie was flirting with you.

Niles: You're right, Guy. She didn't like it, did she?

Guy: No. In fact, she dragged Annie right off to her bedroom.

Niles: Well, I think I know what *that* means.

WE HEAR ANNIE'S <u>GIRLISH SHRIEK OF LAUGHTER</u> FROM DAPHNE'S ROOM. GUY GAZES UP AT THE BEDROOM WITH GALLIC SUAVITY.

Guy: I think we both know. Daphne was jealous.

Niles: She was jealous, wasn't she? (DELIGHTED) Well who would have thought it?

Guy: I am surprised by nothing. You know, I think you did not like Annie's flirting either.

Niles: I certainly didn't. It made my skin crawl.

Guy: Annie is not your . . . cup of tea?

Niles: (LEANS IN; CONFIDENTIALLY) Just between us, my interests lie elsewhere this weekend.

Guy: (SMILES) Really?

<u>FRASIER ENTERS FROM THE KITCHEN</u>.

Frasier: Rum's ready.

Niles: (TO GET RID OF HIM) Guy, perhaps you can give my dad a hand with the drinks.

Guy: I am at your service.

<u>GUY EXITS TO THE KITCHEN</u>. NILES TURNS EXCITEDLY TO FRASIER.

Niles: Daphne wants me!

Frasier: She told you that?

Niles: No. But Annie was flirting with me and Daphne dragged her away in a jealous rage.

Frasier: You're imagining things. Annie was not flirting with you – I'm the one she's hot for.

Niles: I think I know when I'm being flirted with.

Frasier: It's sheer vanity. Next thing you'll be thinking Guy's after you.

RESET TO:

<u>INT. KITCHEN – CONTINUOUS</u>

MARTIN STANDS LADLING THE RUM INTO CUPS AND HANDING THEM TO GUY. MARTIN TAKES A SIP FROM ONE.

Guy: How do you like your rum?

Martin: It's kinda small, but the view's nice.

Guy: No, your *rum*.

Martin: Oh. Yeah. Could you speak up a little?

Guy: I like your rum too. But I wonder if it's clouded my judgment about something. Your son Niles – is it just me, or is he attracted to –?

Martin: Stop right there. It's not just you. He's got it bad.

Guy: Really? This is not a delicate subject for you?

Martin: Nah. I've known Niles has had those feelings for years. I didn't encourage it during that so-called marriage of his, but now that he's free, whatever makes him happy – I say go for it.

Guy: You are a wonderful father.

RESET TO:

<u>INT. SKI LODGE LIVING ROOM – CONTINUOUS</u>

<u>GUY AND MARTIN ENTER FROM THE KITCHEN</u>, GUY CARRYING A TRAY WITH SIX STEAMING CUPS OF MARTIN'S HOT BUTTERED RUM AND A JUG WITH THE LEFTOVERS. <u>DAPHNE AND ANNIE RE-ENTER</u> FROM DAPHNE'S ROOM. BOTH WEAR NIGHTGOWNS. FRASIER AND NILES FETCH THEM DRINKS.

Martin: Okay, everybody, come and get it.

Niles: Daphne, just in time.

Frasier: Annie, what a lovely gown.

Annie: Daphne just gave it to me.

GUY GIVES NILES A "THERE, SEE?" LOOK AS HE TAKES TWO DRINKS.

Frasier: (TASTING HIS DRINK) Whoa! That's even stronger than the last batch.

Martin: You might want to go easy – it can have some pretty powerful effects. First time I made it was for your mom. I'd been wanting to pop the question but I was afraid she'd say no. This gave me the nerve to ask her and I got myself a great big yes – and it wasn't the last yes I got from her that night either. Scares me to think how close I came to chickening out that night. You know, as you get older it's not your failures you regret, or the times you make an ass of yourself. It's the times you didn't even try, when you just lost your nerve.

Frasier: Wise words, Dad. Faint heart never won fair lady.

Annie: I'd certainly hope that if a man fancied me, he wouldn't be afraid to take a chance, go for a bold gesture.

Niles: Yes. We must never be too timid to pursue our heart's desire.

Guy: And not give a damn what the world thinks . . . right Miss Moon?

Daphne: Indeed.

Martin: This is my best batch ever. It takes an hour to make each one, but it's worth it just to sit and savor every sip.

GENERAL AGREEMENT. THEN DAPHNE DOWNS HERS. THEY ALL FOLLOW SUIT.

Daphne: Well, I'm done.

Niles: Time for bed.

Guy: I'm ready.

Annie: Me too.

Frasier: 'Night, Dad.

Martin: What, already? You sure? You're young people. What do you wanna go to bed for? (REALIZING) Oh. Goodnight.

MARTIN HEADS FOR HIS ROOM AS FRASIER, NILES, DAPHNE, GUY AND ANNIE REACH THEIR RESPECTIVE DOORS. NOTE: DAPHNE AND ANNIE, SLIGHTLY IN THEIR CUPS, SWITCH ROOMS. ANNIE, DAPHNE AND GUY EXIT INTO THEIR ROOMS. NILES AND FRASIER STOP.

Niles: I thought Daphne's room was –

Frasier: I guess they switched.

FRASIER AND NILES EXIT TO THEIR ROOMS. A MOMENT. DAPHNE AND ANNIE BOTH EMERGE INTO THE HALL AND CROSS TO THEIR CORRECT ROOMS.

Annie: Sorry, I took the wrong room.

Daphne: Yes – I thought we'd gotten that backwards.

Annie: Oh well, no harm done.

ANNIE AND DAPHNE GO INTO THEIR CORRECT ROOMS. FRASIER, HAVING HEARD ANNIE'S VOICE, PEERS OUT OF HIS DOOR.

Frasier: (WHISPERS) Annie?

NILES, HAVING HEARD DAPHNE, OPENS HIS DOOR.

Niles: (WHISPERING) Daphne?

FRASIER AND NILES, SEEING THERE'S NO ONE THERE BUT EACH OTHER, WAVE LIMP GOODNIGHTS.

Frasier: 'Night, Niles.

Niles: Goodnight.

THEY CLOSE THEIR DOORS. GUY, HEARING NILES' VOICE, OPENS HIS DOOR.

Guy: 'Allo!

DAPHNE, HEARING GUY'S VOICE, OPENS HER DOOR.

Daphne: Oh, hello.

Guy: (WHISPERS) I know what you want. Don't be timid – go for it!

HE DISAPPEARS BACK INTO HIS ROOM. DAPHNE, ATWITTER, DISAPPEARS BEHIND HER DOOR.

CUT TO:

Scene E

INT. NILES' BEDROOM/ANNIE'S BEDROOM – CONTINUOUS – NIGHT/2
(Niles, Annie, Guy)

A SMALL BEDROOM. NILES NOTICES THAT THERE ARE CONNECTING DOORS TO THE BEDROOMS ON EITHER SIDE OF HIM. HE KNOCKS GENTLY ON THE DOOR INTO WHAT HE THINKS IS DAPHNE'S ROOM BUT IS NOW ANNIE'S ROOM. HEARING NO REPLY, HE OPENS THE DOOR AND PEERS IN.

RESET TO:

INT. ANNIE'S BEDROOM – CONTINUOUS

NILES ENTERS. THERE'S NO ONE IN THE BEDROOM, BUT A HALF-OPEN DOOR LEADS TO THE BATHROOM FROM WHICH WE CAN HEAR WATER RUNNING AND THE SOUND OF SOMEONE GARGLING.

Niles: (CALLS TO THE BATHROOM) Hello? It's me, Niles.

The Ski Lodge

Annie (O.C.): (GARGLING) Wait.

Niles: I can't wait. I may lose my nerve and not say what I came to say. I need you. I've wanted you since the moment I laid eyes on you.

ANNIE EMERGES FROM THE BATHROOM.

Annie: I feel the exact same way.

Niles: Annie!

Annie: I see you're surprised. I've tried to send you signals tonight, but as usual I was too damned subtle. Just promise you won't mention this to Daphne.

Niles: My lips are sealed.

Annie: (ADVANCING) Not for long I hope.

SFX: KNOCK ON ANNIE'S DOOR. NILES, THRILLED AT ANY INTERRUPTION, TURNS TO THE DOOR.

Niles: Come in!

GUY ENTERS.

Niles (CONT'D): (SAVED) Guy!

Guy: Niles. I thought I heard your voice in here.

Annie: What do you want?

Guy: Niles – you told me you wanted to see that thing. You know – in my room.

Niles: Oh yes! Thank you . . . for reminding me.

Annie: What thing?

Niles: Won't take long. We'll catch up later.

NILES AND GUY EXIT ANNIE'S BEDROOM.

CUT TO:

Scene H

INT. SKI LODGE LIVING ROOM – CONTINUOUS – NIGHT/2
(Niles, Guy)

NILES AND GUY SPEAK IN WHISPERS.

Niles: Boy, that was close. I owe you a big one.

GUY STARTS FOR HIS ROOM, NILES CROSSES TO HIS OWN BEDROOM DOOR.

Guy: Your room?

Niles: You're right – of course. My room's out. She's bound to hear me in there.

Guy: Oh, you are the type who makes noise. We could still go to my room.

Niles: It's as good a place as any.

THEY HURRY TO GUY'S ROOM. GUY OPENS THE DOOR.

Guy: *Entrez.*

NILES AND GUY EXIT INTO GUY'S BEDROOM.

CUT TO:

Scene J

INT. GUY'S BEDROOM – CONTINUOUS – NIGHT/2
(Niles, Daphne, Guy)

NILES AND GUY ENTER TO FIND DAPHNE THERE WAITING ON GUY'S BED.

Niles: Daphne!

Daphne: Dr. Crane!

Guy: Miss Moon. Is your room not satisfactory?

Daphne: (MORTIFIED) Oh, dear. I seem to have made a dreadful mistake.

Niles: What are you doing in Guy's room?

Daphne: (A WAY OUT) Is this Guy's room then? I was looking for Annie's room.

Guy: Ah, now it makes sense.

Daphne: I'll just go.

Niles: Wait for me! That hall is horribly dark. I'll show you the way. (TO GUY) My room should be safe now.

Guy: Ah, very well. I'll see you later.

Niles: Excellent. Come along, Daphne.

NILES AND DAPHNE EXIT GUY'S ROOM.

CUT TO:

The Ski Lodge

Scene K

INT. SKI LODGE LIVING ROOM – CONTINUOUS – NIGHT/2
(Daphne, Frasier, Niles)

NILES AND DAPHNE EXIT GUY'S ROOM JUST AS FRASIER EMERGES FROM
HIS ROOM. HE IS NOW NAKED UNDER HIS BATHROBE AND CARRIES A
BOTTLE OF DOM PERIGNON.

Daphne: Dr. Crane?

Frasier: (EMBARRASSED; SUDDENLY NONCHALANT) Oh. Hello.

Niles: Frasier!

Frasier: Was that Guy's room you were both in?

Niles: Yes. You see Daphne was just –

Daphne: Looking for Annie. I need to talk to her.

Frasier: To Annie? For how long?

Daphne: Two minutes.

Frasier: Right.

Daphne: (TO FRASIER) Is that champagne?

Frasier: Yes. I was just – bringing it . . . to . . . Dad. (THEN) Carry on.

FRASIER CROSSES DOWN TOWARD MARTIN'S ROOM. NILES HUSTLES
DAPHNE UP THE FEW STAIRS TO HIS DOOR.

Niles: Before you see Annie could you come to my room?

Daphne: What for?

Niles: There's something I need to tell you.

THEY GO INTO NILES' ROOM.

CUT TO:

Scene L

INT. NILES' BEDROOM/DAPHNE'S BEDROOM – CONTINUOUS – NIGHT/2
(Niles, Daphne, Annie, Frasier, Guy, Martin)

THE ROOM IS DARK. NILES AND DAPHNE ENTER.

Niles: This may come as a surprise to you –

NILES TURNS ON THE LIGHT. <u>ANNIE</u> IS WAITING IN NILES' BED.

Daphne: Annie!

Annie: Daphne!

Daphne: Didn't I tell you to leave Dr. Crane alone?

Annie: And now I see why. You wanted him all to yourself!

Daphne: I do not want him all to myself!

Annie: Oh, I see! It's a threesome you're after. Well, I don't do those any more.

Niles: Annie, I think there's been a misunderstanding here.

Annie: I don't see how. You barged into my room not five minutes ago and told me how much you wanted me.

Daphne: (TO NILES) You did?

Niles: Well, technically, yes –

Annie: Then as soon as this one bats her eyes it's shove off, Annie. (TO DAPHNE) This is the worst birthday I've ever had!

<u>ANNIE RUNS INTO HER ROOM</u> THROUGH THE CONNECTING DOOR.

Daphne: I'm sorry, Dr. Crane. I've ruined everything for you.

Niles: No, you haven't. Those things I said to Annie, I can explain –

Daphne: No, it's none of my business. I've had enough embarrassment for one evening.

<u>DAPHNE HURRIES BACK INTO HER OWN BEDROOM</u> FOLLOWED BY <u>NILES</u>.

RESET TO:

<u>INT. DAPHNE'S BEDROOM – CONTINUOUS</u>

<u>DAPHNE AND NILES ENTER</u>. SHE TURNS ON THE LIGHT. <u>FRASIER</u> LOLLS ON HER BED, NAKED UNDER A SHEET, A GLASS OF CHAMPAGNE IN HIS HAND.

Daphne (CONT'D): Dr. Crane!!

Frasier: (AGHAST; COVERING HIMSELF) Daphne!

Niles: Frasier! You snake!

The Ski Lodge

Frasier: Sorry! Wrong room!

Daphne: Get out of here! Right now!

Frasier: Right. Just give me a second and off I go. Is it next door I want then?

Daphne: Just go!

Frasier: Right. Sorry again!

RESET TO:

INT. NILES' BEDROOM - CONTINUOUS

THE ROOM'S NOW DARK. FRASIER, A TOWEL AROUND HIM, RACES IN FROM DAPHNE'S ROOM AND CLOSES THE DOOR BEHIND HIM. IN THE DARKNESS WE HEAR:

Guy: *Bonsoir, chéri.*

GUY TURNS ON THE LIGHT. HE IS NAKED IN NILES' BED.

Frasier: Guy!

Guy: You are not the Crane I want!

Frasier: You're not even the sex I want!

Guy: Where is Niles?

FRASIER OPENS THE DOOR TO DAPHNE'S ROOM.

Frasier: Oh, Niles! Company!

NILES ENTERS.

Niles: (SPOTTING GUY; TO FRASIER) My God, what are you doing in here with Guy?

Guy: Don't be jealous, Niles. It's not how it looks.

Niles: Excuse me!?

Frasier: Well, much as I'd love to stay and help you two sort this out, there happens to be a beautiful woman on the other side of this door who wants me desperately.

HE FLINGS OPEN THE CONNECTING DOOR TO ANNIE'S ROOM.

Frasier (CONT'D): Hello, Annie.

Annie (O.C.): (SHRIEKS, THEN) Go away! Get out! Get out! Get out!

Frasier: Sorry!

HE CLOSES THE DOOR AS <u>DAPHNE</u>, ALARMED, <u>ENTERS</u> FROM HER ROOM.

Daphne: What's going on? (SEES HIM) Guy!

<u>ANNIE ENTERS</u> FROM HER ROOM CLAD ONLY IN A TOWEL.

Annie: (TO FRASIER) How dare you barge in on me when I'm naked!

Frasier: I'm sorry. I was misled. My father told me you wanted me.

Annie: Your father did?

Frasier: Blame Daphne. She told him.

Daphne: I did not. I said she wanted your brother.

Guy: Could Niles and I please have some privacy?

Annie: (TO NILES) You're just putting the moves on everyone, aren't you?!

Niles: (TO GUY) Would you kindly get out of my bed. I am not gay, Guy.

Guy: Oh, please! Acknowledge your true nature and stop chasing these lesbians!

Daphne: Lesbians!

Guy: Your father himself said you were gay.

Niles: (INCREDULOUS) My father?!

PANDEMONIUM. THERE'S A FIVE-WAY OVERLAP. "MY FATHER SAID THAT?", "WHO ARE YOU CALLING LESBIANS?", "YOU'RE THE MOST HORRIBLE FAMILY I'VE EVER MET," "WOULD EVERYONE PLEASE JUST GO TO BED," "I'VE NEVER BEEN SO HUMILIATED IN MY LIFE!", ETC., ETC.,

FINALLY <u>MARTIN ENTERS</u>.

Martin: Hey you want to keep it down in here? Some of us are trying to sleep! . . . (REALIZES) Hey, my ears must've popped. I can hear again! Well, goodnight all.

<u>MARTIN EXITS</u>.

Niles: All right. We could discuss this till we've figured out every detail of what went on here tonight, but if you ask me, breakfast will be embarrassing enough as it is. I say we go to bed and forget any of this ever happened.

THEY ALL MUMBLE THEIR ASSENT AND HEAD FOR THE VARIOUS DOORS. JUST BEFORE THEY GO:

Frasier: Wait. Let me make sure I have this straight . . . All the lust coursing through this lodge tonight . . . all the hormones virtually ricocheting off these walls . . . and *no one* was chasing me?

Daphne: Goodnight, Dr. Crane.

Frasier: Goodnight.

GUY, ANNIE AND DAPHNE EXIT TO THEIR ROOMS. FRASIER WEARILY FOLLOWS, AS WE:

FADE OUT.

END OF ACT TWO

SEASON SIX

Three Valentines

THREE VALENTINES

#40570-136

Written by Rob Hanning
Created and Developed by David Angell, Peter Casey & David Lee
Directed by Kelsey Grammer

ACT ONE

Scene A

FADE IN:

INT. FRASIER'S LIVING ROOM – VALENTINE'S DAY – DAY/1
(Niles, Delivery Guy, Eddie)

NILES, DRESSED IMPECCABLY IN A SUIT AND TIE, ENTERS FROM THE KITCHEN CARRYING A BOTTLE OF CHAMPAGNE AND TWO CHAMPAGNE FLUTES. HE IS ALONE IN THE APARTMENT. HE PLACES THE FLUTES ON THE DINING TABLE NEXT TO A SPREAD OF GOURMET HORS D'OEUVRES AND AN ICE BUCKET, BUT IN THE PROCESS OF NESTLING THE CHAMPAGNE BOTTLE INTO THE ICE, HE NOTICES SOMETHING ON THE LABEL THAT GREATLY DISPLEASES HIM. EXASPERATED, HE MARCHES OVER TO THE PHONE AND DIALS.

(DURING THE FOLLOWING PHONE CALL, HE TIDIES AN ALREADY TIDY LIVING ROOM, REPOSITIONING A FEW COUCH PILLOWS, MOVING A BEAUTIFUL FLORAL ARRANGEMENT A FEW INCHES TO THE LEFT, SNATCHING A NEAR-INVISIBLE PIECE OF LINT OFF THE FLOOR, AND ADJUSTING THE LARGE, DECORATIVE QUILT THAT IS DRAPED OVER MARTIN'S CHAIR.)

Niles: (INTO PHONE) Hello, François, this is Niles Crane. You delivered some Champagne earlier for Valentine's Day – only you brought me the 1990 and I asked for an '88 rose . . . I'm glad you're sorry but I will be needing the '88 . . . My date will know the difference. She happens to be president of our wine club . . . Remember, I'm not at home, I would never entertain at the Shangri-La. My brother was kind enough to let me use his place . . . (LOOKING AT MARTIN'S CHAIR) What could I do? I threw a quilt over it. Now hurry – that bottle is all that stands between this night and perfection!

NILES HANGS UP, GOES TO THE STEREO AND TURNS ON SOME MUSIC. HE SURVEYS THE APARTMENT AND, CONTENT WITH WHAT HE SEES, SITS ON THE COUCH. AS HE SETTLES IN, HE NOTICES THAT THE CREASE IN ONE TROUSER LEG ISN'T QUITE RIGHT. HE TRIES ADJUSTING IT. HE STANDS UP, SHAKES HIS LEG OUT, SITS DOWN AGAIN – STILL NO GOOD. CHECKING HIS WATCH, HE HESITATES FOR A SECOND, THEN GETS UP AND DISAPPEARS INTO THE KITCHEN . . .

. . . RETURNING A MOMENT LATER WITH AN IRON AND AN IRONING BOARD. HE PLUGS IN THE IRON AND SETS IT DOWN AND THEN, WITH DIFFICULTY, SETS UP THE IRONING BOARD. AS HE FINISHES AND BEGINS TO TAKE HIS TROUSERS OFF, HE NOTICES EDDIE, WHO HAS RUN IN FROM MARTIN'S ROOM. HE PERCHES SOMEWHERE AND STARES AT NILES.

Niles (CONT'D): (TO EDDIE) What are you staring at?

HE FINISHES TAKING HIS TROUSERS OFF AND STARTS TO IRON THE CREASE. HE CHECKS HIS WATCH, AND IRONS MORE QUICKLY.

AS HE IRONS, HE NOTICES A LOOSE THREAD ON ONE OF THE TROUSER CUFFS. HE PULLS GENTLY ON THE THREAD, BUT IT JUST GETS LONGER, SO HE PUTS DOWN THE IRON, CROSSES TO THE DESK BY THE KITCHEN DOOR, GETS A PAIR OF SCISSORS OUT OF A DRAWER, AND CROSSES BACK TO THE IRONING BOARD. AS HE BENDS OVER THE PANTS LEG TO TRIM THE THREAD HE LOOKS AT EDDIE AGAIN.

Niles (CONT'D): (TO EDDIE) Don't get too comfortable there. The minute she comes you're going to have to – Ow!

HE'S CUT THE TIP OF HIS FINGER WITH THE SCISSORS.

Niles (CONT'D): (TO EDDIE) Now look what you made me do. I'm bleeding.

NILES LOOKS AT THE CUT AND THE SIGHT OF THE BLOOD MAKES HIM WOOZY. HE STARTS TO SWOON, BUT HE CATCHES HIMSELF. HE QUICKLY LOOKS AWAY, STEADIES HIMSELF ON THE IRONING BOARD, AND HOLDS HIS CUT FINGER IN THE AIR ABOVE HIS HEAD.

Niles (CONT'D): (TO EDDIE) Will you just get out of here?

NILES ATTEMPTS TO SHOO EDDIE OUT OF THE ROOM BY SNAPPING HIS FINGERS AND POINTING TO THE HALL, BUT THIS CAUSES HIM TO NOTICE HIS BLOODY FINGER. HE GETS WOOZY AGAIN AND FALLS OVER ONTO THE COUCH AND PASSES OUT. EDDIE JUMPS ONTO THE COUCH AND LICKS NILES' FACE. AFTER A FEW SECONDS, NILES COMES TO. HE REMEMBERS ABOUT HIS FINGER AND HOLDS IT OVER HIS HEAD, OUT OF SIGHT.

NILES NOTICES THAT WHILE HE WAS PASSED OUT, HIS FINGER BLED ONTO THE ARM OF THE COUCH, LEAVING A SMALL STAIN. HORRIFIED, HE TRIES TO CLEAN THE STAIN WITH HIS HANDKERCHIEF, BUT IT WON'T COME OUT. HE GETS UP, SHOOS EDDIE OUT OF THE ROOM, AND AS EDDIE EXITS TO THE HALLWAY, NILES WRAPS HIS HANDKERCHIEF AROUND HIS CUT FINGER, CAREFUL TO LOOK AWAY WHILE DOING SO. HE THEN EXITS TO THE KITCHEN.

IMMEDIATELY, EDDIE RUNS BACK INTO THE ROOM, JUMPS UP ON MARTIN'S CHAIR AND WATCHES EVERYTHING THAT FOLLOWS. NILES RETURNS FROM THE KITCHEN CARRYING A RAG AND A TIN OF CLEANING FLUID. HE SITS AND SCANS THE DIRECTIONS ON THE SIDE OF THE CAN.

AFTER DOING SO, HE CAUTIOUSLY MOVES A NEARBY LIT CANDLE AWAY FROM THE STAIN AND THE CLEANING FLUID. THEN, HE POURS SOME OF THE CLEANER ONTO THE RAG AND RUBS THE STAIN.

NILES STANDS TO LOOK AT THE SOFA AND SMILES – SATISFIED. THEN, AS HE GOES TO PUT THE LID BACK ON THE CLEANING FLUID, HIS HANDKERCHIEF FALLS OFF THE CUT FINGER. SEEING THE BLOOD, HE AGAIN BECOMES WOOZY AND FAINTS, FALLING ONTO THE COUCH WHILE STILL HOLDING THE OPEN CAN OF CLEANING FLUID. IT EMPTIES OUT ONTO THE SOFA NEXT TO HIM.

AFTER A FEW SECONDS NILES COMES TO, PUTS THE CLEANING FLUID DOWN ON THE COFFEE TABLE, AGAIN REMEMBERS HIS FINGER AND QUICKLY PUTS IT IN THE AIR. WHILE STILL HOLDING IT ABOVE HIS HEAD AND OUT OF SIGHT, HE WRAPS THE HANDKERCHIEF AROUND IT AND HASTILY CROSSES . . .

INTO THE KITCHEN. AS HE PUTS THE CLEANER AND RAG AWAY, HE PAUSES TO SNIFF THE AIR. CONCERNED BY SOMETHING HE SMELLS, HE CHECKS THE POTS ON THE STOVE – THEY'RE OKAY. HE CHECKS THE OVEN – FINE. HE SHRUGS, THEN WANDERS BACK . . .

INTO THE LIVING ROOM, WHERE HE FINDS HIS PANTS ARE NOW ON FIRE ON THE IRONING BOARD. PANICKED, HE RUNS OVER AND TRIES TO SMOTHER THE FLAMES WITH ONE PANT LEG – SUCCEEDING ONLY TO SPREAD THE FIRE TO THE OTHER PANT LEG. HE INSTINCTIVELY FLINGS THE TROUSERS AWAY FROM HIM, CAUSING THEM TO LAND . . .

. . . ON THE SECTION OF THE COUCH SOAKED WITH CLEANING FLUID, WHICH IMMEDIATELY IGNITES. AN ALARMED EDDIE BARKS AS NILES QUICKLY EXITS TO THE HALLWAY, RETURNING WITH A LARGE FIRE EXTINGUISHER. HE AIMS IT AT THE COUCH AND SQUEEZES THE HANDLE, BUT NOTHING HAPPENS. REALIZING THAT THE SAFETY PIN MUST BE REMOVED, NILES TRIES TO PULL IT OUT, BUT CAN'T GET IT TO BUDGE. FINALLY, THE PIN COMES FREE, CAUSING THE FIRE EXTINGUISHER TO START DISCHARGING WITH SUCH FORCE THAT NILES IS UNABLE TO CONTROL IT. FOAM SPRAYS IN EVERY DIRECTION COVERING THE WALLS AND EVERY PIECE OF FURNITURE – BUT THE COUCH – AS NILES BATTLES TO GET THE THING UNDER CONTROL. HE FINALLY MANAGES TO AIM IT AT THE COUCH, BUT BY THEN THE NOZZLE JUST SPUTTERS A LITTLE AND THE LAST OF THE FOAM DRIBBLES OUT AND ONTO THE RUG.

TOSSING ASIDE THE EMPTY CANISTER, HE EXITS TO THE KITCHEN AGAIN, RETURNING AFTER A MOMENT WEARING OVEN MITTS ON EACH HAND AND CARRYING TWO OF THE POTS THAT WERE ON THE STOVE. HE GETS AS CLOSE AS HE CAN TO THE COUCH AND DUMPS THE CONTENTS OF THE TWO POTS ONTO THE FLAMES, DOUSING THEM WITH A LOT OF BOILING WATER, SOME SPAGHETTI AND A BIG PILE OF SHRIMP. THIS DOES THE TRICK – THE FLAMES ARE EXTINGUISHED.

COUGHING A LITTLE FROM THE SMOKE, NILES CROSSES TO THE FRONT

DOOR AND OPENS IT TO AIR OUT THE APARTMENT. HE FANS THE DOOR BACK AND FORTH TO GET SOME AIR CIRCULATING. NOT SATISFIED WITH THE RESULT, HE OPENS THE DOOR WIDE AND TRIES TO PUSH OUT THE SMOKE BY WAVING HIS ARMS. HE WAVES THEM SO WILDLY, HOWEVER, THAT THE HANDKERCHIEF FLIES OFF HIS FINGER. WHEN HE GOES TO RETRIEVE IT, IT IS NOW SUFFICIENTLY BLOODY THAT IT CAUSES HIM TO FAINT YET AGAIN, THIS TIME ON THE FLOOR. AS SOON AS NILES FAINTS, EDDIE JUMPS UP ONTO THE STILL-SMOKING COUCH AND STARTS EATING THE SHRIMP.

A BEAT LATER, A <u>DELIVERY MAN</u> CARRYING THE CHAMPAGNE, APPEARS AT THE DOOR AND STOPS TO TAKE IN THE TABLEAU: FOAM EVERYWHERE, THE CHARRED COUCH COVERED IN SHRIMP AND SPAGHETTI, AND A PASSED-OUT, PANT-LESS NILES SPRAWLED ON THE FLOOR.

AND WE . . .

FADE OUT.

<u>END OF ACT ONE</u>

ACT TWO

Scene B

FADE IN:

<u>INT. RADIO STUDIO – VALENTINE'S DAY – DAY/1</u>
(Frasier, Cassandra Stone, Roz)

<u>FRASIER</u> IS ON THE AIR. <u>ROZ IS IN HER BOOTH.</u>

Frasier: That's all for today, listeners. Goodbye and good mental health.

CASSANDRA STONE ENTERS FRASIER'S BOOTH.

Cassandra: Hello, Frasier.

Frasier: Ah, Cassandra.

Cassandra: I just had to say how much I loved your show today. Well, okay, every day.

Frasier: (MODEST) Thank you. You're too kind, as I tell you every day. How's that new publicity campaign going?

Cassandra: Oh, great. It'd be a lot easier if I had a few more like you to promote. Cultured, charming, photogenic . . .

Frasier: I'm also a wizard with a crêpe pan if you want to work that in somehow.

AS THEY SHARE A LAUGH, CASSANDRA FIXES FRASIER'S JACKET COLLAR,

SMOOTHING HIS LAPELS WHILE SHE'S AT IT. THEIR MOMENT IS
INTERRUPTED WHEN SOMEONE WAVES TO CASSANDRA FROM THE
HALLWAY.

Cassandra: Oh, I've got to speak to my copywriter. I'll stop by again sometime, okay?

CASSANDRA QUICKLY EXITS.

Frasier: My jacket and I look forward to it.

HE BEGINS TO HUM AS ROZ CROSSES INTO FRASIER'S BOOTH.

Roz: All right, what happened?

Frasier: What do you mean?

Roz: You're doing your humming. The happy humming – not to be confused with the
sad humming, or that aria you sing after you get lucky.

Frasier: What aria?

Roz: I didn't catch the title. I'd need to hear it a second time.

Frasier: Very amusing, Roz. It happens there's someone new at the station who's quite
taken with me, and it's none other than that lovely little peach in publicity, Cassandra.

Roz: Oh, poor Frasier.

Frasier: What?

Roz: I hate to be the one to tell you this, but . . . that woman's just, well . . . a flirt.

Frasier: Obviously you haven't seen how she virtually accosts me in the hallway every
day.

Roz: She's been treating everyone that way. She even flirted with me her first day until I
took off my baseball cap and parka.

ROZ MOVES BACK INTO HER BOOTH AS CASSANDRA RE-ENTERS FRASIER'S
BOOTH.

Cassandra: Frasier, you have a second?

Frasier: Oh. Certainly, Cassandra.

Cassandra: I was just wondering if you might want to have dinner with me.

Frasier: Dinner? Really?

Cassandra: Yeah, I thought it'd be nice to get to know each other a little. (REALIZING)
Oh, gosh, tonight's Valentine's Day, isn't it? You probably have other plans.

Frasier: As it happens, I don't. Dinner would be lovely.

Cassandra: Great.

SHE GIVES HIM A BIG SMILE, SQUEEZES HIS ARM, AND GOES. FRASIER, WATCHING HER WALK AWAY, STARTS HUMMING AND CROSSES INTO ROZ'S BOOTH.

Frasier: Well, I certainly didn't misread the signals that time. She just asked me out to dinner.

Roz: Really?

Frasier: Yes. She coquettishly pretended to forget it was Valentine's Day, but I saw right through that.

Roz: You're sure this is a date-date, right, and not a business dinner?

Frasier: Reasonably sure.

Roz: Then, good for you.

Frasier: Then again . . . she has mentioned wanting to talk about her new marketing campaign. I suppose it is possible she really did forget it was Valentine's Day. I guess I'll just have to ask her if she's viewing me in, you know, a romantic way.

Roz: Are you crazy? What if the answer is no? Then it's awkward all through dinner, and it'll be weird every time you see her at the office – not to mention how embarrassing it'll be when everyone else around here finds out.

Frasier: You're right, I can't just ask her. I guess I should just go to dinner and see how the evening plays out. I'll know what she has in mind by the way she acts, how she dresses, the way she treats me.

Roz: Much better.

Frasier: So, I'm sure you have plans tonight.

Roz: I'm going out with Bob – y'know, the tax accountant.

Frasier: Oh, Roz – isn't he the one who drones on so incessantly you call him "the cricket"?

Roz: No. (THEN) I call him "the cricket" because he rubs his hands together really fast during sex. (OFF HIS LOOK) Hey, it beats being alone.

OFF FRASIER'S REACTION, WE:

FADE OUT.

Scene C

FADE IN:

<u>INT. RESTAURANT – THAT EVENING – NIGHT/1</u>
(Frasier, Cassandra, Violinist, Mario)

FRASIER SITS ALONE AT A TABLE. <u>CASSANDRA ENTERS</u> AND APPROACHES FRASIER.

Frasier: Ah, Cassandra. Our plans were so last minute, I thought maybe I'd misunderstood somehow.

CASSANDRA PLANTS A BIG KISS HELLO RIGHT ON FRASIER'S MOUTH.

Frasier (CONT'D): But your arrival certainly has cleared things up . . .

CASSANDRA SLIPS OFF HER COAT – SHE LOOKS STUNNING.

Cassandra: You don't think I'd pass up dinner with the sexiest man in radio, do you?

NEARBY, A TUXEDOED <u>VIOLINIST</u> FINISHES SERENADING A COUPLE AND PRESENTS A RED ROSE TO THE WOMAN.

Violinist: Compliments of the gentleman.

THE WOMAN IS DELIGHTED, AND GIVES HER DATE A BIG KISS.

Cassandra: Oh, that is so romantic. Will you excuse me for a second?

<u>CASSANDRA MOVES OFF</u> TO THE COAT CHECK. FRASIER MAKES SURE CASSANDRA ISN'T WATCHING, THEN SIGNALS THE VIOLINIST.

Frasier: Excuse me – you see that woman over there by the coat check? We're on a first date, and I want to make sure she knows I'm interested.

Violinist: Then you should have offered to check her coat.

Frasier: Just come over and play something romantic when she gets back.

FRASIER GIVES HIM MONEY, AND THE <u>VIOLINIST MOVES OFF</u>. <u>CASSANDRA RETURNS</u> TO THE TABLE. THE MAITRE D', <u>MARIO, APPROACHES</u>, HER.

Mario: Miss Cassandra, so nice to see you again.

Cassandra: You too, Mario. How's the sexiest maître d' in Seattle?

SHE GIVES MARIO THE SAME BIG KISS ON THE MOUTH THAT SHE GAVE FRASIER. FRASIER REACTS TO THIS. THE <u>MAITRE D'</u> HANDS THEM THE WINE LIST AND <u>MOVES OFF</u>. THE <u>VIOLINIST STARTS TO APPROACH THEM</u>. AS CASSANDRA LOOKS DOWN AT THE WINE LIST, FRASIER WAVES AWAY

THE VIOLINIST. THE <u>VIOLINIST</u> SHRUGS AND <u>MOVES OFF</u>.

Cassandra: Oh, they have the best wine list here. You feel like sharing a bottle?

Frasier: If you like.

Cassandra: Good thing I took a cab here – I'm a real lightweight. Then again, I'm sure a gentleman like you won't mind escorting me back to my room after dinner, will you?

Frasier: I think that can be arranged.

AS CASSANDRA OPENS THE MENU, FRASIER SIGNALS CONFIDENTLY FOR THE <u>VIOLINIST TO COME BACK</u> TO THE TABLE.

Cassandra: They have a great menu here.

Frasier: What do you recommend?

Cassandra: (OFF MENU) Oh, I don't know. I think I'll start with the tomato and onion salad and then have the garlic chicken with scallions.

Frasier: Really? Interesting choice.

FRASIER WAVES OFF THE VIOLINIST AGAIN.

Cassandra: And for you, let's see . . . are you in the mood for oysters?

Frasier: Actually, I'm not sure.

AND WE:

FADE OUT.

Scene D

FADE IN:

<u>INT. HOTEL ROOM – LATER THAT EVENING – NIGHT/1</u>
(Frasier, Cassandra)

CASSANDRA OPENS THE HOTEL ROOM DOOR. FRASIER JUST STANDS OUT IN THE HALLWAY.

Frasier: Well, here we are. Last stop. Your hotel.

Cassandra: I can't wait until I find an apartment. Come on in.

CASSANDRA PULLS HIM IN AND CLOSES THE DOOR.

Cassandra (CONT'D): God, I can't believe we got caught in the rain like that – I'm freezing. Of course, there is a way we can warm up fast.

Frasier: Yes, all we have to do is . . .?

Cassandra: Have a brandy.

Frasier: Yes, have a brandy.

Cassandra: The mini-bar's over there. I'll be right out.

SHE SQUEEZES HIS SHOULDER AS SHE EXITS INTO THE BATHROOM. FRASIER GOES TO THE MINI-BAR AND TAKES OUT HIS CEL PHONE AND DIALS. AND WE:

CUT TO:

INT. ROZ'S APARTMENT – CONTINUOUS
(Roz)

SFX: PHONE RINGING

THE ROOM IS DARK. A BEDSIDE LAMP GOES ON AND ROZ REACHES FOR THE PHONE.

Roz: Hello?

DURING THE FOLLOWING WE INTERCUT BETWEEN FRASIER AND ROZ:

Frasier: Roz, I'm in Cassandra's hotel room.

Roz: Well, I guess things are going well.

Frasier: I think they are, but I'm not sure. She does keep bringing the conversation back to business. I'm just waiting for a totally clear, unambiguous sign.

Roz: Oh for God's sake, Frasier, the woman invited you back to her hotel room. The only sign you're going to need is "Do Not Disturb."

CASSANDRA RE-ENTERS WEARING A BATHROBE. FRASIER CONCEALS HIS PHONE.

Cassandra: I just had to get out of that dress.

Frasier: Here's your brandy.

HE HANDS HER A GLASS OF BRANDY.

Cassandra: I'll just go dry my hair.

SHE EXITS BACK INTO THE BATHROOM.

Frasier: (INTO PHONE) All right, I'm back. What should I do?

Roz: Let's see, she ditched her dress and she's hitting the sauce – what do you need, runway lights on the mattress?

Frasier: It's not as clear cut as it seems.

Roz: Frasier, she's way out on a limb here. You know how rejected she'll feel if you don't make a move? You're going to blow it forever.

Frasier: You're right. I probably should take off my jacket and tie.

Roz: Yeah, go get her, cowboy.

ROZ HANGS UP. FRASIER PUTS HIS PHONE AWAY. CASSANDRA OPENS THE BATHROOM DOOR A CRACK AND CALLS TO HIM.

Cassandra (O.S.): Frasier, are you making yourself comfortable?

FRASIER TENTATIVELY REMOVES HIS JACKET AND HANGS IT ON THE BACK OF A CHAIR, THEN LOOSENS HIS TIE A TINY BIT.

Frasier: Yes.

Cassandra (O.S.): If it's okay, I still have a few questions about the ad campaign I'd like to ask you.

Frasier: Of course. That's what I'm here for.

FRASIER GRABS HIS JACKET AND STARTS TO PUT IT BACK ON.

Cassandra (O.S.): Or, if you prefer, we could just talk about it over breakfast tomorrow.

Frasier: Breakfast you say?

FRASIER SMILES, TAKES OFF HIS JACKET AND REMOVES HIS TIE.

Cassandra (O.S.): I hope I wasn't being presumptuous. We will be having breakfast together, won't we?

Frasier: Absolutely.

HE PULLS HIS SWEATER HALFWAY OVER HIS HEAD, WHEN . . .

Cassandra (O.S.): Great. So, who else is supposed to be there?

Frasier: Where?

Cassandra (O.S.): At the breakfast meeting. The one for the sponsors here at the hotel tomorrow. You just said you were going, right?

Frasier: The meeting, of course.

FRASIER QUICKLY PULLS HIS SWEATER BACK ON AND IS STILL STRAIGHTENING HIMSELF AS CASSANDRA RE-ENTERS.

Cassandra: Frasier, what are you doing?

Frasier: Well, I . . .

Cassandra: I thought you were going to make yourself comfortable? Check the closet, I think you'll find something in there you can slip on.

Frasier: All right.

Cassandra: I'm just going to take my lenses out.

CASSANDRA EXITS TO THE BATHROOM AGAIN. FRASIER GOES TO THE CLOSET AND FINDS A BATHROBE HANGING INSIDE THE DOOR. CHUCKLING TO HIMSELF, HE STARTS GETTING UNDRESSED, NOW INCLUDING HIS PANTS.

Cassandra (O.S.) (CONT'D): Y'know, I'm really glad I asked you to dinner.

Frasier: Oh, so am I.

Cassandra (O.S.): You may not believe this, but I almost chickened out at the last minute. It just goes to show, it's always better to take the risk. I mean, so you say no. I'm an adult, what's a little embarrassment.

Frasier: I couldn't agree more.

FRASIER IS JUST STEPPING OUT OF HIS TROUSERS, WHEN . . .

Cassandra (O.S.): Did you find the slippers?

Frasier: What?

Cassandra (O.S.): In the closet. You stepped in that puddle after dinner, I figured you might want to get out of those wet socks. I mean, it's up to you – I know some people feel funny about taking their shoes off in someone else's room.

FRASIER SCRAMBLES FRANTICALLY TO PUT HIS CLOTHES BACK ON.

Cassandra (O.S.) (CONT'D): My gosh, it's really starting to come down out there. You know what I'm thinking?

Frasier: No, I truly don't.

Cassandra (O.S.): You are coming back for breakfast anyway. Why don't you stay the night?

Frasier: Well, ah . . . All right.

CASSANDRA ENTERS.

Cassandra: It's funny, when I got up this morning, I never imagined you and I would end up doing this tonight.

Frasier: You know, when you say "doing this," you of course mean . . .

SHE GETS INTO BED.

Cassandra: Spending the night together. Oh, you're going to love this bed. It's so comfortable.

Frasier: Oh, good.

FRASIER QUICKLY DISROBES.

Cassandra: Would you mind turning off the lights?

Frasier: No, not at all.

FRASIER CLICKS OFF THE LIGHTS AND GETS INTO BED. IT IS VERY DARK.

Frasier (CONT'D): Ah, this is nice. (THEN) You know, Cassandra, I have to make a confession. I'm sure you'll find this amusing – especially seeing where we've ended up. All night, I've been desperately trying to figure out if we were on a romantic date or a business date. Isn't that silly? But I guess all's well that ends well. So, let the games begin.

THERE IS THE UNMISTAKABLE SOUND OF SNORING.

Frasier (CONT'D): Cassandra . . . Cassandra?

BUT FRASIER'S ONLY REPLY IS MORE SNORING. AND WE:

FADE OUT.

END OF ACT TWO

ACT THREE

Scene E

FADE IN:

INT. RESTAURANT – VALENTINE'S DAY – NIGHT/1
(Martin, Daphne, Maître D', Waiter)

MARTIN AND DAPHNE ARE WAITING TO BE SEATED AT A RESTAURANT.

Daphne: You know, there was really no need to do this. I would've been perfectly happy going to the movies by myself.

Martin: Come on, I couldn't have you sitting alone in some dusty old theater on Valentine's Day. Now, I want you to know that tonight's on me. You order anything you like. Cost is no object. This night only comes around once a year.

Daphne: This is all very nice, but Valentine's Day really doesn't mean that much to me.

Martin: In that case, they got a nice chicken cordon bleu for $8.95. But you gotta order it in the next seven minutes.

THE HOSTESS SIGNALS THAT THEIR TABLE IS READY AND LEADS THEM TO IT. AS THEY CROSS THROUGH THE CROWDED ROOM . . .

Martin (CONT'D): Y'know, I'm impressed with you, Daph. A lot of women get to the point where they can't stand being alone on any night, let alone Valentine's Day. But you got a good head on your shoulders. Here let me take your coat.

THEY GET TO THEIR TABLE. MARTIN TAKES DAPHNE'S COAT.

Daphne: No, no, I'll keep it.

Martin: It's better to hang it up. I noticed a rack over there.

Daphne: So did I, and it's on the coat check girl.

MARTIN GRABS THEIR COATS AND HEADS OFF TO THE COAT CHECK AS THE MAITRE D' COMES OVER.

Maître D': Happy Valentine's Day, and welcome to Russano's.

Daphne: Thank you.

Maître D': The waiter will be by to take your drink order when your husband gets back.

Daphne: Oh, he's not my husband. I don't have a –

BUT THE MAITRE D' IS GONE. DAPHNE LOOKS AROUND THE RESTAURANT. THE MOOD IS INTIMATE. COUPLES TALK SOFTLY, SOME HOLDING HANDS. DAPHNE TAKES ON A REFLECTIVE LOOK. MARTIN RETURNS.

Martin: I wish there was something else I could check. Besides my blood pressure. (LAUGHS AT HIS JOKE, THEN) Hey, I noticed a couple over there splitting a real beaut of a steak. (OFF MENU) Here it is – "T for Two. A thirty-ounce T-bone. Perfect for lovers or just plain steak-lovers." What do you think, Daph?

DAPHNE BEGINS TO CRY.

Martin (CONT'D): Look if you'd rather have the lamb chops . . .

Daphne: Oh, it's not the food, it's my whole life.

Martin: What happened?

Daphne: Look around you, nothing but couples in love. It's never going to be me. I'm just going to wind up a dried-up old maid in a quilted robe with a smelly, deaf cat on my lap.

Martin: I thought you said you were okay with that.

DAPHNE CRIES A LITTLE LOUDER. MARTIN LOOKS AROUND NERVOUSLY.

Martin (CONT'D): Now, Daph, come on. There's no need to get all upset.

DAPHNE TRIES TO PULL HERSELF TOGETHER.

Daphne: I'm sorry. I don't know what came over me.

Martin: That's all right. It's all over now.

Daphne: I haven't cried like that since, well . . . New Year's Eve.

SHE STARTS CRYING AGAIN.

Martin: Aw, Daph, you'll find someone. You have a lot of great qualities, and don't you ever doubt that.

Daphne: Thank you, Mr. Crane. I know it's not easy for you to say these sorts of things.

Martin: That's okay. (THEN) So, ready to order?

Daphne: What kind of qualities?

Martin: Uh, you know . . . you're smart . . . nice looking . . . fun to be with. (THEN) So, you going with the soup or the salad?

Daphne: You really think I'm nice looking?

Martin: Well, sure.

Daphne: (TEARING UP) That's so sweet of you. I'm getting emotional again.

Martin: Ah, jeez.

Daphne: Oh, don't worry. I'm fine. Let's change the subject.

Martin: Fine. Now take a sip of water and we'll start this evening all over again.

Daphne: Nice looking how?

Martin: Well, pretty, and tall, and you take care of your hair . . . You know, attractive. What do you want from me?

Daphne: Sorry, I just don't hear this sort of thing much these days.

Three Valentines

Martin: Well, you're just in a slump. That's all.

THE WAITER APPROACHES.

Martin (CONT'D): If you ask me, you're a pretty great catch.

Waiter: It's not my place to say so, Miss, but I think your father's right. You're a very attractive woman.

THE WAITER MOVES OFF.

Daphne: Well, how about that? That's a nice little ego boost.

Martin: Yeah.

Daphne: I feel so silly all of a sudden, getting upset out of nowhere like that. Well, I feel better now. (THEN) Ready to share a nice steak?

Martin: What the hell made him say that – "your father"?

Daphne: What?

Martin: Why'd he assume that I was your father? There are plenty of guys my age who go out with women like you. What's he saying, I could never attract someone young and pretty?

Daphne: Oh, thank you, Mr. Crane.

Martin: Does this all have to be about you?

Daphne: Oh for heaven's sake, you're a very attractive man with many wonderful qualities.

Martin: Yeah, I know, I know. Let's just order.

THEY BOTH START LOOKING AT THEIR MENUS. AFTER A BEAT:

Martin (CONT'D): Like what?

Daphne: Oh, I don't know. The veal piccata or –

Martin: Not that.

Daphne: I know. Well, let's see, you're honest, gentle, kind, you have a good sense of humor. Still have all your hair and I believe all your teeth. (OFF MARTIN'S LOOK) Now, come on, where's that sense of humor? (THEN) And most of all, you're good company. I enjoy living with you.

Martin: Thank you, Daphne. I like living with you too.

Daphne: Thank you.

THEY AGAIN START READING THEIR MENUS. AFTER A BEAT.

Daphne (CONT'D): So, why do you like living with me?

Martin: Oh for God's sake, let's just both agree to cut this out.

Daphne: All right, I'm wonderful, you're wonderful. (THEN) You know, it's funny when I think about the two of us. Sure, we have our little fights, but for the most part we get along so well together. And when I think about how I enjoy looking after you and how you always cheer me up when I'm blue, it's sorta like you're my –

Martin: What?

Daphne: No, it might sound funny to say it.

Martin: Go on, you can say it.

Daphne: All right. It's sort of like you're my pet.

Martin: What?

Daphne: In a good sense. Like you and Eddie.

Martin: I'm not crazy about this comparison.

Daphne: Well, I take you for walks. I give you your dinner.

Martin: I only wish I ate as well as Eddie.

AS THE BICKERING CONTINUES, "ARE YOU COMPLAINING ABOUT MY COOKING?" "WHY'D YOU REALLY THINK I WANTED TO GO OUT TONIGHT?" "I'M GOING TO FEED YOU REAL DOG FOOD ONE OF THESE DAYS, AND WE'LL SEE HOW YOU LIKE IT," "IT'LL PROBABLY BE A NICE CHANGE OF PACE," "YOU DON'T THINK I'D REALLY DO IT, BUT I WILL," ETC. WE . . .

FADE OUT.

END OF ACT THREE